LOST
RAILWAYS
OF THE WORLD

LOST RAILWAYS
OF THE WORLD

NIGEL WELBOURN

PEN & SWORD
TRANSPORT

AN IMPRINT OF PEN & SWORD BOOKS LTD.
YORKSHIRE – PHILADELPHIA

First published in Great Britain in 2022 by
Pen and Sword Transport
An imprint of
Pen & Sword Books Ltd.
Yorkshire - Philadelphia

ISBN 978 1 39909 617 1

Typeset in Palatino 10.5/14 by SJmagic DESIGN SERVICES, India.

Printed and bound by Printworks Global Ltd, London/Hong Kong.

Pen & Sword Books Ltd incorporates the imprints of Pen & Sword Books Archaeology, Atlas, Aviation, Battleground, Discovery, Family History, History, Maritime, Military, Naval, Politics, Railways, Select, Transport, True Crime, Fiction, Frontline Books, Leo Cooper, Praetorian Press, Seaforth Publishing, Wharncliffe and White Owl.

For a complete list of Pen & Sword titles please contact

PEN & SWORD BOOKS LIMITED
47 Church Street, Barnsley, South Yorkshire, S70 2AS, England
E-mail: enquiries@pen-and-sword.co.uk
Website: www.pen-and-sword.co.uk

or

PEN AND SWORD BOOKS
1950 Lawrence Rd, Havertown, PA 19083, USA
E-mail: Uspen-and-sword@casematepublishers.com
Website: www.penandswordbooks.com

CONTENTS

PREFACE

After examining every country in the world with significant lengths of lost railways, over a period of half a century, some of the most interesting lost lines have been selected. Whilst some countries may have more coverage than others, this reflects the number of closed lines, or lost railways of particular interest.

In order to keep the book to a manageable length, islands and countries with short sections of lost line are not included. In the context of the huge number of closed railway lines in the world, the book cannot be comprehensive, but a representative selection of individual lost lines and stations is included. The author's personal favourites of ten great lost railways in the world are highlighted.

Some of the well-established geographical regions have been changed in order to more suitably reflect railway links between countries, or lost lines of a similar nature. Some narrow-gauge conversions from metric to imperial have been rounded. Mainland countries and islands are shown with bold headings for ease of reference. Finally, whilst apolitical and simply aiming to reflect historical railway facts, any impoliteness to any of the countries mentioned in this book is entirely unintentional.

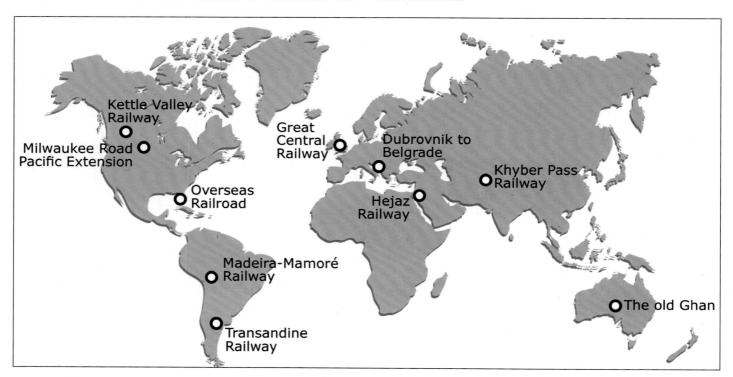

Map of the author's top ten lost railways of the world.

ACKNOWLEDGEMENTS

I am indebted to those who have helped me with this book and to those who willingly made their photographs and other material available to me from around the world. Every effort has been made to acknowledge the source of all illustrations in this book, but please contact the publisher if for some reason you have not been given full credit. Map outlines were by FreeVectorMaps.com, https://freevectormaps.com and Vecteezy.com for the world map outline. This book is dedicated to my partner Rob who has been a constant support.

INTRODUCTION

Lost railways can be found at the top of mountains, deep underground, in freezing Arctic areas, in the densest jungle and in the scorching heat of deserts. Whilst in remote rural areas lost lines might be expected, they can also be found in city areas of dense population.

While there may be local differences, lost railways follow a global pattern. Where extensive railway networks were established, such as those built during the Industrial Revolution, the greatest number of closed lines can often be found. Large numbers of lost railways are to be found from South Wales to New South Wales in Australia. Huge swathes of lost lines are to be found in the USA. In Africa and South America, long stretches of line sometimes remain, but many are no longer used. In Asia and elsewhere in the world, large numbers of closed lines are to be found. The one thing that almost all countries in the world have in common is lost railway lines.

Throughout the world, lost railways can be instantly recognised, with overgrown trackbeds and abandoned structures, as they often have a haunting and romantic charm. Many lost lines are narrow-gauge, but they also include standard and other gauge main lines, sometimes with huge, abandoned engineering works. There are countless thousands of lines that have been lost over many years.

Where it has been economically viable, closed railways and their buildings have been converted to other uses, but in weaker economies more lost railway remains are usually to be found, often just left abandoned from the time of closure. Difficult, or too large to demolish, structures remain, as do many former station residential houses, but viaducts of metal and other valuable items have mostly been sold off after closure. The process of dismantlement after closure can be slow, sometimes leading to hope of a revival, but sadly, few lines ever spring back into life.

During the First World War, lines and stations were closed, some in Europe by damage and sabotage, whilst a number of lesser-used lines were closed to save on staff and provide track and equipment for the war effort. The first closures stem back to this period, as a number

Many railways were originally built for the transport of coal. A disused railway coal pier that once served shipping is seen at Punta Arenas in Chile in March 2020. Opened in 1902, the pier remained in use until the 1940s. *Author*

of lines never reopened. Nevertheless, most lines were eventually restored back to use after the war and it was not until the worldwide depression of the 1930s, coupled with the growth of road traffic, that closures started to increase.

During the Second World War, in Europe, Asia and North America some duplicated or little-used lines again had their tracks torn up for use elsewhere in the war effort. A number of new wartime lines were also built by forced labour at enormous human cost such as the Burma Railway. Once again, the railways were damaged, while the destruction of viaducts in France led to a few

In some countries, railways declined into an ever-dilapidated state. Here in Paraguay a British built 2-6-0 locomotive No 102, dating from 1911, is seen on the Abai branch in August 1994. Steam traction remained in use until the end of most railway operations in 1999. *Vincent Corasi*

lines never reopening. Many stations, including those in Berlin and London Docklands, were damaged beyond repair and some never saw passenger services again. The lack of maintenance and huge additional usage during the Second World War enfeebled the railways.

At the end of the war, there was a surplus of army lorries that were sold off cheaply. The end of petrol rationing saw the rapid growth of use of the car, whilst the development of airliners all resulted in a worldwide decline in rail use and a steady increase in the numbers of lost railway lines. Decreasing passengers and freight, resulting in lack of funds, in turn resulted in years of underinvestment and this was the root cause of many future closures.

In some instances, powerful unions harmed the railway industry with strikes, making customers wary of reliability, or resulted in the retention of outdated working practices. Equally, in some instances, management extracted quick profits, putting greed and shareholders' returns before freight users, passengers and staff and without returning proper levels of investment for the future.

A number of closures have been caused by extreme natural events. Sections of line have been closed in Cuba, Florida and Jamaica due to damage by hurricanes. Earthquakes have closed lines in the Americas, while tsunamis have closed lines in Sri Lanka and Japan. Fire led to the closure of railways in Jersey and washouts to the closure of the old Ghan line in Australia.

Some lines have been closed by theft and looting such as in Egypt, South Africa and Zambia, and metal bridges have been stolen after closure in Guatemala, Sierra Leone and Russia. There are no electric trains in Pakistan because the overhead copper wires were repeatedly stolen. There have even been closures caused by an invisible enemy, coronavirus, and subsequent consequences for passenger railways have already resulted in some closures.

The organisation and sometimes endless restructuring of railways have not prevented closures. Railways have been nationalised, privatised, or a mixture of the two. Nationalised railways sometimes fail to understand the realities of business viability. Privatised railways sometimes fail to understand the realities of anything other than shareholder profit making.

Populist politics and corruption have played a role. In Britain in the 1960s, the Beeching Report, which recommended mass closures, was instigated by a transport minister with vested road interests and huge swathes of railway went on to be closed. The government opposition said that, if elected, they would stop the closures; they were elected and then went on to close even more railways. In Africa, aid for railway improvement was spirited away by officials, whilst a transport minister, with a fleet of lorries, managed to close down some competing freight railways. A report recommending closures in Australia was led by a former car firm executive.

Politicians sometimes try and shift responsibility for closures from the centre to the local level, knowing there is not the money at the local level to provide subsidies. Examples of this could be found in America, Russia and Japan. Politicians can make wild promises about the retention of routes closed for possible reopening, but this is mostly to try to mitigate the political damage closures can cause.

In Poland in the 1990s, subsidies to the railway were cut by over 40 per cent, resulting in widespread closures. At the same time, Argentina simply decreed the end of all long-distance trains. Political decisions to try to save money continue, while the financial crisis of 2008 sped up the closures of almost all the remaining narrow-gauge lines in Portugal and Greece.

Lost railways are found everywhere, from small island narrow-gauge railways to former main lines. Numerous early lines were built before national networks were eventually formed and lost their original purpose. Many were originally built for freight flows that have ceased, particularly coal. Others were built cheaply, often resulting in winding routes with speed restrictions and inconveniently located stations. Duplication of privately owned lines and new high-speed lines have also resulted in the closure of a number of formerly important sections of main line.

In the post-war years, in addition to narrow and secondary lines, numerous small freight depots have also closed throughout the world, together with many links to industries and ports. The closures of huge city freight depots have also taken place. Modernism in the 1960s led to the destruction of fine buildings, even if the station remained open, such as London Euston and its Doric Arch and Penn Central station in New York.

In some of the poorer countries, the general role of railways has declined in the last few decades. Their market share has weakened, there has been underinvestment, and assets have deteriorated. If this continues, they are likely to make an ever-smaller contribution towards the transport needs of such countries and eventually become no match for subsidised roads with the air-conditioned buses and heavy lorries.

In some parts of the world, railways are seen as relics of the past. They are also seen in many instances as a priceless asset, which was emphasised by the oil crisis of the 1970s. Heavy freight, commuter lines and intercity routes were thriving as the most sustainable form of transport in a world of climate change. However, in 2020 the coronavirus pandemic severely cut railway passenger use in particular, and the consequent enfeeblement of railway finances will most likely lead to future closures.

Closures caused by terrorism, war, politics within and between countries, strikes, bad management, underinvestment, floods, fires, earthquakes, tsunamis, hurricanes, economic depressions, road lobbies and corruption are amongst many issues that have all played a part. In some ways, it is perhaps surprising that railways have survived at all.

Island railways have seen many closures. A two-car Wickham diesel multiple unit in Trinidad. Before export to the island, the units had been used in Britain for a short time. The railway closed in 1968, but the disused coach is seen here in 1973. *Colour-Rail*

EUROPE

Europe was the birthplace of railways and an extensive network of lines developed. As such, when decline in use came there developed an equally extensive network of lost lines. The world's earliest lost passenger lines are to be found in Europe, some closures even dating from the 1820s, but significant closures began in the 1930s and continued apace right through to the 1970s and beyond, albeit at a slower rate.

Rural lines, particularly those originally inexpensively built and often inconveniently located to the settlements they served, together with isolated narrow-gauge lines, sometimes on islands, have been particularly susceptible to closure, particularly as road transport developed after the Second World War. Former coal lines and a number of once important secondary routes are also to be found abandoned throughout Europe.

Although there is still a relatively high-density network, with passenger services pre-coronavirus being the second busiest in the world, closures continue, and subsidies are required for lines that remain. Rationalisation, particularly in cities, has resulted in many splendid former railway buildings becoming surplus to requirements. A surprising number have survived and have been put to new uses, whilst elsewhere some remarkable former railway infrastructure can be found throughout the continent.

The door into Birkirkara narrow-gauge station on the Malta Railway, which closed in 1931, seen in October 2009. *Author*

CHAPTER 1

BRITAIN'S LOST LINKS TO THE WORLD

Bradshaw's railway guide for 1910 indicated that passengers could once travel to almost anywhere in the world from British ports. Cunard provided services from Liverpool to North America, whilst through tickets from London to Australia, via India with P&O, or via Canada with Canadian Pacific (CP), competed for passengers. Each of the main railway companies had their own port stations and many ran boat trains connecting with shipping services.

Before the current Channel Tunnel, train ferries allowed Britain's railway rolling stock to travel directly to other destinations in Europe. The train ferries were intensively used to transport freight during the First World War, but all services were disrupted and the Great Eastern Railway's Captain Fryatt was captured and shot by the Germans for attempting to ram a submarine with his railway ship.

The wagon-loading equipment from a new port built at Richborough for the war effort was, after the war, bought second-hand and moved to Harwich, operating there between 1924 and 1987. A similar train ferry transfer was also provided between Dover and Dunkerque and ran between 1936 and 1988. At one time, this link was used to convey the stock of the famous 'Night Ferry' direct sleeping car service from London to Paris.

Over a century after work on the first Channel Tunnel was stopped, 1994 was to see the opening of the current Channel Tunnel. This had implications for nearby ports. Dover Marine, later renamed Dover Western Docks, was when built the largest in Britain; opening at the end of the First World War it was once the main gateway to the continent. The 'Golden Arrow' passengers used the station until 1972. The station closed in 1994, but the main building was converted into a cruise terminal.

At neighbouring Folkestone Harbour, the original station had been rebuilt and, as with other south coast ports, saw heavy usage in both world wars. Although not used for regular passenger services since 2001, when a hovercraft Channel connection ceased, British Pullman excursion trains ran until 2009. The station was officially closed in 2014 and it has been incorporated into a new walkway using the closed line.

Newhaven Marine was also once an important cross-Channel link to Dieppe but closed to passengers in 2006. Empty stock trains then used the station tracks to avoid the lengthy closure process, which was not invoked until 2020.

The development of transatlantic crossings had seen RMS *Titanic* depart from Southampton Docks, with passengers passing through the original railway terminal to board the fateful maiden voyage. This terminal was later extended by the Southern Railway before it closed in September 1966, but the original buildings still survive.

WORLD'S FIRST LOST INTERNATIONAL RAILWAY UNDER THE SEA

A fixed rail link to Europe under the English Channel was an early railway ambition. Several ideas were proposed, including a combined tunnel and bridge using steam trains, but compressed air traction and later electricity were suggested as ways of solving the problem of ventilation in such a long tunnel. The original channel tunnel was started by the visionary Sir Edward Watkin in 1881 and ran for over 6,000ft (1,830m) under the sea near Dover. It was designed to meet a French counterpart tunnel being built from Sangatte.

The plan was for the Channel Tunnel to also connect to the Great Central Railway, whose London extension line was built to accept the larger continental loading gauge. The forward-thinking plan would have directly connected Paris, London, Manchester and Liverpool. Work continued on the tunnel without government agreement, but there were growing concerns about the military implications of a fixed link to France and work was eventually forced to stop by the government in 1883.

Above: Harwich train ferry gantry had a hinged section of track that allowed rolling stock to access ships at any state of the tide and provided a direct rail service to the continent. It was erected at Harwich in 1923 and after closure in 1987 is seen in November 2012. *Author*

Right: Dover Marine, later renamed Western Docks, was once the largest maritime railway station in Britain and the main passenger gateway for the continent. It is seen here just before closure in September 1994. *Author*

A new Ocean Terminal, which provided a short walk from the London–Southampton boat trains to the transatlantic liners and opened in 1950, was mostly demolished in 1983. This modern structure was short-lived, as transatlantic traffic went increasingly by air from the 1950s onwards. Connecting railway shipping services also ran from Southampton Docks to the Channel Islands, Le Havre and St Malo.

Liverpool's Riverside terminus opened in 1895 and was used as the departure point for transatlantic crossings, including ships run by the Canadian Pacific. Boat trains once served this station from London and northern cities. No fewer than 4,648 troop trains used the Riverside station during the Second World War.

The huge scale of Southampton Ocean Terminal building is seen with a Lord Nelson class No 30857 heading the 'Cunarder' boat train at the platform in 1956. Opened in 1950, it was superseded by transatlantic air travel and was demolished after a short life in 1983. Pat Whitehouse. *Colour-Rail*

Regular transatlantic crossings to and from Liverpool ended in 1968; the station closed in February 1971 and was finally demolished in the 1990s.

In Scotland, a new and enlarged port station opened at Greenock Princes Pier station on the Firth of Clyde in 1894. A quayside connection provided boat train links from Glasgow and Edinburgh to ships departing to North America until closure in 1965. Local Clyde steamers also operated from the station.

Whilst European links from Newcastle, Hull and Harwich Parkeston Quay were a success, a number of potential international port terminals on the east coast of England failed. Tollesbury Pier closed in 1921 and Southwold Harbour in 1929; both were originally considered good port locations for trade with Europe but silting up contributed to their demise as commercial ports and closure of their rail links.

On the Thames Estuary, both Gravesend and Tilbury competed for European traffic. Gravesend West station was located on a pier and served by boat trains from London Victoria, but these ended in 1953 and the station closed in 1968. On the north bank of the Thames, Tilbury Riverside station was rebuilt on a grand scale and opened in 1930. It was complete with a floating pontoon landing stage and was part of wider connecting train services between London, Rotterdam and Gothenburg. An increase in cheap air travel and problems berthing the largest of ships resulted in closure in 1992.

Weymouth Quay station was connected by a street tramway to the main line that enabled boat trains to run direct from Waterloo to the quayside, with connecting ships to Cherbourg and the Channel Islands. Opened in 1865, the tramway was last used for regular boat trains in September 1987. Although some use continued until 1999, it was not officially closed until 2016 with track being removed in 2021.

Above: After transatlantic passenger services from Liverpool ceased, none of the original passenger stations in the dock area survived. However, many buildings once associated with freight remain such as this preserved dockside warehouse seen in front of the Three Graces in July 2000. *Author*

Right: Part of the extensive Tilbury Riverside station, seen in poor condition, in December 1997. The station closed in 1992, but the building remains as a cruise terminal as does the Thames ferry to Gravesend. *Author*

Street running with flagmen through Weymouth with a class 33/1 diesel hauling a boat train to the Quay station, for onward links to the Channel Islands, in September 1983. The line was last used in 1999, but track removal was not until 2020-2021. *Author*

Whilst several railways had a wider strategic importance, the Great Central Railway in particular had a visionary international ambition of providing a fixed railway link with France. The railway aimed to provide a direct, modern and high-speed link between many of the cities of Britain and the continent, together with links to east and west-coast ports and other parts of the world.

Elsewhere in Britain, on the freight side, numerous ports have lost their railway connections. Coal was once exported worldwide and the closed coal lines in the North East of the Tanfield and Stockton & Darlington railways are of particular historic significance. Coal is no longer exported, and hardly extracted in Britain, leading to the loss of coal exports from ports such as Newcastle and Hull. Methil was once the largest coal-exporting port in Scotland but ceased this trade in 1977. The same was the case in South Wales. Newport once had over 100 miles (160km) of coal sidings, while Cardiff saw the last coal train in 1964, Barry in 1976 and Swansea in 1987.

TEN GREAT LOST RAILWAYS OF THE WORLD – THE GREAT CENTRAL MAIN LINE

The foremost main line to have been lost in England was the ex-Great Central Railway route from London Marylebone running over 200 miles (320km) of double-track along the industrial heartlands of England, via Leicester, Nottingham and Sheffield to Manchester. The London extension from Nottingham, opening in 1899, was built with no level crossings, slight gradients no steeper than 1 in 176, and curves of less than 1-mile radius, all designed for high-speed running.

Much of the section of line into London was built so that it could, if required, be quadrupled and also accommodate larger continental stock, as there was a visionary plan for trains to run from this line directly to France, via a Channel railway tunnel. This wider continental use never came to fruition, but the line developed as a long-distance trunk route for freight, coal in particular, whilst it also became known for its high-speed and luxurious passenger trains. In 1953, the Manchester–Sheffield section of line was electrified at enormous cost, including a new 3-mile (4.8km) tunnel under the Pennines.

In 1958, the line was transferred to the Midland Region of British Railways, who already ran the competing ex-Midland Main Line. They neglected the ex-Great Central main line and cut the express passenger services in 1960. In 1963, the Beeching Report suggested that much of the route was duplicated by other lines. It was deliberately starved of traffic, resulting in the most modern and last main line in Britain, built during the Victorian period, being controversially closed as a main line and through route in 1966. Some local sections remain open, including that operated by the heritage Great Central Railway.

Map of the Great Central Railway as a main line and its proposed connection to France.

Freight was important on the Great Central Railway and a preserved freight train is seen on the heritage section in April 2015, hauled by a Stanier 4-6-0 class 5 No 45305. *Alan Axcell*

WORLD'S LARGEST SURVIVING WOODEN RAILWAY COAL PIER

As the coal industry developed, some huge piers were built to transfer coal from rail to seagoing vessels. Although other large wooden structures were built on the North East coast and elsewhere in the world, such as by the Baltimore & Ohio Railway, the largest surviving example is to be found at Dunston Staithes. This huge wooden pier on the River Tyne near Newcastle was completed in 1903 and is some 66ft (20m) high and 1,725ft (526m) long. It closed in 1980 and, although damaged by fire, much of the wooden pier remains.

Dunston Staithes near Newcastle is the largest remaining wooden pier in the world in terms of overall bulk and was once used to transfer millions of tons of coal from trains to ships. Closed in 1980, part is seen here in September 2016. *Author*

In the mountainous area of North Wales, massive slate quarries were established and those at Dinorwic and Penrhyn were the largest in the world. Elsewhere, such as at Nantlle and Blaenau Ffestiniog, the landscape was also scarred by huge slate workings. Narrow-gauge lines such as the innovative Ffestiniog Railway were established to enable the slate to reach local ports and Welsh slate was once exported worldwide.

General goods were also transported by the railways to and from the ports. The Port of London Authority once ran a network of 140 miles (225km) of line, but the last original London Docks and freight lines closed in 1980, replaced by docks capable of handling larger ships downriver at Tilbury. Numerous smaller ports have lost their railway connections and disused quayside sidings can still be found at many ports.

CHAPTER 2

MARITIME STATIONS AND SEA CROSSINGS

Once tidal issues were overcome by constructing dredged harbours, timetabled ship arrivals and departures were in many cases served by connecting boat trains. Whilst some original port stations were expanded, a number of fine purpose-built maritime passenger stations were constructed at the busier quayside locations to allow passengers to transfer between train and ship. Long-distance journeys by ship were slow and the development of international air travel has seen the demise of most railway-served maritime stations.

The Irish Sea

A number of well-known ports provided links across the Irish Sea. Others were less successful, such as the ferries that ran for a short time from Aberdovey in Wales. Other ports also had problems, for example Port Carlisle that had silted up by 1853, and the exposed Portpatrick Harbour in Scotland that closed for services to Ireland in 1874. Whilst the ports of Silloth, Preston, Fleetwood and Cairnryan survive, they have all lost their railway connections. Trains remain to Stranraer, although the ferry service ceased in 2011.

On the Irish side, the North Wall terminus at Dublin was provided to directly connect with Holyhead in Wales and scheduled railway-connected shipping services operated until 1922. The port station at Greenore also connected to Holyhead until the ferry crossing to Britain ceased in 1926. Both of the closed Irish port stations were directly attached to railway hotels which are also closed, but the buildings survive at Dublin.

The North Wall station at Dublin opened in 1877 and regular passenger trains used the station, connecting with steamers to Britain, until 1922. A freight container service used the old goods yard until May 2001. The station is seen here in August 2005 and still survives. *Author*

The Channel

A regular and reliable cross-Channel service developed with mostly British, French and Belgian steamers being used. Boat trains connected London with Paris and Brussels. Services developed and the 'Golden Arrow', becoming from Calais Maritime the 'Fleche d'Or', ran until 1972.

The main British Channel ports are mentioned in the previous chapter, but there were of course several railway-served complementary Channel ports in the north of France. Some of the major French ports also provided transatlantic services such as Le Havre. Just as the opening of the Channel Tunnel affected ports in Britain, it had a similar influence in France. The maritime stations at Dieppe, Calais and Boulogne, the latter once the second busiest port station in France, lost their rail services in 1995, whilst freight on the St Malo Maritime line ran until 2008.

France's largest maritime station

Cherbourg Maritime station was opened in 1933 and consisted of a huge transatlantic hallway some 787ft (240m) long, through which railway passengers linked to ocean liners, for all parts of the world, via mechanised gangways that could be used at all states of the tide. Thirty-four concrete arches supported an overall copper and glass train shed, and at the time of opening it was the largest maritime station in the world and the second largest building in France. It included a spectacular 230ft (70m) high clock tower. On the transatlantic quayside, two ocean liners could berth and a thousand passengers could be transferred between ships and trains in an hour. Up to seven trains a day would take passengers directly to Paris.

The station was partly destroyed during the Second World War, including the clock tower, but by 1952 had been repaired, although the remains of the clock tower

Quayside track at Le Havre in July 1999 with the *QE2*. The rail served French port had regular transatlantic links until 1974. The *Normandie*, launched in 1935, ran from the port to New York and the *Queen Mary*, launched in 1936, also called at the port en route to the USA. *Author*

Right: The Art Deco Cherbourg Maritime station was damaged during the Second World War and the huge 70m (230ft) high clock tower was destroyed. The station closed in the early 1990s, but the building remains and is seen here in September 2012. *Author*

Below: On opening in 1933, Cherbourg Maritime was one of the largest buildings in France and at its peak up to 1,000 passengers an hour could be transferred between ships and boat trains. The luggage reclaim is seen here in September 2012. *Author*

were demolished. By 1968, regular scheduled trains no longer used the terminal, although a museum opened in the station after the final closure, and cruise ships still use the quayside and part of the station building.

The North Sea

In Scotland, the need to cross the Firth of Forth resulted in the first ever railway freight ferry in 1850, which ran until the Forth Bridge was opened in 1890. Wider North Sea ferry services developed and a number of port stations survive, particularly in estuaries and inlets.

On the tidal Thames Estuary, a ferry remains between Gravesend West and Tilbury Riverside, although both stations are closed. Tilbury Riverside buildings survive at this former rail-served station. At Hamburg, the St Pauli Piers buildings on the tidal Elb also survive, together with the former Gare Maritime at the inland port of Brussels.

On a smaller scale, the Humber estuary ferry service opened in 1848 from Hull Corporation Pier to New Holland Pier. The service was withdrawn in 1981 after the Humber road bridge was opened. However, two of the Humber paddle steamers, *Tattershall Castle* and *Wingfield Castle*, are still in existence, as are the coastal stations.

The Mediterranean Sea

Shipping services once connected all the main Mediterranean ports and islands, carrying mail and passengers. There were regular steamer services with first, second and third class fares. It was possible to forward heavy baggage on some routes, and rail connections were provided to and from the main ports.

At Naples, a new maritime station was completed in 1936, with two almost identical buildings connected to each other by a large, covered area. A direct railway connection ran from the Centrale station for passengers. The complex could accommodate four transatlantic liners which could allow up to 4,000 people to use the station at busy periods. The station originally divided the travelling passengers according to rail class and cabin categories, both on departure and on arrival. Smaller steam ships also provided passenger services to other Mediterranean ports and to the island of Sardinia. The building was mostly destroyed during the Second World War but was rebuilt in the same style by 1947. Rail services became infrequent and were gradually withdrawn, but the building remains as a cruise terminal.

Naples with the maritime terminus, once served directly by trains from Centrale station, that in turn connected with a number of scheduled shipping services. The maritime station was severely damaged during the Second World War, but was rebuilt and is seen here in October 2008. *Author*

At the port of Genoa, a large and opulent Art Nouveau-styled maritime station was started in 1914 and only completed in 1930. Trains once provided quayside connections to liners that, in turn, ran links to other Mediterranean ports and North America. The rail line was closed, but the building was restored in the 1990s and remains in use by cruise ships.

Marseilles once provided ship connections to many world destinations and most key ports in the Mediterranean, including Corsica and North Africa, where connecting passenger rail links were provided at Port Said and Alexandria. A once-busy rail line ran down from the main station at Marseilles to a maritime station in the dock area and remains open for freight, but the passenger station itself has been demolished.

Extensive rail-served warehousing was provided at Barcelona docks and an ornate maritime station opened in 1907. It was converted to offices in 1918, but the building still remains. Passenger ships ran to many Mediterranean ports and, in particular, to the Balearic Islands. Redevelopment in the 1990s saw the loss of many railway buildings and surrounding tracks.

The Adriatic Sea

On the Italian coast, an imposing maritime station building survives at Trieste, but train services are now confined to the nearby main line station. Passenger shipping services from the port at one time ran to America. At Venice, a line once served the main dock area, but freight was then delivered to the city by barge and a maritime passenger station was not provided. Elsewhere on the Italian coast, lines ran into the dock areas at a number of ports, including to Brindisi Maritime. The station once boasted of a 45-hour railway link to London providing connections for India, but it was closed in 2006 and was demolished.

On the Dalmatian coast, trains at one time ran from Belgrade to Dubrovnik on the coast, where ship connections ran to offshore islands and across the Adriatic to Italy. Eventually, the narrow-gauge line was closed in favour of a new standard-gauge line that was built to connect with the Adriatic at Ploče instead. This led to the closure of the quayside railway terminal at Dubrovnik in 1976.

Dubrovnik Croatia, in October 2009, with the terminus of the Bosnian-gauge line that twisted through the mountains from Sarajevo. Located on the waterfront, nearby ferry services operated to a number of Adriatic ports, the station closed in 1976. *Author*

The Baltic Sea

Although impressive maritime stations were not built on the more domestic Baltic routes, passenger ferry services operated from a number of mainland railheads to Baltic islands and also between the major ports of most countries bordering the Baltic. In the 1960s, seven passenger train ferries and connecting train services operated in the Baltic area. In Denmark, the railways of Zealand were linked to those in Jutland by train ferries, which also provided wider railway links between Denmark, Germany and Sweden. Replacement bridges and tunnels have made passenger train ferries redundant. In 2020, the last passenger train ferry between Trelleborg and Sassnitz, providing part of a Malmö–Berlin service, ceased.

Train ferries reduced the need for passengers to wait at grand Maritime stations. Copenhagen–Hamburg trains used a train ferry between Rødby and Puttgarden until December 2019. A high speed train is seen on the ferry in March 2014. *Dr Alan Grundy*

CHAPTER 3

TRACKS TO IRELAND

The island of Ireland, a near neighbour with several railway ferry links to and from mainland Britain, was surprisingly different, having some most unusual railways, whilst the main-line gauge adopted was 5ft 3in, unlike the standard-gauge of mainland Britain. Being a relatively lightly populated country, the railways have seen significant cutbacks. About half of all the original lines are closed. In the south, Valentina became the terminus of the most westerly closed line in Europe.

A number of early railway accidents were the result of ineffective signalling, culminating in the now closed ex-Great Northern Railway of Ireland's Armagh–Warrenpoint line in Northern Ireland. In 1889, two trains were running in the same direction on the same single line, when the first one stalled on a gradient. The coaches of the first train were divided into two sections, but the divided rear coaches, not linked to the locomotive, simply rolled back into the second oncoming train, killing eventually over 80 people and injuring many more.

The terrible scale of deaths and injuries caused by the accident led, within a very short space of time, to the legal requirement for what is known as 'block signalling' on railways. This working allows just one train on a

An old enamel advert showing the Irish–British ferry service from Rosslare, Waterford and Cobh (Queenstown) to Fishguard, the latter port opened in 1906 giving a date for the advert, which also shows a number of connecting lines that have since closed. *Author*

Stranraer once operated a ferry service to Larne in Northern Ireland and a main-line ran from Carlisle, through Scotland, to reach the port. Most of the line closed in 1965 and the disused Big Water of Fleet Viaduct is seen here in July 2009. *Author*

section, or block, of line at a time. The principles of the system are still used worldwide today and immensely improved the safety of railways. By 1965, the remaining section of the line where the accident happened was closed.

Of all the railways in Ireland, the Great Northern Railway of Ireland suffered most due to Partition. Its network of lines crossed the border between Northern Ireland and the Republic, requiring checks at fourteen stations, seven on each side of the border. There was little coordination; when a line was closed in the north by the Ulster Transport Authority, the remaining line in the south soon became uneconomic and also had to be closed. There were even plans to close the entire network in the north, but the main line between Belfast and Dublin and some other sections still survive.

In addition to the main lines, a network of narrow-gauge secondary lines developed. The narrow-gauge passenger lines, although all of 3ft gauge, were highly individualistic, but sadly all have closed. On the wider network, since the substantial closures during the 1960s there have been no significant closures for many years, but there are some concerns about the long-term future of some of the secondary routes.

WORLD'S FIRST HYDRO-ELECTRIC LOST RAILWAY

The Giant's Causeway Electric Railway was the first long line in the world to use hydro-electric power, opening in 1883 with electric traction powered from water turbine generators at Bushmills. The 9¼-mile (15km) 3ft narrow-gauge tramway was also the longest electrified line at the time. The power for the trains was originally provided by a ground-level conductor rail; however, a cyclist was electrocuted due to fluctuating currents and subsequently the line was converted to obtain power from an overhead wire. After this modification, the line's assets were never updated; it ran into financial difficulties during the Second World War and closed in 1949.

The innovative Donegal

The County Donegal Railways developed a 125-mile (200km) 3ft narrow-gauge network, which became the largest narrow-gauge system in the British Isles. The final branch to Ballyshannon was opened in 1905. It was an innovative railway, pioneering the introduction of the first diesel railcars in the British Isles in 1931, integrating

Above: The iconic red-liveried engines of the County Donegal Railways that ran in the north of Ireland. The narrow-gauge system survived until January 1960. Preserved Baltic tank No 5 *Drumboe* headed the last passenger train and is seen at Donegal in August 2005. *Author*

Right: The plush seats of a County Donegal Railways railcar. The Donegal line was at the forefront of attracting passengers with modern railcars and integrated bus and train services. The railcar is seen in the Derry/Londonderry museum in July 2010. *Author*

bus and train services and retaining steam stock for excursions.

The Glenties branch was the first to be closed in 1947 and the Strabane–Londonderry line was closed by the Ulster Transport Authority in 1955. Large-scale track replacement had been endlessly postponed and 1959 proved to be the last full year of operation.

On the last day, so many passengers turned up to say farewell that the regular railcar service could not cope and steam stock was pressed into use. To the sounds of exploding detonators, the last passenger train arrived in the drizzle and darkness at Stranorlar, with staff overcome with emotion. Amidst many a tearful eye, the 'Wee Donegal' finally died.

A frail looking road over bridge on the narrow-gauge Tralee & Dingle Light Railway which closed in June 1953, seen in August 2005. Many structures on the line were economically built including a viaduct which necessitated a 2½mph speed limit. *Author*

Dingle cattle fair

The 32-mile (50km) 3ft Tralee & Dingle Light Railway opened in 1891 and was the most westerly closed narrow-gauge line in Europe. The railway was cheaply built, but still did not cover its operating expenses in this remote area. In the 1930s, the adjacent road was improved and the railway became increasingly dilapidated. The year 1939 saw the railway closed to passengers and the Castlegregory branch was closed completely. Regular freight continued until 1947. After this, a special cattle train operated once a month in connection with the cattle fair at Dingle. Filthy looking and worn-out locomotives toiled over rotting, overgrown track and frail viaducts to the delight of enthusiasts. These trains ended in 1953. A short section was restored to use as a heritage line but is currently out of use.

Are ye right there, Michael?

The West Clare Railway opened in 1887 from Ennis and, by 1892, some 53 miles (85km) of 3ft line were operating to Kilrush and Kilkee on the coast. It was a prosperous line until the Second World War, when road improvements cut into its revenue. The railway was made famous by the Percy French song, 'Are ye right there, Michael?' which was not too flattering about the

punctual operation of the line. In 1952–3, seven new diesel engines were supplied and steam haulage ended. It thus became the first diesel-only run narrow-gauge railway in Britain. However, it continued to operate at a loss and all services ceased in 1961.

A unique monorail

The Listowel & Ballybunion Railway was a one-off 9-mile (14km) monorail opened in 1888. The system used was invented by a Frenchman, Charles Lartigue, the line was built by a German engineer, opened by an English company and operated in Ireland. The twin boiler Mallet-designed locomotives, together with the rolling stock, straddled the single elevated rail that was supported from the ground on 'A' frame trestles. Changing from one line to another, road level crossings and balancing the weight in goods vehicles all presented unique problems.

The riding quality left something to be desired and, on a few occasions, passengers were obliged to help push trains on the final gradient up to Ballybunion. Yet, the line worked, unlike a similar project at Feurs in France that was much less of a success. Unfortunately, the line was damaged during the Irish Civil War and, together with a refusal of the main line railway to absorb the route, the distinctive monorail closed in October 1924.

The Listowel & Ballybunion Railway was a successful steam worked passenger monorail. It was built to the French Lartigue system which had a raised central running rail. Closed in October 1924, a replica of the unique locomotives that would have used the line is seen here at Listowel in May 2005. *Author*

Liffey water

The Guinness brewery at Dublin once had the largest industrial railway in Ireland. Much of the 1ft 10in narrow-gauge system was constructed between 1873 and 1877 and eventually consisted of an 8-mile (13km) network. Some lines were located in public streets, linking the brewery to the main line exchange sidings and to a quay on the River Liffey. The layout was a forerunner of the 'merry-go-round' principle. The line also included a spiral tunnel, 865ft (264m) long, of over two and a half turns, on a 1 in 39 grade. This enabled the network to link the two levels of the brewery.

A fleet of Dublin-built narrow-gauge locomotives operated on the system. They were unique in that they could be hoisted into a wider Irish-gauge truck and drive along this as well. This innovative device was used on the standard Irish-gauge sidings. The remaining narrow-gauge brewery lines closed in 1975. A number of locomotives survive in preservation and the Guinness brewery remains in operation – *sláinte!*

The Dublin St James's Gate Brewery railways closed in 1975. Locomotive No 23 found its way to the Amberley Museum in the UK and is seen here in June 1999, together with lifting gear used to transfer the locomotive between narrow and broad gauges. *Author*

CHAPTER 4

SOME CITY CLOSURES

European railways and their architects often sought to make their city passenger stations a symbol of importance and enterprise. Train sheds had to deal with smoke and steam and many large stations were rightly known as 'cathedrals of the railway age'. London's Euston Arch was an example of the grandeur of a number of main-line city stations. Some stations tried to harmonise the building with the city itself, but an imposing distinction could also be aimed for and, whilst Italian and Gothic styles were popular, a whole range of architectural designs were used.

In almost all major European cities, lost railway stations are to be found. Expansion prior to the First World War made some smaller buildings unfit for purpose, while destruction during the Second World War and rationalisation beginning in the 1960s due to declining use, the duplication of facilities, or high city land values have all resulted in the closure of some spectacular city station buildings.

Barcelona has seen rationalisation of rail services that resulted in the closure of the North Station in 1972. The building, dating from 1861, remains and was turned into a bus station, whilst the former station yard was converted into the North Station Park.

Belgrade's original main terminus was positioned alongside the River Danube and in the centre of the city in 1884. In June 2018, it was closed, and trains were transferred to a newer, but far less central, station. Once a stop on the 'Orient Express', the value of the station's prime riverside estate seems to have been a factor in its closure.

In Berlin, as with London and Paris, the railways were planned so that the main terminal stations skirted the historic city centre. The earliest terminal, known as the Hamburger Bahnhof and dating from 1846, was the first to close, as early as 1888. Remarkably, it still survives and is one of the oldest former railway buildings in Germany. Services were diverted to nearby Lehrter Bahnhof, itself closed in 1952, to eventually become what is now Berlin's Central Hauptbahnhof station.

A disused Belgrade Central station city exit in October 2018. The station closed, amidst protest, in 2018 to allow for redevelopment. Parts will be repurposed as a museum, whilst an alternative station away from the city centre is now used instead. *Author*

Anhalter Bahnhof opened in 1880 but was severely damaged during the Second World War, as were many other German city stations, surviving in a derelict form until 1952, when services ceased. Part of the main entrance still exists and highlights the once vast scale of the station.

Potsdamer Bahnhof closed in 1946, again due to extensive war damage. After the war, the railways suffered from the division of Berlin between the Soviet Union and the West. Görlizer Bahnhof, damaged during the war, closed in 1951. North Bahnhof, formally known as Stettiner Bahnhof, closed to most services in 1952 and the remaining underground platforms stayed closed from 1961 until 1990 when the Berlin Wall, that once divided the city, was pulled down.

Berlin's Anhalter Bahnhof, seen in May 2014, was for a time the largest station in Europe. It was damaged during the Second World War and closed in 1952, when services were switched to the Russian sector. Demolition began in 1960, but part of the smashed front entrance seen here has survived. *Author*

Bristol is home to two interesting disused stations. The stone-built Bristol Old Terminus, designed by I.K. Brunel and dating back to 1839, was the western terminus of the Great Western Railway. The nearby Bristol & Exeter buildings, dating from 1845, also survive and show that sometimes age is no bar to urban survival.

Bristol Old Station dating from 1839 and designed by I.K. Brunel was built for the Great Western Railway. The iron Tudor-styled hammer beam roof was the largest of its type in the world on opening. The station closed in 1965 and is seen here in June 1993. *Author*

WORLD'S EARLIEST SURVIVING MONUMENTAL CLOSED RAILWAY STATION

Birmingham Curzon Street station building, unlike the Euston Arch at the other end of the line, has mostly survived in spite of the station closing to the majority of passenger trains in 1854 and completely as a freight depot in 1966. The remaining stone building once included a hotel and is to be incorporated into the new HS2 terminal at Birmingham. It is the world's earliest large surviving piece of monumental railway architecture, dating from 1838.

Birmingham Curzon Street station was designed by Phillip Hardwick and is seen in August 2001. The site closed to remaining freight in 1966, but fortunately, unlike the Euston Arch, the building survived and will form part of a new HS2 station. *Author*

Dublin Broadstone station was an Egyptian-styled building opened in 1847. In 1937 trains were transferred to the present Connolly station, although Broadstone was still used for railway purposes until April 1961. It is seen here in August 2005. *Author*

Dublin has two interesting former main line stations. The Egyptian-styled terminus at Broadstone, not being that central to the city, was closed to passengers in 1937. Harcourt Street station was closed in 1959. A spectacular accident occurred at the latter station in 1900 when a train failed stop at the terminus and smashed through a wall at the end of the high-level platforms and down onto the street below.

Edinburgh once had a comprehensive suburban network of railways, but this gradually withered away without much protest. The largest station to close was Edinburgh Princes Street. The imposing station was situated at the west end of the famous street of that name. The main line terminus closed in 1965, when trains were diverted to Waverley station, once terminus of the Waverley route. Princes Street's train shed was demolished, but the imposing hotel survived and is still open.

Glasgow St Enoch station was a handsome collection of buildings incorporating twelve platforms located under two huge barrelled, glazed train sheds and included a hotel. The station closed in 1966, the hotel in 1974 and, amidst protests, all the buildings were demolished in 1977.

WORLD'S FIRST CITY PASSENGER STATION TO CLOSE

Liverpool's purpose-built passenger railway station, with an overall glass train shed, was the first in the world of this scale to close. Crown Street station opened in 1830 but closed in 1836 when the larger Liverpool Lime Street station opened. The buildings did not survive, but the site remained open for freight until 1972.

The London Necropolis Railway station opened in 1854 and funeral trains once conveyed over 2,000 bodies a year to Brookwood Cemetery in Surrey. The station was damaged during the Second World War and closed, but the frontage survived and is seen here in April 2015. *Author*

London saw its graveyards become full and some railways were used to convey the dead to cemeteries outside the city. The most famous was the London Necropolis Railway, running its own trains to Brookwood Cemetery in Surrey. The railway opened its terminus next to Waterloo station in 1854 and, at one time, over 2,000 bodies were carried from London to Brookwood each year. There were even 1st, 2nd and 3rd class tickets according to the type of funeral arrangements made. The London station was severely damaged in the Blitz of 1941 and funeral trains never ran again, but the station frontage still survives.

WORLD'S GREATEST LOST HISTORICAL RAILWAY MONUMENT

London's Euston Arch was an early and huge monumental entrance to the London & Birmingham Railway. Designed by Phillip Hardwick with stone Doric columns and opened in 1837, it stood some 70ft (21m) high and was a key London landmark. It was demolished amidst protest in 1962 in an act of disgraceful and mindless vandalism. Even the demolition contractor offered to store the arch for free. Smashed sections of the stone structure were dumped in the River Lea, but the ornamental iron gates once provided as part of the structure survive. There have been plans for its reconstruction, and I was once told in a letter that it would be re-erected as part of the HS2 project. We will see.

Although modernisation saw the demolition of the original Euston station, together with most of the original buildings at Holborn Viaduct, Blackfriars and much of London Bridge, these stations remain open. London Broad Street station was the only major terminal in London to be completely closed. Being in the heart of the City, its commercial value was high and closure came in 1986.

As for London's underground passenger railways, these started with the opening of the Metropolitan Railway in London in 1863, which provided the word 'Metro' throughout the world.

The Tower Hill Subway closure was followed by the short underground link to a terminus at King William Street, which closed in 1900 when the line was extended northward. In terms of significant tube

WORLD'S FIRST LOST TUBE TUNNEL

The Tower Subway in London under the River Thames, opened in 1869, had a 2ft 6in narrow-gauge track that boasted of a single 12-seat coach operated by a cable that ran in a tube tunnel made from cast iron sections. The limitation of this single coach proved unworkable and the company went bankrupt, but the line was converted to a footpath. However, once the adjoining toll-free Tower Bridge opened, this resulted in the former tube route closing in 1898.

lines, the next closure in London was Aldwych. Whilst again a short passenger link, this was closed in 1994, an unusual occurrence at such a late date in the heart of a congested city.

The 2ft-gauge Post Office Railway in London operated for almost 8 miles (13km) between Paddington and Whitechapel and was the longest non-mining underground freight railway in Europe. It was also the first significant railway to use driverless trains from its opening in 1927. The line was gradually run-down and not fully utilised after Travelling Post Office trains on the main lines ceased. The line closed in 2003, adding a further eighty lorries to London streets. A short section has since reopened as a tourist attraction at the Post Office Museum.

Madrid's Delicias station was opened by the Spanish royal family in 1880. Soon after opening, the station was taken over by a larger rival railway, which already had its own station in Madrid. An international service to Portugal developed, but usage was low and the station closed in 1969. The main station buildings survived and became a railway museum in 1984.

Manchester has two very contrasting closed stations. The Midland Railway's Central station opened in 1880. It is the largest surviving closed station in the British Isles. Closed in 1969, after a period of dereliction, much remained and its 90ft (27m) high train shed, sitting above a labyrinth of subterranean arches and next to the Midland Hotel, is now used as a conference centre.

Manchester Central with its train shed, now used as a conference centre, sits above a labyrinth of subterranean arches and next to the Midland Hotel. The station is the largest surviving closed railway terminal in Britain and is seen in August 2016. *Author*

WORLD'S OLDEST SURVIVING PURPOSE-BUILT CLOSED RAILWAY PASSENGER STATION

Manchester Liverpool Road station, the original terminus of the Liverpool & Manchester Railway, remains. Dating from 1830, it is the oldest surviving purpose-built passenger station in the world. It was only used by passengers until 1844 when increasing passenger numbers were transferred to the larger Manchester Victoria station. The old station site survived for freight until 1975 and tracks to it were only cut in 2015. The site has been used as a museum for many years.

Manchester Liverpool Road station's frontage seen in August 2016. Dating from 1830, it was the terminus of George Stephenson's first intercity railway in the world. Passengers using the doors once proceeded upstairs to the trains. The buildings are now a museum. *Author*

Milan's Porta Nuova station closed in 1931, whilst the current Centrale station had the original buildings replaced at the same time. Centrale station still contains lost lines that once served its subterranean post office platforms. During the Second World War, Jews in Italy were deported to the death camps from these platforms in appallingly overcrowded conditions inside enclosed freight trucks, which were hoisted up to the surface on railway lifts.

Oslo's railways were altered when a new tunnel was built in 1980 through central Oslo and enabled the east and west rail networks serving the city to be linked. This, in turn, led to the closure of Oslo West station in 1989 and changes to Oslo East station, now called Oslo Central.

Paris is home to a number of interesting former stations. The huge and decorative Gare d'Orsay was opened in 1900. By 1939, as a result of the station's short platforms,

it was used only by local trains, which still use lower levels today. The station hotel closed in 1973 and, after closure as a main line station, the buildings opened as a museum in 1986.

Another famous closed station building in Paris was Gare Lisch, which was designed by Gustave Eiffel and originally located directly under the Eiffel Tower. The station was removed from this site and is currently in a Paris suburb, with plans for refurbishment.

Elsewhere in Paris, the 3-mile (4.7km) Promenade Plantée was a viaduct serving the Paris Bastille terminus, which closed in 1969 and was demolished, after protest, in 1984. The original Montparnasse station became famous for a runaway train in 1895 which crashed through the terminus and fell 33ft (10m) into the street below. The original station building was demolished in 1969 and replaced by a nearby newer station.

La Petite Ceinture, or the Little Belt, was an orbital railway around the centre of Paris and was completed

Oslo West station closed when a new underground line linked the West and East stations, but the building remains in good condition, as seen here in September 2004, part being used by the Nobel Peace Centre. *Author*

Paris Gare d'Orsay station, was closed as a main line because of the difficulties in extending its short platforms. The elegant station is now used as a museum. One of the two large illuminated station clocks is seen here in January 1997, from within the works. *Author*

in 1869 before the Paris Metro was built. It was closed to passengers in 1934 and for freight in the late 1980s. The tracks were never removed and today some sections are used by more recent lines and a small part acts as an urban park.

Rome's original centrally located station was demolished and the new station set further back. Of interest, the city also contains the world's smallest national railway in the Vatican City, which is still linked to the main network. Papal visits by train were few and far between, but excursion trains have been run from the Vatican station since 2015.

Rotterdam's Delftse Poort station was severely damaged during the Second World War. The Maas terminus closed in 1953 and trains were diverted to a new Central station which was completed in 1957. Hofplein station was closed in 2010 and services were also diverted into Central station. A new enlarged Central station opened in 2014.

Utrecht has a modern central station, the largest in the Netherlands, that runs an hourly service to Maliebann station that, after closure to regular services, eventually became a railway museum.

Warsaw over the years has had several stations served from a loop line around the city. Kowel station was damaged during the First World War and is now known as Warsaw Gdanska. The Vienna station closed in the 1920s and a new cross city line opened in the 1930s. Two central stations were seriously damaged during the Second World War, with only a goods station building surviving. Temporary arrangements were made until a largely concrete 'Central' passenger station replacement was constructed in the communist era. A number of modern stations now serve the city.

Vienna's Südbahnhof was demolished and modernised the 1960s but closed in 2009 and the replacement station building was demolished without complaint and replaced by the new Hauptbahnhof. A building in complete contrast was Karlsplatz underground station; it also was proposed for demolition, but after an outcry was saved.

Zurich, again as a result of reorganisation of the railways, a stretch of line and Lenten station are closed in the centre of the city. It is just one of many smaller closed stations that are found in cities.

Above: Utrecht Maliebaan station closed in 1939 and became a railway museum. The exhibits include a War Department locomotive *Longmoor* which was ferried into Europe after D-Day. The station frontage is seen in September 2012. *Author*

Right: Vienna with Karlsplatz underground station, seen in September 2019. The attractive building was designed by Otto Wagner and dates from 1899. When scheduled for demolition in 1981 there was outcry and the buildings were renovated and saved. *Author*

Some other city closures

The demolition of city station buildings can be traced back over many years. Hamburg's Berliner Bahnhof closed in 1903 and its wooden trainshed was demolished. Even stations that remained open such as Antwerp South were to see their beautiful buildings demolished in the 1960s, often replaced with cheaply built modern utilitarian structures.

Elsewhere, many buildings survived closure and some have been put to new uses. Examples include Bergslagsbanans station at Gothenburg that closed in 1930, and Malmo West that closed in 1955. Prague's Art Nouveau Vyšehrad terminus closed in 1960 and Katowice old station closed in 1972; whilst the two buildings remain, they are in poor condition. In later years, Seville's old station closed in 1992 and was refurbished for retail use. St Petersburg's Varshavsky (Warsaw) station closed in 2001, when trains moved to a more central site and, for a time, the old station became a railway museum.

CHAPTER 5

FORGOTTEN FRENCH CONNECTIONS

Rural France was not heavily populated, and the greater distances and lower population resulted in a slower development of railways than in Britain. Unlike Britain, a national plan was established by the French government to serve every key town and region with a standard-gauge line; however, with metre-gauge branches filling the gaps, a huge network eventually developed.

The French Decauville engineering firm produced portable narrow-gauge light railway track, stock and equipment, originally mainly for industrial or agricultural use, but this was widely used during the First World War and provided a crucial role in serving the troops on the Western Front. After the end of hostilities in 1918, much of this railway infrastructure was sold for civilian use. In particular, stock was used to serve both the French and German sugar beet industry and worked up until the closure of many of these operations in the 1960s.

The First World War resulted in both heavy use and damage to French railways, particularly on the eastern border with Germany. Lines were later restored, but construction of the mountain line from le Puy to Lalevade d'Ardèche was suspended in 1914, never to resume, leaving the extensive disused summit tunnel at St Cirgues as one of the first abandonments.

After the First World War, more general decline occurred over many years and France lost about half of its network of lines by closures that first started in the 1920s. To protect the remaining lines, the government nationalised the network in 1938 and the Societe Nationale des Chemins de Fer Francais (SNCF) still survives.

The almost complete loss of French metre and narrow-gauge railways is a key feature of France's

Narrow-gauge railways in France have almost totally disappeared. Le Cheylard station, on the narrow-gauge Vivarais lines that ran in the Rhône Valley, is seen here in October 1959. The network closed in 1968, but a section has reopened as a heritage railway. *Colour-Rail*

railways. Before the First World War, about 13,000 miles (21,000km) of narrow-gauge line was built, mostly to metre-gauge, but also to 2ft gauge. After the war, building continued, but at a slower rate due to the impoverishment of the country. The last new narrow-gauge line opened in 1925, but soon after closures began as road transport made greater incursions into railway revenue. Some new lines were short-lived, with one surviving for just six years.

France also has a number of closed rack railways. The first to close was the rack line from Monaco to La Turbie in 1932 after an accident, but much of the disused route remains. An original line at Clermont Ferrand opened in 1907 and used the Fell system until closure in 1926. At Langres, a rack line linking the station to the town above was opened in 1887 and survived until 1971.

The railways again suffered much damage during the Second World War. There was the destruction of stations and infrastructure, particularly in the north and east of France. Yet, other regions of France also suffered, including the French Riviera, where a network of secondary routes ran from Nice. Railcars had been introduced on these lines in the 1930s, but damage, including to the huge Loup Viaduct, on these routes made reinstatement after the war prohibitively expensive.

The Second World War did at least see a temporary halt to closures and about 7,000 miles (11,260km) of narrow-gauge line survived until 1947. However, the scale of metre-gauge closures after the Second World War was remarkable, and some examples will make this clear. The Finistère Railway in north-west Brittany

The Monte Carlo–La Turbie rack railway closed in 1932, after two passengers were killed. The station, seen here in October 2015, was the first at La Turbie and still survived in relatively good condition. *Author*

comprised 133 miles (214km) of metre-gauge line. Opened in stages by 1907, it was closed in 1946. A 269-mile (433km) network opened in the Morbihan area in 1902, but this was closed by 1948. The Reseau Albert was a 120-mile (190km) network of lines that ran between 1889 and 1955. The Côtes-d'Armor network was metre-gauge, opening from 1905 and eventually comprising of some 264 miles (457km) of line. The final section closed in 1956.

Train des Pignes comprised four lines that once operated in southern France. The lines from Toulon to St Raphael and Cogolin to St Tropez, both over 50 miles (80km) in length, are closed, but the Nice to Digne line remains open. It was one of the very few narrow-gauge lines to survive, together with those in the Pyrenees and Alps. The few surviving lines are of a tourist nature, whilst a number of heritage lines such as at Baie de Somme and the Vivarais Railway are also to be found.

The standard-gauge network has also suffered losses; branch lines went first, particularly in the 1930s, 1950s and again in the 1980s. The original state financing of railway construction, particularly in mountainous areas, resulted in some spectacular engineering on lines that were never that well used. On the Lapeyrouse–Volvic line at Fades, a viaduct rising some 430ft (131m) above the valley was built and was once the highest in the world. The line was a state requirement rather than a commercial necessity and closed in 2007, mainly because the viaduct, that had been allowed to rust and decay, required costly maintenance.

Whilst many buildings, stone viaducts and tunnels are still to be discovered after closure, particularly station houses and buildings, a few spectacular structures have also sadly been destroyed. The Souleuvre Viaduct was built by Gustave Eiffel and opened in 1893. It was set on five stone pillars which remain, but the metal girders between them were blown up and destroyed, in spite of protests.

The local branch line terminus at Cherbourg on the line to Barfleur, seen in September 2010. Opened in 1911, the line closed in 1950 and buses now use the former station site. *Author*

Above: Saint-Vaast-la-Hougue seen in September 2010. Many of the stations on the line were of a similar standard size and easily recognisable design, particularly the window surrounds. The station was a terminus, closing in 1954. *Author*

Right: The coastal resort station of Bretteville in September 2010 on the Cherbourg–St Vaast line on the Cotentin Peninsular. The line, which saw the early use of diesel railcars, was severely damaged during the Second World War and closed in 1954. *Author*

The Champagne region once used the railways to convey its wines. Crézancy station was on the Mézy–Romilly-sur-Seine line that closed to most traffic in 1999. A section of the track remained as a siding for occasional freight, the station is seen in September 2008. *Author*

Canfranc International station

A trans-Pyrenean international line ran between France and Spain and was provided with a huge and opulent interchange station at the border at Canfranc. The completed line from Bedous in France opened in 1928 after years of construction, climbing into the Pyrenees with steep gradients of up to 1 in 25, and hydroelectricity being used for the electrified French section of the route.

A 1-mile (1.6km) spiral tunnel was amongst the more unusual tunnels on the French section from Bedous, whilst the Somport Tunnel, at almost 5 miles (8km) in length, was the longest closed passenger tunnel in France.

At Canfranc, a change from the standard-gauge of France to the wider gauge of Spain required the transhipment of all passengers and freight traffic. The huge interchange facilities of the passenger station,

being 790ft (240m) long, together with other facilities and goods sheds at one time involved some 2,000 staff.

The station has a rich history, particularly during the Second World War when spies, Jews, Nazis and the Resistance, together with smuggled gold, all used the

Canfranc is the longest disused international station in world and is seen in June 2012. It is said the station has some 365 windows and 52 doors. After the Second World War the station's use declined and damage to a bridge on the French line ended its international status. *Phil Carey*

Canfranc with an old coach seen in June 2012. During the Second World War the station firstly witnessed Jews escaping from occupied France, whilst at the end of war, Nazis were also escaping from Germany. The international status of the station ceased in 1970. *Phil Carey*

route. The French line closed in 1970 due to damage caused to Estanguet Bridge by a double-headed electrically hauled freight train that failed and ran away, gathering speed on what was the steepest standard-gauge main line gradient in France.

Today, part of the French route is used as a footpath. Canfranc itself is in Spain and the line on the Spanish side remains open with local trains. Plans to reopen the French line and turn the station into a hotel are underway.

An uncertain future?

Great as the high-speed lines for the Trains à Grande Vitesse are, they have in turn resulted in a legacy of neglect and starved investment for some other parts of the network. Half of France's branch lines already operate at low speeds because the track is worn, parts of it dating back to the 1930s, and many secondary lines have become increasingly unreliable.

In 2015, a nationwide plan was revealed to close a number of routes which had been neglected for many years. Huge anger ensued and the plan was temporarily shelved. However, closures continued, as the SNCF has a policy of 'suspending' routes rather than closing them, but this effectively amounts to closure by stealth. Any unforeseen expenditure to secondary lines can also simply result in closure. A programme of abandonment is again possible after a further study in 2019 of 5,590 miles (9,000km) of little-used lines recommended closure.

There was indignation at the recommendations to close lines and measures to reduce costs for remaining lines have been put forward. Strikes in 2019 and the coronavirus pandemic in 2020 may not have assisted, but in 2021 the regional governments were given the option of taking control of rural lines. Although some investment is proposed, it is considered that a number of lines may not last too long as the regions are increasingly cash strapped. The south-west of France and the Massif Central may be the worst affected.

Many secondary and branch lines have closed, but it is clear that a number of French lines that have been proposed for closure teeter on the edge, such as the Ligne des Causses that runs from Clermont Ferrand to the Beziers near the Mediterranean. Its daily passenger train travels through breathtaking scenery, past already closed stations and over the Garabit Viaduct designed by Gustaf Eiffel.

Finally, the country is already covered with a web of disused railway lines, many of which have been converted to footpaths and over 50 rail trails. An influx of tourists and travellers has given these lost railways a new lease of life in both rural and urban areas.

Monte Carlo station opened in 1867. The old line ran through the town and the station, close to the harbour, closed in 1965 when new inland tunnels and a later station were built and part of the old line was turned into road. The road is viewed in October 2015. *Author*

This viaduct on the former Grasse–Vence route in the south of France, seen in October 2015, is now used as a footway. The railway opened in 1911, but closed after damage to viaducts on the line during the Second World War. *Author*

CHAPTER 6

NARROW-GAUGE NECROSIS

Throughout Europe there developed a number of different gauges, but narrow-gauge is generally recognised as anything below 4ft 8½ins, (1,435mm) which is known as standard-gauge. Narrow-gauge lines had the advantage of being cheaper, easier to build and more flexible, particularly in mountainous areas. Europe once had a huge number of narrow-gauge, mostly secondary passenger lines. Narrow-gauge forestry, peat, agricultural, mining and industrial railways were also once found extensively throughout Europe.

The savings in building a narrow-gauge railway were considerable. Yet, in some ways this was a false economy as competition from the roads grew, while the disadvantages of transhipping freight and even cross-platform changes for passengers added to the costs and inconvenience. Furthermore, the saving in construction costs often resulted in sharp curves, steep gradients and slow services.

The survival of isolated narrow-gauge lines, once road transport became more reliable and economical, became increasingly insecure and they have been in decline for years. They often served less-prosperous, or smaller, communities with stations sometimes not that convenient to town centres. A large number of such lines were destined for either conversion to standard-gauge or closure by the end of the 1960s. Numerous buildings and structures remained after lines closed, whilst many routes have been converted into long-distance footpaths, rail trails and cycle ways.

Austria once operated an extensive number of narrow-gauge lines, many in difficult mountainous terrain. The defeat of the Austro-Hungarian Empire during the First World War resulted in boundary changes and a number of lost lines are now located in other countries. Transporter wagons were used on some routes to convey standard-gauge wagons, but this innovation was unable to save lines.

There have been closures over a number of years and the attractive line to Bezau closed in 1982. The Salzburg–Bad Ischl line ran through the scenic Austrian lake district but was closed despite a petition signed by over 50,000 people. One of the last lines to close, the Thörlerbahn in 1995, also served the iron industry, but attempts to save the railway were sadly unsuccessful. The Mariazell line was the only long route to be electrified and remains open, together with a number of secondary and heritage lines, many taking advantage of spectacular scenery.

Austria's mountain terrain also resulted in a number of rack railways. The first at Kahlenberg opened in 1874 and was well used, but was damaged during the First World War with the remaining sections closing in 1920. The Iron Mountain Railway to Eisenerz closed in 1986, whilst he Achenseebahn line was threatened with closure in 2020 but should reopen in 2022.

A typical Austrian narrow-gauge four wheeled coach with wooden seats operating on the Welshpool & Llanfair Welsh heritage railway and seen in September 2018. The spartan and rather hard sprung coaches were hardly the height of luxury. *Author*

TEN GREAT LOST RAILWAYS OF THE WORLD – DUBROVNIK TO BELGRADE

The narrow Bosnian-gauge lines from Dubrovnik on the Dalmatian coast to Belgrade, via Mostar and Sarajevo, were some 470 miles (756km) in length, although it was only about 200 miles (322km) between the centres as the crow flies. This was because the line was forced to twist and turn through spectacular Balkan mountain scenery. The section between Sarajevo and Pale had some 99 tunnels and was hugely expensive to build. The 26-hour journey included rack and pinion sections and a figure-of-eight spiral. Narrow-gauge, sleeping and restaurant cars were provided.

The line was part of the largest interconnected narrow-gauge network in Europe, that was once mostly part of former Yugoslavia. In 1968 and 1970, diesel locomotives and DMUs were introduced, but the construction of new standard-gauge sections on some of the former narrow-gauge routes, a change in government policy, a resultant gauge break and new roads all conspired to result in closure of the narrow-gauge Adriatic network in 1975–6. The narrow-gauge link to Belgrade was closed by 1979 and any remaining passenger sections were closed by subsequent conflicts that resulted in the break-up of Yugoslavia.

Today, the narrow-gauge links to Dubrovnik and the coastal lines, together with the line east from Sarajevo, no longer contain any rails. However, at Mokra Gora a section of line has reopened as the Šargan Eight heritage railway and is famous for its convoluted route and stunning mountain scenery.

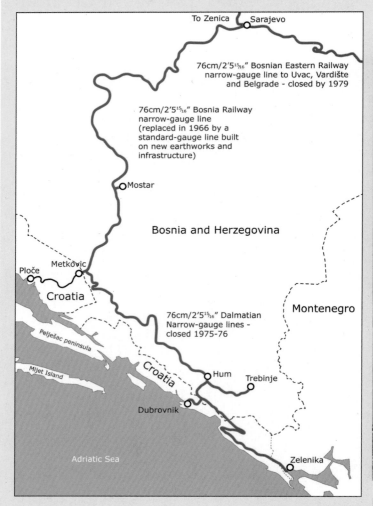

Map of Bosnian-gauge railways from Dubrovnik and on the Adriatic coast.

Bosnian-gauge track runs through solid rock tunnels number 3, 4 and 5 located in the gorge of the Drina River east of Sarajevo, part of the spectacular route is seen from this 1906 postcard.

Belgium with its crowded population resulted in it once also having the densest interurban railway network in the world. The network of metre narrow-gauge lines was once more extensive than the main line network. In 1945, it was estimated that there were about 2,800 miles (4,500km) of narrow-gauge passenger lines in existence, and much was electrified. By 1960, this had been reduced to about 600 miles (960km). Today, just one line remains, a 42-mile (68km) coastal route, together with a few heritage lines. A greenway network of footpaths and cycleways of over 560 miles (900km) uses the closed lines.

Bosnia Herzegovina, Croatia and Serbia had a unique 2ft 5⅓in (760mm) Bosnian-gauge network that could trace its roots back to military railways. The railway developed and was once worked by over 650 steam locomotives on what was the largest network in the world laid to this small gauge. Some lines were converted to standard-gauge and others were closed in the 1960s and 1970s. The last Serbian narrow-gauge passenger link was the Lajkovac–Mladenovac line which closed in 1983, but steam locomotives still operated part of a coal line at Banović in Bosnia in 2020.

Bulgaria had several 2ft narrow-gauge lines that were built up to the 1920s. Some of the narrow-gauge lines were later converted to standard-gauge, including the international line from Sofia to Greece, via Rila. Others were closed such as that to the Rila Monastery in 1960, and by 2021 just one narrow-gauge line survived at Septemvri, running through mountain ranges and serving the highest station in the Balkans.

The Czech Republic had a number of Bosnian and metre-gauge lines, including some that crossed new borders after the First World War, together with industrial, forestry and agricultural lines. Most served remote areas and almost all passenger narrow-gauge lines had closed by 1976. However, two lines have survived several threats of closure and a number of tourist railways remain, including one at Nové Údoli.

Germany at one time had a large number of narrow-gauge railways. For example, lines near Dresden had almost a main-line feel with large 0-10-0T locomotives, whilst Saxony alone had over 300 miles (500km) of metre and 2ft 6in gauge lines, linking many of the small towns

A typical small industrial 0-4-0T locomotive seen at Ruse in Bulgaria in October 2018. It was located at Bulgaria's first railway station which closed in 1954 and was subsequently turned into a railway museum. *Author*

in the area. Although the last line was not completed until 1948, closure of Germany's once numerous narrow-gauge lines first started in the 1920s, due to increasing bus competition and high inflation, but closures during this period were not extensive.

After the Second World War, because of the poor condition of the track and stock, the decision was taken in the 1960s to close all the remaining narrow-gauge lines in communist East Germany by 1975. Many closures ensued, including the surviving section of the 2ft-gauge line between Anklam and Friedlam in 1969, which saw a locomotive subsequently used on the Welsh Brecon Mountain Railway. However, there were protests and, at first, this led to closures being undertaken with little or no notice, but eventually seven lines were reprieved and remained busy during the 'Cold War', particularly when oil supplies were cut to East Germany.

A narrow-gauge 0-6-2T No 99 253, built in Munich in 1908 for the Walhalla Railway and seen preserved at Regensburg in September 2019. The locomotive was withdrawn in 1960 and the German line closed in 1968. *Author*

Closures also continued in West Germany and the only 'commercial' narrow-gauge lines remaining are on the North Sea Islands of Wangerooge and Borkum, but the reunification in 1990 was a lifeline for remaining lines in East Germany as controls were reduced, subsidies were paid by local authorities and tourism grew. The lines that survived the unification of Germany are now in a generally good condition, but most rely on tourism and only one is operated by Deutsche Bahn on Wangerooge. Investment in East German lines had been limited, but this resulted in the largest steam-operated narrow-gauge network in the world surviving in the Harz Mountains. Elsewhere, there are numerous narrow-gauge heritage railways.

Greece witnessed its first major closures due to damage during the Second World War, with some lines never reopening. An extensive metre-gauge network existed, particularly from Athens and extending into the Attica region, until it was closed in 1957, due in part to lobbying by bus owners.

There was also once a network in the Thessaly region. When the narrow-gauge line to Vólos was converted from narrow to standard-gauge, it resulted in Vólos, for a time, having some lengths of triple-gauge track, this included the standard-gauge line for Larissa, the metre-gauge line for Kanalia and the 2ft-gauge line for Pelion. The latter lasted until 1971, the remaining metre-gauge line was converted to standard-gauge, and today just standard-gauge lines remain. The last major narrow-gauge network was on the Peloponnese, see Chapter 7.

Hungary once had a large narrow-gauge network of lines, including those serving forestry and industrial complexes. The Austro-Hungarian Empire was dissolved after the First World War and some lines ended up in other countries when borders changed. In 1979, it was estimated that there were 176 miles (283km) of Bosnian-gauge line remaining; however, by 1990 there were only two significant networks still open and, by 2009, these had all but disappeared, except for one remaining line run by the Hungarian State Railways. A few forestry lines and a number of heritage tourist lines also survive, whilst any future destruction of railway infrastructure and stock has been prohibited.

Italy's narrow-gauge railways were mostly built to the Italian metre-gauge (which is 950mm not 1 metre) and a number were electrified. Several closed lines are to be found in the north of the country. One such line connected the town of Menaggio on Lake Como with Porlezza on Lake Lugano, with links being made by connecting steamboats. The line closed in 1939, but there was hoped for a revival and track was not all removed until 1966. Elsewhere, a number of diverse narrow-gauge railways continued operation and one line was not completed until 1956, being the last significant narrow-gauge line to be built in Europe. Almost at the same time, an endless list of closures was also taking place, the 40-mile (65km) Dolomites Railway closed in 1962, several lines in Calabria and parts of the Bari system also closed in the 1960s.

A poster for the Stresa–Mottarone electrified mountain railway in Italy. Opening in 1911, the metre-gauge rack railway ran to a hotel at a height of 4,890 ft (1,491) metres. The line closed in 1963, but some remains are still to be found. *M. Borgoni*

Italy has the largest number of closed narrow-gauge rack railways, with sixteen lines closing between the 1920s and 1970s. The Mont Cenis Pass Railway opened in 1868 and was the first mountain railway in the world, using the Fell system; the route linked Italy to France, but closed in 1871 when the Fréjus Tunnel was opened through the Alps. Much of the equipment was reused to create a rack railway near Rio de Janeiro, which survived until 1965. An early rack railway in Italy ran between St'Ellero and Saltino, opening in 1892, but closed as early as 1922. The Rocchette–Asiago line opened in 1910; rising to 3,435ft (1,047m), it was amongst the highest Italian rack railways until its closure in 1958.

The Mount Vesuvius railway

In 1903, a 5-mile (7.7km) metre-gauge railway was opened from Pugliano to a terminus below the top of Mount Vesuvius. The steep central section of the electrified railway was rack operated. The line was financed with the assistance of Thomas Cook, who was also involved with a hotel and a funicular that was located at the top terminus of the rack railway and which ran to the very edge of the volcano crater.

Vesuvius is an active volcano and in 1906 the stock and parts of the railway were destroyed by an eruption. The railway was repaired, but another eruption in 1911 caused renewed damage. Inevitably, even the stone-built stations were destroyed by yet another eruption in 1944 and Thomas Cook sold its interests in the railway. By 1947, the railway was again in operation, but in 1955 a competing road was built and the railway closed.

The Netherlands once had a large number of industrial narrow-gauge lines, including those for conveying peat, which were some of the last to close in the 1980s, when supplies were exhausted. Most passenger lines took the form of street tramways, many originally with skirted steam traction and served a similar function to the light railways in Britain. The once comprehensive network of lines increasingly suffered from road competition. After a short reprieve during fuel shortages after the Second World War, lines had mostly closed by the 1950s and the last to go was in the mid-1960s. A number of heritage sites have preserved some sections of lines.

Poland once had hundreds of miles of differing narrow-gauged railways. In general terms, there were 2ft and metre-gauge lines, whilst 2ft 5½in was the most common narrow-gauge used. The networks suffered appalling damage during the Second World War. Much was restored to use after the war, but often with track and stock in poor condition, although a number of lines were also converted to standard-gauge.

The lines have been drastically reduced since the 1970s; for example, about 90 miles (146km) of line around Gdansk closed in 1986. Closures accelerated after the collapse of communism until the narrow-gauge lines became shadows of their former extent. Most industrial, forestry and sugar beet lines have also closed, but some of the latter survived longest. At the beginning of the twenty-first century, Polish Railways sold its remaining narrow-gauge lines to local authorities. By 2021, no non-tourist lines were operating, but there were equally increasing numbers of heritage and tourist sections of line. On the closed routes, many remains of stations and railway structures are still to be found and some have been registered as monuments, whilst disused stock has been exported to other countries.

Portugal's metre-gauge railways were found mostly towards the north of the country. Four lines were based north of the Douro Valley and a group of lines centred on the remote junction of Serenada. They were busy until the 1960s, particularly with passengers employed to pick grapes in the autumn.

Many trains conveyed first class and these seats were protected by white linen covers. The lines were often originally built to help development in remote areas and some were not completed until the late 1930s. They became seen increasingly as an anachronism and, although railcars had generally replaced steam, after the financial crisis of 2008 most remaining lines were closed.

There was a strange lack of interest in capitalising on the tourist potential of a number of lines, such as the highly scenic Tua line, the last section which closed in 2018. By 2020, only part of the Vouga line remained; however, steam returned to this line in 2019 and locomotives, some that have been rusting away for years, may yet be restored. Elsewhere, disused trackbeds have been turned into foot and cycle ways.

A short heritage narrow-gauge service operated between Tralee and Blennerville in Ireland until 2013. A number of coaches for the line were purchased from closed narrow-gauge lines in Poland and two are seen rusting here in May 2005. *Author*

Beyer Peacock 2-6-0T Mallets E86 and E84 dating from 1889 and seen in 1969 on narrow-gauge lines that once operated from Porto in Portugal. Almost all lines have closed, but a number of locomotives and stock have been preserved at a railway museum at Lousado. *Colour-Rail*

Romania had about 370 miles (500km) of mostly Bosnian-gauge line in 1979, but other narrow-gauges also existed. Lines in the mountains that were used primarily for logging were known as Mocăniță. Today, only one traditional such narrow-gauge line remains open, but some sections of other lines have become tourist routes such as at Vişeu and Moldoviţa, the latter running a former forestry steam locomotive through attractive scenery.

The Transylvania region of Romania with a narrow-gauge forestry railway 0-8-0T locomotive seen in June 1995 at Borsec, when the railway was still in operation. The line had been extended to the mineral water bottling plant at Borsec in 1955. *Vincent Corasi*

Slovakia's forestry railways were once important with over 745 miles (1,200km) of lines in some 40 locations. An 82-mile (132km) network of forestry lines based around Čierny Balog was one of the last to close in 1982, but the tourist potential of such lines has been recognised and a section reopened as a heritage railway using steam traction.

Slovenia had a number of lines of various gauges, including an international line that once connected Trieste in Italy to Isola d'IstrIa in Slovenia that closed in 1935. Other shorter lines have also closed.

Spain had a number of important narrow-gauge industrial lines, which included the Orconera iron ore line running to Bilbao's docks and the Ojos Negros mine line running to Sagunto steelworks near Valencia. One of the larger networks was the Rio Tinto Railway, which consisted of 186 miles (300km) of 3ft 6in line that ran to a sea pier at Huelva. The pier closed in 1975, but is still in existence, whilst the remaining rail routes closed in 1984. Although primarily a freight line, the railway once conveyed miners and the general public between its 12 stations, and most of its 143 locomotives were British built. A number of locomotives survive, and a section has been retained as a heritage railway.

On the passenger side, lines in the Basque Country had been proposed for closure by General Franco, but he died before this could be implemented. Today, the luxury 'El Transcantábrico Gran Lujo' runs over these lines. Elsewhere, with the exception of some mostly commuter routes, passenger lines became run-down and there have been many closures, with some routes being turned into the 'Via Verde' network of paths and greenways.

Catalonian records (see 1974 table page 54) provide examples of the many closed narrow-gauge railways once found at that time in just one part of Spain. Girona (Gerona) was the starting point of three narrow-gauge railways, each of which had their own station in the city and two were of different narrow-gauges. Both were of a different gauge to the main line, which itself was of a different gauge to that of most of Europe. Perhaps only the Edmondson tickets were consistent. Narrow-gauge lines outside the main urban areas were mostly closed, beginning from the Spanish Civil War in the 1930s. The opportunity for some railways to become tourist attractions in this popular holiday region was not taken.

Gerona (Girona) station in Spain showing the 'Jefe de Estacion' station masters office, station bell hook and clock mount. Although closed in July 1969 and narrow-gauge track to Olot removed, the building seen here in September 1982 still survives. *Author*

A grand doorway to the impressive Tortosa–la Cava Railway station building at Tortosa in Spain seen in September 1982. The 16-mile (26km) metre-gauge line opened in 1926 and was an early user of diesel railcars but closed in January 1968. *Author*

An unlined tunnel on the metre gauge rack railway that led to the Spanish abbey at Montserrat, seen in September 1989. The railway opened in 1892 and closed in 1957, but traffic congestion led to a new line being opened in 2003. *Author*

Line	Gauge	Length	Opened	Closed
Manresa–Olvan	Metre	28m (46km)	1885	1974
Olvan–Guardiola	Metre	13m (21km)	1904	1972
Guardiola–el Clot del Moro	2ft	7m (11km)	1924	1963
Sant Feliu de Guíxols–Girona	2ft 6in	25m (40km)	1924	1969
Girona–Flaçà–Palamós	2ft 6in	30m (49km)	1921	1956
El Pont Major–Banyoles	2ft 6in	9m (14km)	1928	1956
Girona–Olot	Metre	34m (55km)	1911	1969
Mollerssa–Balaguer–Menàrguens	Metre	17m (28km)	1905	1951
Reus–Salou	Metre	5m (8km)	1887	1970
Tortosa–la Cava	Metre	17m (27km)	1926	1968
Montserrat rack railway (original line)	Metre	6m (9km)	1892	1957
Arles–Prats de Molló	Metre	12m (20km)	n/a	1936–9
Manyaques–Sant Llorenç de Cerdans	Metre	6m (9km)	n/a	1936–9
Perpignan (Perpinyà)–Tuïr	Metre	10m (16km)	n/a	1936–9
Perpignan (Perpinyà)–el Barcarès	Metre	14m (23km)	n/a	1936–9
Pià–Ribesaltes	Metre	13m (21km)	n/a	1936–9
Onda–el Grau de Castelló	2ft 6in	18m (29km)	1890	1963
Vila-real–el Grau de Borriana	2ft 6in	7m (11km)	1907	1963
Borriana–la Vilavella	Metre	6m (9km)	1926	1939
Vaiència–Natzaret	Metre	4m (6km)	1912	1957
Castelló de la Ribera–la Pobla Llarga	Metre	4m (6km)	1893	1931
Carcaixent–Dénia	Metre	41m (66km)	1884	1974
Alcoi–Gandia	Metre	33m (53km)	1893	1969
Jumilla-Villena–Muro del Comtat	Metre	62m (100km)	1909	1969

Switzerland provided a network of narrow-gauge lines and there have been few significant closures compared to many neighbouring countries. However, a handful of mostly electric urban lines have closed, together with a small number of rural lines such as the Rigi Scheidegg Railway, which closed in 1931. The 'Glacier Express' originally used a route through the Furka Pass that passed the Rhone Glacier until a new tunnel was opened in 1981. A heritage railway has reopened the abandoned pass route.

Ukraine had many narrow-gauge lines converted to the broad Soviet gauge after the Second World War, whilst remaining narrow-gauge lines used Soviet equipment. By the 1990s, most remaining loss-making narrow-gauge lines had been closed, but three narrow-gauge routes, including the 80-mile (130km) line from Haivoron, remained. In March 2020, all regular passenger services were suspended and complete closure of the remaining lines is likely after the Russian invasion.

Forestry railways were once extensive, one having a network of lines covering over 280 miles (450km) of track. A couple remain and, at Skole, a logging railway known as the 'Carpathian Tram' is still used to convey forestry workers and some tourists in motorised converted road vehicles. Almost all industrial lines, with the exception of some peat railways, are closed. Children's railways survive and a few tourist sections are proposed, but in 2022 there were few remaining operating railways.

Wales and England had many industrial and mineral narrow-gauge lines, and the Woolwich Arsenal Railway

The Talyllyn Railway in Wales was the first line in the world to be preserved as a heritage railway by volunteers in 1951. A train is seen here at Towyn, in June 1999, with a coach from the Gyn Valley Tramway, a defunct Welsh line that closed in 1935. *Author*

was the largest and most complex narrow-gauge railway network in Britain, with about 150 miles (241km) of line. There were only a few narrow-gauge public passenger lines, of various gauges and distinctive character. All the narrow-gauge passenger lines eventually closed, starting with the original Ravenglass & Eskdale Railway in 1913, the Southwold Railway in 1929 and ending with the Ashover line in 1950. One of the most famous lines to close was the Ffestiniog Railway, which, together with many others, starting with the Talyllyn Railway, have subsequently been restored and reopened as a heritage line.

The iconic lost Lynton & Barnstaple Railway

The most significant narrow-gauge line yet to be fully reopened in Britain is the Lynton & Barnstaple Railway. The 19½-mile (31km) 1ft 11½in line ran from Lynton on the North Devon coast to Barnstaple. The railway opened in 1898, but as a result of the rugged terrain

encountered, crossing the shoulder of Exmoor, this resulted in construction costs being twice what had been anticipated with many engineering works. This bankrupted the contractor, but provided a delightfully scenic railway.

Winter traffic was disappointing, and closure came with real sadness in September 1935. A note at the time said, 'Perchance the railway is not dead but sleepeth'. A section of the line has since been reopened at Woody Bay, with long-term plans to reopen much more of this iconic railway.

The mystery of *Lew* the disappearing locomotive

After the closure of the Lynton & Barnstaple Railway, one locomotive survived. This was the Manning Wardle-built 2-6-2T called *Lew*. Just ten years old, it was sold in 1935 and, following its use in dismantling track, it was transported in 1936 on the SS *Sabor* to the railway-connected port of Pernambuco, now called Recife, in Brazil. Mysteriously, *Lew* then disappeared and was never seen again.

The letters 'ALC' had been painted on the locomotive for its transhipment. There are a number of possible interpretations of these initials, including a generic shipping term for Latin America, an Argentinian importing company and a Brazilian sugar company.

There were sugar mills in the Recife region and, until 1935, there had been growth in the Brazilian sugar industry, but *Lew* had a relatively small coal bunker and sugar plantation locomotives in this area ran on bagasse, a waste product of sugar cane. Bagasse has a smaller energy value than coal and ideally required a large tender, together with a spark-arresting chimney. *Lew* therefore may not have been ideally suited for use at a sugar mill without modifications.

As soon as *Lew* arrived in Brazil, statistics also show that, due largely to the Great Depression, sugar output declined and by 1938 had almost halved. It was, therefore, likely that if *Lew* was ever used on such a railway, it soon became surplus to requirements. A similar decline beset the coffee industry and support the conjecture that *Lew* was sold on again in 1939.

There are other possible leads as to what might have eventually happened to *Lew* after it arrived at Recife. One was a report that it worked on a coffee plantation near São Louís in Brazil until it was finally scrapped, after years of disuse, in 1957. The facts do not entirely substantiate this, as this was not a coffee-producing area and appears to have had no such railway-served plantations. Whilst the port of Recife was a staging post and it would have been possible for *Lew* to be shipped back north to São Louís, it is more likely it would have gone south to Salvador or Rio de Janeiro, which were the final ports of call for the SS *Sabor*.

Another possible lead is that *Lew* was sold on to a forestry or timber railway in Argentina, is supported by a number of wider factors. Recife was an important staging post for port destinations in Argentina. Forestry was not regulated, and statistics show forestry production was rapidly increasing in 1939 as Argentina geared its industry up to being more self-sufficient during the Second World War.

About 10 tons of wood were required to obtain one ton of charcoal and large amounts of charcoal were being used in the blast furnaces of Argentina's iron and steel industry. Whilst charcoal was an inefficient fuel, at this time Argentinian coal supplies were mostly low grade and some distance from the industrial areas. Consequently, vast tracts of forest were being felled.

Increasing numbers of small producers with short narrow-gauge lines were the result of the growing timber demand. They frequently used second-hand locomotives and stock, because their lifespan was limited by the local supply of trees. Some had rough track, weak structures and sharp bends, unsuited for a locomotive such as *Lew*. However, the majority of lines were ideally suited and 1ft 11½in was the most commonly used forestry railway gauge.

The lines were worked by wood-burning locomotives. Wood also has a smaller energy value than coal and *Lew* would again have had a limited range without modification, so use on one of the many relatively short logging lines would have matched its wood-burning capabilities.

Argentinian iron ore was of low quality and the iron and steel industries were heavily dependent on the use of scrap metal. Argentina developed a serious shortage and records for 1939 show large amounts of scrap metal being imported. *Lew* could have been amongst those statistics.

A reputable report of the locomotive's frame being seen on a loaded freight train, somewhere in South America, is of significance. It is questionable whether the locomotive would have been taken apart to this extent simply for transportation, but more probable that the boiler may have been separated from the frame for new use at an establishment requiring steam power and may therefore have survived longer than the rest of the locomotive.

There has been a lack of actual photographic evidence of *Lew*, including in any modified, or disassembled form, anywhere in South America. Early scrapping of the locomotive may be one reason, but equally this may well be due to *Lew* operating in areas where photography was not commonplace, particularly during the Second World War.

In early 2020, I visited some former logging railways in Argentina that were once served by 1ft 11½ins tracks. At one site, a steam operated saw mill building retained some difficult-to-extract equipment, but elsewhere nothing remained. At all sites, the railway elements had long been completely removed, and even the sleepers had been taken up for firewood. There was no railway stock of any significance, or any abandoned boilers to be seen. It became evident that, unlike some of the closed main line railways, logging railway stock and equipment had been comprehensively sold off after closure.

Today, a number of preserved narrow-gauge locomotives can be found in South America. These do not include *Lew* and one fact is sadly very likely – that however, or wherever, the locomotive ended its days, it has in my view been scrapped, but perchance it sleepeth somewhere and may yet be found. A replica locomotive called *Lyd* was built in Britain and a lookalike called *Camila* can be seen working on the 'End of the World Railway' in Argentina.

Very few British built narrow-gauge locomotives are still to be found in various conditions in South America. Sadly, this is not the cab of *Lew* but of a German narrow-gauge locomotive once used in remote Patagonia and seen near Punta Arenas in March 2020. *Author*

CHAPTER 7

LOST ISLAND RAILWAYS

Unique railways were often developed on islands as the sea divide meant that there was often no real need to conform with the mainland railways. As many islands were not heavily populated, lines were sometimes relatively cheaply built and frequently to narrow-gauge. The lines on some islands were of a relatively short distance and, whilst island railways have undergone differing fortunes, many small islands have lost their railways.

Baltic islands

The railways on the Swedish island of Gotland were completed by 1921 and consisted of a network of 2ft 11ins narrow-gauge lines linking to the main port at Visby. In 1962, the last section on Gotland closed. Öland, which was just off the coast of Sweden, also had a similar narrow-gauge line running from tip to toe and a causeway section still links to the mainland. Although no longer a public passenger line, residents can run their own stock on the remaining part of this route, but a new road connection has resulted in the loss of rail traffic.

A network of metre-gauge lines was built on the Danish island of Bornholm, but all had closed by 1968.

A number of military railways can also be found, for example on the island of Saaremaa. German lines were built during the First World War and survived until 1940. The island of Usedom is now divided between Germany and Poland, but much of the original main railway bridge to the island was destroyed during the Second World War. The German island of Rügen had two separate narrow-gauge lines until closure of most remaining lines by 1970, although a section survives as a heritage railway.

A railway that has been closed for many years was the unique line to the Russian island of Kotlin. The railway linked to St Petersburg, some 20 miles (48km) away, and ran, in part, over the relatively shallow frozen Baltic Sea in this area during the winter months. In the spring, as the ice melted, the railway was closed and the track removed.

Channel Islands

In Jersey, the Jersey Eastern Railway was a 6¾-mile (11km) standard-gauge line that closed in 1929. The 7¾-mile (12km) 3ft 6in gauge Jersey Railway ran from a separate station in St Helier and closed in 1936. Many of the well-built stations on this line have survived.

St Aubin station in Jersey seen in October 1998. The building survived a devastating fire that destroyed most of the coaching stock and resulted in the closure of the railway in 1936. Railway connecting ferries once ran from both France and England. *Author*

The Guernsey Railway opened with steam trams in 1879 and was converted to electric traction in 1892. Bus services cut into revenue and the line closed in 1934. At St Peter Port, a window in the remaining tram shed is seen in May 2015. *Author*

A number of military railways were built during the German occupation during the Second World War, but all lines are now closed.

At St Peter Port in Guernsey, the standard-gauge Guernsey Railway, which was mostly a roadside tramway, closed in 1934. On Alderney, a quarry line, opened in 1847, is now used as a heritage railway.

Corsica

The island still has a metre-gauge system, much of it passing through stunning scenery. A line along the east coast from Casamozza to Porto-Vecchio, where the old terminus still survives, was damaged in 1943 during the Second World War, when eighteen bridges were blown up and never reopened. A number of proposals to close the entire network have been resisted.

Cyprus

The 2ft 6in Cyprus Government Railway operated along the north of the island. Opening in its entirety by 1905, the 67-mile (108km) line ran from Famagusta on the east coast and served Nicosia, by a stone built central station, en route to Morphou, before terminating at Evrychou. The line was well used during the Second World War, but the section west of Nicosia Airport closed in 1948 and the remaining section to Famagusta was closed in 1951. Two separate mineral railways survived until the 1970s. Evrychou station survives and houses the Cyprus Railway Museum.

Isle of Man

Douglas is the main port of entry to the Isle of Man and the 3ft narrow-gauge steam railway once ran boat trains to connect with passenger ships. At its peak, about 70 miles (113km) of narrow-gauge tramway and railway were in operation on the island. Railway lines from Douglas to Peel and Ramsey were closed in September 1968, but the remaining Douglas–Port Erin steam line, the Douglas-Ramsey electric tramway, together with the Snaefell Mountain Railway and a few other short heritage routes, are amongst lines that remain open with remarkable historic stock.

Corsica has a number of lightly used stations, whilst some stock on the island was purchased second hand from narrow-gauge lines that closed in France. A Billiard trailer dating from 1938 was still surviving at L'Île-Rousse in April 2003. *Author*

Isle of Wight

Ryde Pier developed as the key entry to the island, which became a popular holiday destination in Victorian times. There was once a network of about 55 miles (90km) of standard-gauge railway, but with a restricted loading gauge serving the main settlements. Closures began in the 1950s and all remaining lines were proposed for closure in the Beeching Report, with surviving lines closing at the end of 1966. However, the Ryde Pier–Shanklin link was reprieved and electrified, whilst the Isle of Wight Steam Railway's Smallbrook Junction–Wootton line was brought back into service as a heritage railway.

Malta

The 7½-mile (12km) metre-gauge line opened in 1883 from Valletta to Notable and was extended to Museum in 1900. The line had some significant engineering works, including tunnels to enable the railway to serve the centre of Valletta. Many of the stations were also substantial stone buildings. Ten locomotives were used over the lifetime of the railway, which for many years was busy and was used by an army barracks located beside the line. The railway closed in 1931, an early victim to a competing tram line for part of the route and to Malta's buses.

The Isle of Wight's main railway link to the mainland is via Ryde. The pier once covered a larger area and until 1969 provided a tramway in addition to the railway. This has resulted in rusting iron beams and legs no longer in use. The pier is seen here in August 2011. *Author*

Valletta with the Floriana Tunnel seen from the old terminus station in September 2000. The tunnel ran under Malta's capital's fortifications. After closure in 1931 the tunnel was used as an air raid shelter during the Second World War. *Author*

Birkirkara, originally called Birchircara, in Malta seen October 2009, the station was enlarged in 1910 to become the only two-storey station on the line. In 1884 a feast day celebration saw almost 7,000 passengers use the station. A carriage located here is the lone surviving stock of the railway. *Author*

Majorca

Some lines remain, but an extensive network of mostly metre-gauge railways once served the island, centring on Palma's old terminus, where British signalling equipment from Ransom & Rapier of Ipswich could still be seen in operation in 1974. Agricultural freight once used the lines, before tourism became important. The 38-mile (62km) service to Santanyí closed in 1964. The 27-mile (43km)

The island railway in Majorca once ran rather frail looking 4 wheeled railcars and four wheeled trailers, as seen at this unrecorded rural location on the island. New diesel railcars had replaced these by the 1970s. *Colour-Rail*

El Arenal with a substantial disused single span bridge built in 1917 over a dry gorge and seen in September 1980. The nearby 65ft (20m) high seven-arched viaduct at Llucmajor is the largest abandoned railway structure on Majorca. *Author*

Above: The Peloponnesus in October 2008 at Isthmos. The metre-gauge line was a casualty of the financial crisis in Greece this led to the cessation of regular services on most of the remaining network by 2011. *Author*

Below: The Corinth Canal bridge in Greece, which opened in 1892, seen here in October 2008. The original bridge was destroyed by Germans in 1942 and railway stock deliberately crashed into the canal. By 1948 the bridge and canal were restored to use. *Author*

line to Felanitx closed in 1968 and the 19-mile (30km) Manacor–Artà line closed in 1977. At this time, the remaining railways were life expired and further closures were a real possibility. The surviving lines were subsequently modernised and routes to Manacor and Sa Pobla reopened in 2001, whilst the scenic railway to Sóller also remains.

North Sea islands
A number of islands in the North Sea are located close to the mainland and once operated narrow-gauge railways. Off the German coast, a line ran from 1893 to 1939 on the island of Amrum. A wooden causeway with a railway linked to the island of Juist from 1899 to 1982, whilst a freight line on the island of Baltrum ran from 1949 to 1985. Off the British coast, the island of Orford Ness incorporated a secret military establishment and a railway, opened during the First World War, served part of the island until it was closed in 1971.

The Peloponnese
This part of Greece technically became an island when the Corinth Canal cut it from the mainland. The area once contained the largest metre-gauge system in Europe of over 500 miles (800km), with a line skirting the entire

region. The Greek government spent money refurbishing and updating the narrow-gauge railway, but then the financial crisis effectively closed it down by 2011. In 2020, a new standard-gauge line on the north coast opened.

Sardinia

Until 2009, a train freight ferry ran from Italy to Golfo Aranci, where rail sidings still exist, but elsewhere the links to the docks at Cagliari have been severed. Some lines through beautiful and remote parts of the island lost regular services in 1997, but four lines extending to about 250 miles (400km) still retain infrequent summer tourist trains. Much of the overall network of standard

In Sardinia at Cagliari, disused track is seen leading to dock quaysides in April 2003. Train ferry links once connected the island to Italy and whilst much of the network remains, most port connections have been removed, such as seen here. *Author*

and narrow-gauge lines remains, although some link and branch lines have been closed including to Ozieri, Calasetta and Ales. A number of closed station buildings survive, together with many other railway remains, including some attractive viaducts, throughout the island.

Sicily

This largest of the Mediterranean islands was once served by an extensive standard-gauge main line, secondary and narrow-gauge network. Several lines were originally constructed to convey sulphur from numerous mines. Most of the dozen or so narrow-gauge railways had closed by 1985, including two long lines leading from Palermo. Surprisingly, even in the 1990s some remaining narrow-gauge steam locomotives were still awaiting dismantling, but unfortunately no line was to reopen as a tourist route.

Palermo in Sicily with the overall roof supports at the terminus of the Palermo–San Carlo narrow-gauge line. This was the first narrow-gauge railway on the island opening in 1886 but closed in 1959. The building remains are seen in October 2009. *Author*

On the remaining standard-gauge network freight is much reduced, whilst some secondary lines are rather run-down and may be threatened with closure. In spite of volcanic damage on occasions, the only remaining narrow-gauge railway runs on a circular route around Mount Etna. The last remaining passenger train ferry in the Mediterranean still operates on the short crossing to Italy at Messina and, in 2022, sleeping cars still linked Palermo with Rome.

WORLD'S MOST NORTHERLY LOST RAILWAY

Spitsbergen

The most northerly lost railway of significance in the world was a 1½-mile (2.4km) Norwegian-owned line at Kings Bay on the island of Spitsbergen. The steam-operated railway connected coal mines to the harbour, but due to Arctic weather was only used during the summer. Opened in 1917, the line closed in 1963, after an accident in the coal mine. A locomotive and some wagons still survive.

Spitsbergen, part of Svalbard in northern Norway, is the most northerly island with a significant disused railway. The line closed in 1963, but a remaining narrow-gauge 0-4-0T locomotive dating from 1909 and some stock are seen here in August 2013. *Rob Oo*

CHAPTER 8

THE BALTIC AND BEYOND

Freezing winter conditions, including heavy snow, short daylight hours and mountain terrain made railway construction difficult in some of the more remote environments of northern Europe. The harsh operating conditions and scant population enfeebled the finances of a number of lines, but some also served isolated rural needs, or tapped into timber and mineral reserves, and a network of lines developed.

Denmark

The higher population density makes Denmark different from other Scandinavian countries, and the ease of construction on generally flat countryside resulted in an extensive standard-gauge network being established. Denmark's islands were connected in the 1960s by five passenger train ferries, but new fixed links connecting the chief islands to the mainland have replaced the earlier train ferries.

The railways were economically managed; for example, dieselisation began in 1927, but was not completed until 1970 when most remaining steam locomotives were worn out. At the same time, railcars were introduced on secondary lines. Nevertheless, the previously extensive network has seen many closures over the years, particularly in rural areas. By way of example, the railways on the island of Langeland closed

Before a fixed link between Denmark and Sweden was opened, Copenhagen had train ferries. A Copenhagen port building and clock tower, once surrounded by railways, survived the regeneration of this part of the port. The building is seen in September 2001. *Author*

in 1962 and a line that once conveyed human waste from Copenhagen to the island of Amager closed in 1992.

Whilst attempts by private operators were made to reopen some lines for freight in the 1990s, these were mostly unsuccessful. After closure, many station buildings, some of which were relatively modern, have been used as dwellings. Several closed branch lines use rail cycles for recreational use on the old track.

Relatively few narrow-gauge passenger lines were constructed, but a number of narrow-gauge industrial and agricultural lines once operated, including networks associated with peat extraction and sugar beet factories. All were closed by the 1960s, including the Faxe Railway which shared part of its route with the standard-gauge line.

Left: Copenhagen with a disused freight train ferry berth, seen in September 2001. The use of train ferries was once considerable and railway services crossed from the harbour tracks here in Denmark to Sweden. *Author*

Below: Aarhus in Denmark with a goods building that was closed in 2000. The attractive administrative building, associated with the adjoining closed freight yard is seen in June 2000 and still remains. *Author*

Finland

Finland was until 1917 part of the Russian Empire and adopted the 5ft gauge. Finland's population is sparse, but forests provided timber freight and poor roads resulted in a network of railways radiating out from what became, in 1919, the architectural masterpiece of Helsinki station.

There was only a handful of narrow-gauge lines and most of these were privately owned. They provided isolated lines to fill gaps in the railway network, sometimes connecting rivers and lakes. All are closed, but a few were converted to the 5ft Russian-gauge and a section of one is used as a heritage railway.

Some of the 5ft lines are closed, some have axle-load restrictions and others are freight only, including three lines crossing into northern Russia and to a number of Baltic ports. Whilst by 2020 there had been relatively few complete line closures, the line north of Savonlinna was severed by a new road and the Nurmes line is threatened with closure. A line to Kemijärvi in Lapland was closed in 2006, but protests saw it reopened in 2008.

Germany, Estonia, Latvia, Lithuania, Poland and Russia

The coasts of Germany, Poland and, at one time, much of the Soviet Union, abut the Baltic and a relatively dense and partly strategic network of lines developed. This included a number of narrow-gauge lines, some of which were converted to standard-gauge. In addition to freight use, the lines also enabled troops and supplies to be sent to some of the ice-free Baltic ports. The Second World War saw damage to the railways and also resulted in suspension of international services.

A Finnish 5ft broad-gauge 4-6-2 locomotive No 1008 seen in a rusting condition at Ongar in September 2016. The locomotive was withdrawn in the 1970s and was one of a dozen Finnish locomotives that were imported into the UK; they were mostly never used due to their gauge difference. *Author*

Haapsalu station with a locomotive on the rusting track seen in March 2021. The Estonian coastal resort and spa town was once a favourite with the Russian tsars. The station closed to passengers in 1995 and freight in 2014 but remains as a museum. *Andrei Nekrassov/Almy*

After the war, through services did not run to East Germany for a while, whilst the current Baltic states of Estonia, Latvia and Lithuania became independent of the Soviet Union in 1991. Since that time, many branch lines to the smaller Baltic coastal towns have closed. By way of just a few examples, in Estonia the narrow-gauge line to Virtsu closed in 1968, that to Tallinn port 1971 and to Ikla in 1975. In 1995, the standard-gauge line to the imperial-styled spa station at Haapsalu closed. The 39-mile (63km) line to Mazirbe in Latvia closed in 1962 and that to Ainaži harbour in 1975. In Poland, a narrow-gauge line to the coast at Mrzeżyno has closed, but at Elblag a broad-gauge canal railway has reopened.

Greenland
The remote area once had a handful of isolated and short mineral lines of various narrow gauges in operation. A line built to transport fish closed in 1971, together with the abandonment of the associated fishing village.

Iceland
The sparsely populated island has never had public passenger services. At Reykjavik, a 2ft 11½in narrow-gauge harbour railway operated between 1913 and 1928, bringing stone from a quarry for the construction of the harbour and breakwaters. Elsewhere, workers were carried on an industrial railway associated with

Reykjavik Harbour Railway was a narrow-gauge line that ran from 1913 until 1928 from a quarry outside the Icelandic city to the harbour. The two German built 0-4-0T locomotives that worked the line have both been preserved. *Minør* is seen here at Reykjavik in June 2013. *Author*

Oslo with a tunnel on a disused branch to the port of Oslo in September 2004; the line closed in 1983. Some tunnels cut through rock in Norway were not lined with bricks, provided the rock was fairly stable. *Author*

the construction of a hydro-electric plant, whilst a large farm was once equipped with an agricultural railway.

Norway

Railway construction through mountainous sections was difficult and some main lines were originally built to a narrow-gauge but have since been converted to standard-gauge. During the Second World War, the German occupation resulted in the construction of new lines, including the planning of a Polar line running south from Narvik to convey iron ore trains to the port

at Oslo, where the ore would be transhipped by sea to Germany. Only about 25 miles (40km) of the line, that was being built by prisoners of war, was completed, but abandoned remains of this section can still be seen.

After the Second World War, there were only about 70 miles (112km) of narrow-gauge line left in operation and in 1962 the last line operated by Norwegian State Railways closed, but a section was converted to heritage use. Closures on the standard-gauge network began in the 1950s and there are now some three dozen or so

Disused track on the 7-mile (12km) Norwegian Ganddal–Ålgård line. Originally a narrow-gauge line, opening in 1924, conversion to standard-gauge failed to save it from closure in 2001. The rusting track is seen at Ganddal in June 2008, although proposals for reopening have been considered. *Author*

The Setesdal Railway was opened in 1896 linking the town of Kristiansand with the Setesdal Valley. The Norwegian line mainly conveyed timber and closed in 1962. A British Dübs locomotive built in 1894 is seen at Beihølen on a heritage section of the line in June 2008. *Author*

closed branch lines. More significant lines were closed in the 1970s and 1980s, whilst closures on a smaller scale continued into the 1990s.

Some lines that have been closed have had bridges removed to assist road transport, although many ex-railway buildings have been retained and some heritage lines have been formed. At the unusually named station at Hell, a new railway bridge has allowed the disused old bridge to be used to experiment with the deterioration of older metal structures.

Sweden

A standard-gauge network developed with a number of railways taking over freight from earlier river and lake ferry routes. Electrification was introduced early on, but branch lines have closed throughout Sweden, including a line at Stockholm that was built during the Second World War to convey wounded troops from the docks to a hospital. The line closures have been more extensive to the south of the country where the network was easier to build and once also more extensive. The remote and lengthy Inland Line to the north of the country was reprieved in the 1990s, after a massive petition against closure. Of the standard-gauge lines that have closed, rail cycles are used on a disused line near Lund and on some other closed branch lines.

The country once had over thirty narrow-gauge passenger lines of various gauges. Decline of the narrow-gauge railways came before the Second World War and lines have either been closed or converted into standard-gauge. Lines at Gothenburg survived until the 1960s, whilst an electrified narrow-gauge network at Stockholm remains in use, together with some heritage lines. A once extensive number of narrow-gauge forestry, industrial and mineral lines conveying copper and iron ore in particular have also closed. It is of interest that a private iron ore line at Oxelösund successfully operated steam turbine locomotives from 1930 to 1970.

When tourist traffic was heavy and hotel accommodation was full at popular resorts, the state railway at one time allowed passengers to use sleeping cars as hotel accommodation. At peak times, as many as twenty sleeping cars parked in sidings could be used as a hotel annexe.

A tunnel through a rock outcrop on the Dellenbanan railway line between Hybo and Hudiksvall in Sweden, seen in August 2008. The branch to Delsbo closed in 1968, but parts are used by a heritage railway and by tourists using cycles converted for use on rails. *Kildor*

CHAPTER 9

RUSSIA AND FORMER COMMUNIST COUNTRIES

Whilst Russia spans both Europe and Asia, I have included it in the European section as most lost lines are here. The Russian network gradually developed and, by 1912, the Trans–Siberian line advertised passenger trains taking 11 days from Moscow, and via a ferry crossing to Tokyo. From 1914, Wagon Lits coaches were used on the route, but the Russian Revolution intervened to close the line to foreigners until 1930.

The Second World War

During the Second World War, Germany invaded the Soviet Union and managed to convert thousands of miles of railway from the Russian 5ft gauge to standard-gauge. As the war continued, lines suffered considerable damage, for example Stalingrad station was almost completely destroyed. However, main lines were reopened once again in Russian-gauge as the tide of war changed in the Soviet Union's favour.

Elsewhere in Eastern Europe during the Second World War, some lines were shrouded in infamy during the German occupation of countries. Large numbers of Jewish prisoners were transported by rail to their death in the Nazi death camps during the Second World War, an estimated 6 million. The most accurate figures of those exterminated rely very much on the records of the German and other railways, with each train of cattle or goods trucks eventually conveying between 4,000 to 7,000 victims to the camps. Without the railways' capacity to transport large numbers to the extermination camps, the shocking scale of the killing would not have been possible.

WORLD'S MOST INFAMOUS LOST RAILWAYS

The first trains of mostly Jewish families arrived at Auschwitz–Birkenau in 1942 and, from then on, several trains arrived daily carrying Jews from almost every country in Europe to the centrally located extermination camps in German-occupied Poland. Initially, arrivals at Auschwitz–Birkenau were unloaded on the main line at Oświęcim station, from where the prisoners were then walked to the extermination camp. However, special sidings and lines were built by prisoners at Auschwitz, in preparation for the arrival of more people destined for forced labour, or extermination, during 1944. Railway tracks were laid through the 'gates of hell' and right into an unloading area in the concentration camp. The track remains today as a shameful reminder of the Holocaust.

Other lines and stations were also used specifically to convey people to their death, and at Treblinka and Buchenwald disused spurs laid directly towards the concentration camps are still visible. A memorial track and platform are to be found at Grunewald station commemorating the 50,000 Jewish prisoners deported from this Berlin station alone during the Second World War, whilst similar memorials are to be found at Łódź and other railway stations throughout Europe.

Auschwitz-Birkenau rail yard in Poland with the 'Gate of Death' in the background seen in May 2011. The railway was built by Jewish prisoners to increase throughput to the gas chambers. Opened in 1940, the camp was liberated by Soviet troops in 1945. *John Benton*

WORLD'S MOST BRUTALLY BUILT TRANS-POLAR RAILWAY – STALIN'S DEATH RAILWAY

What became known as Stalin's Death Railway was planned to run across Siberia from Salekhard to Igarka. This was 806 miles (1,297km) of 5ft-gauge line and some 28 stations and 106 goods sidings were proposed. It was not originally possible to cross the Ob and Yenisei rivers, so ferries were ordered for use in the summer, while tracks on ice embankments were to span the frozen river surfaces in winter.

The line was under construction from 1947 to 1953 but was never completed. Built by prisoners from the Gulag labour camps, it is estimated that perhaps 100,000 prisoners could have died during the railway's construction. Thousands perished in the freezing winter conditions, or from diseases during the summer. There were many problems with the mostly hand-built route. Frost distorted structures in winter, and embankments and bridges settled in boggy ground during the thaw and short hot summer.

Although built in a remote area, there were several reasons for its construction. The railway was designed to facilitate the export of minerals from northern Siberia, to provide better links to the east where there was concern about Japan's influence, to provide work for prisoners, to open up a remote area and to provide an east-west trans-Polar route linking with existing railways.

On Stalin's death in 1953, construction of the line was abandoned, but by this time some 434 miles (700km) had been built. A western part of the line between Salekhard and Nadym was already in use, but sections of track further east, including locomotives and rolling stock, were simply abandoned.

In the 1990s, the Salekhard–Nadym section was dismantled, but frost heave and poor construction had already seen much of the line fall apart after closure and metal bridges were removed for scrap. However, natural gas in the area has led to some parts of the route being rebuilt and reopened, although a branch to Yamburg, that ran over part of the original route, has been out of use since 2015.

A rusting Stalin Soviet era locomotive on the Salekhard–Igarka railway, cut into three to ensure that it was disabled. The remains of the railway are seen at Kranoyarsk Krai in remote Siberia in July 1991. *David Litschel/Alamy*

The damage to the Soviet Union and other Eastern European railways caused by the German invasion resulted in a decline of passenger use for a number of years after the war. However, Stalin was a keen advocate of railways and a number of new lines were built after the war. One of his lines was of particular infamy.

State Control

The railways were a dominant part of the Soviet Union, both for military and economic reasons. They allowed most party comrades to travel at reduced or free rates, whilst trains often had a high complement of staff, including security guards. There were many industrial lines and passenger services were subsidised by freight revenues. The railways were a monopoly, subject to central government five-year plans, and competition was strictly regulated. There was little railway duplication, roads were poor and car ownership low. However, this did not always prevent the closure of some branch lines. Closure decisions were taken by the state and often involved little prior consultation with the rail users of the lines concerned.

The Circum-Baikal Railway

The original Trans-Siberian route was cut by Lake Baikal and a British-built ice-breaking train ferry made the connection across the lake between Port Baikal and Mysovaya in the early 1900s. The lake froze in winter and, when the ice became too thick for the ship to cross, tracks were laid on top of the ice, being removed in the spring thaw. A direct link around the southern shore of the lake was opened by 1905 resulting in closure of the ferry service.

In 1949, a single line across the mountains was upgraded to main-line standards, making the original Circum-Baikal route on the northern shore largely redundant. The section to the north of Port Baikal towards Irkutsk had track removed in 1950 in connection with the Irkutsk dam, which flooded much of the railway, but some embankments remain visible. The remaining section of the original Circum-Baikal Railway route on the northern shore from Kultuk to Port Baikal was retained with a single track used as a scenic branch line.

Disused tunnel No 18 on the Russian Circum-Baikal line seen in August 2011. Closure of this section of line was proposed in the 1980s but reducing the line to a single-track branch has resulted in a number of abandoned railway works. *Artem Svetlov*

Chernobyl

Although originally part of the Soviet Union and now in Ukraine, the Chernobyl disaster of 1986 resulted in the closure of lines in what became the nuclear power station's radioactive exclusion zone. This included a dozen passenger stations that have all remained abandoned since the accident. Radioactive contamination was high and contaminated rolling stock in the area has just been left to rust away, but in 2021 part of the exclusion zone was reconnected to the main network.

Russian narrow-gauge

Some estimates indicate that the Soviet Union once had about 60,000 miles (100,000km) of narrow-gauge railways. Of this, many were of 2ft 5½ins gauge, but there were also metre and 2ft-gauge lines. They were mostly built for industrial, mineral, logging, or the extraction of peat purposes, but passenger services were also provided. The closure of non-passenger lines was not always subject to central state control, but most passenger lines have closed, completely or in part.

The Russian government's main railway operator has also closed all its narrow-gauge lines.

Some industrial, peat and logging narrow-gauge lines remain and a very small number of railways still operate passenger services, often in areas with poor roads, or little other public transport. For example, the Alapayevsk network mainly conveys timber, but in 2020 a sleeping car service ran to the village of Sankino, whilst the system in the town of Kirovo-Chepetsk, once owned by the mining industry, is hoping to develop tourist services. In 2020, Russia still produced new passenger coaches and container flats for narrow-gauge railways and there remain a number of children's railways.

The break-up of the Soviet Union

The dissolution of the Soviet Union in the 1990s saw the division of the former Soviet railways into the new state railways. The upheaval resulted in a decline in railway freight that broadly halved in seven years, partly due to a decline in heavy industry and partly due to the fact that communist policy was

Narrow-gauge towards the end of its life in Russia. Diesel locomotive TU4-1984 at Kupanskoe station on the Pereslavl Railway is seen in October 2002. Although closed in 2004, a railway museum has been created at Pereslavl. *Artem Svetlov*

to use rail transport for freight after the oil crisis of the 1970s. Passenger numbers also fell as traditional links were cut and new international boundaries were established. In some cases, years of central control had done little to improve services and large parts of the network suffered from under investment. Moldova, even in 2020, still had a number of railway carriages with wooden seats.

In many former Soviet Union countries, the new freedoms did not always work in favour of the railways. Roads were improved, deregulation saw competing bus routes expand and car and lorry use increased. As a result, states such as Estonia, Latvia, Lithuania and Ukraine have all seen closures of narrow-gauge railways and standard-gauge branch lines and secondary routes. Whilst abandoned Russian rolling stock was stored in Belarus and disused Soviet railway tunnels are found at Kiev, tensions between Ukraine and Russia elsewhere saw links from Ukraine to Crimea being closed in 2014, following Russia's annexation of Crimea. In the eastern Ukraine border areas, the conflict with Russia has also led to line closures.

The fragmentation of the Soviet Union was also bad news for some railways to the south of Russia when lines were cut by new international frontiers. Several lines in some of the newly formed countries in the Caucasus were closed by civil unrest and a number of cross-border lines were closed. After 1993, Armenia only had one direct international passenger service remaining to Georgia and through services to Azerbaijan, Iran and Turkey were discontinued. Fighting again erupted in 2020 between Armenia and Azerbaijan and the fragmentation and disruption have resulted in a significant loss of both passenger and freight traffic.

A similar situation applied to Georgia where the link to South Ossetia and Black Sea resorts was severed in 1992 as a result of war with Russia in the Abkhazia area, which also saw local services cease and some attractive stations abandoned. The 60-mile (97km) section between Sukhumi and Zugdidi was closed and, thus, Georgia's international link to Russia.

In Kyrgyzstan, rail traffic has declined significantly and, whilst rail freight ferries across the Caspian Sea still connect Azerbaijan with Kazakhstan – where, incidentally, there are two closed children's railways – and Turkmenistan, schedules are not very reliable and ships often run only when they are fully loaded.

Former Soviet satellite states

Railway closures have continued in all of the former Soviet satellite states. The reunification of Germany resulted in closures in East Germany, as this part of the network was in poor condition and second-hand cheap cars became available. Some lines in the Czech Republic and more in Slovakia were closed, whilst Hungary announced the closure of all branch lines, but later drew back from this and even reopened some secondary routes. Bulgaria had allowed much track to become in an increasingly poor condition, whilst Romania announced the closure of about 40% of lines, but this figure was later reconsidered.

At Bratislava in Slovakia a cold-water railway port was established, as this was the furthest ships could once travel along the River Danube in winter as it froze beyond this point. Disused freight buildings are seen in September 2019, as the river no longer freezes beyond here today. *Author*

A Hungarian Railways MÁV M61 006 diesel, preserved in its original 1963 livery, with the five-pointed communist star. Although ordered by a communist country, the locomotives incorporated American technology and were built in Sweden. It is seen here in Budapest in October 2018. *Author*

Above: The Danube riverside station at Giurgiu in Romania. Passenger ferries gradually fell out of use after a nearby bridge was opened in 1954. Disused track and an impressive station building remain and are seen here in September 2019. *Author*

Left: Ruse (Rousse) riverside station in Bulgaria on the opposite side of the Danube to Giurgiu, seen in September 2019. Railway freight to the nearby docks remains, but the station is closed. Paddle steamers once connected the two riverside stations. *Author*

One of the largest networks was in Poland and an extensive number of lines were to be found, particularly to the west of the country in what had formally been part of Germany. The network had a growing number of little-used branch lines, but some secondary lines had been electrified in the 1980s. For a while, closures were resisted, but government funding to the railways was cut. A Western-style Beeching cull was eventually undertaken, and neglected and abandoned lines are today found throughout the country.

Russian changes and closures

In 2014, the Russian government transferred the subsidies for many passenger trains to local authorities or cut services. Closure procedures are required and protests aimed at retaining services to remote areas have seen some lines reprieved, but many local railway stations and several passenger services in Russia have been closed or cut back. As a consequence, disused railways are to be found throughout Russia, not only in former 'Cold War' depots, but even an occasional former electrified route. In some parts, old Soviet stock is stored and is just rusting away, whilst in one remote area a disused metal railway bridge was stolen by scrap merchants.

The break-up of Yugoslavia

The railways in the Balkans have also experienced an endless list of closures to secondary and branch lines. The break-up of former Yugoslavia in the 1990s broadly into Serbia, Croatia, Bosnia, Montenegro, Macedonia and Slovenia resulted in civil wars that directly resulted in the closure of a number of lines. Some remaining lines are in a poor state of repair and almost all narrow-gauge routes have closed. A similar position applied in nearby Albania, where all narrow-gauge lines have long closed, and in 2019 no passenger trains ran for three months due to a lack of funds to buy fuel.

Belgrade freight crane on the River Sava, a tributary of the Danube, seen in October 2018. The concrete freight buildings of the Serbian rail-river interchange are no longer in use, but many of the riverside buildings have been converted to leisure uses. *Author*

Belgrade station in October 2018 with a powerful 4-8-0 locomotive formerly used to convey Yugoslavia's Marshal Tito Blue Train. The station opened in 1884, once a stop on the 'Orient Express', it was the main station in Belgrade until its closure in 2018. *Author*

Conflicts continue, Vukovar with the war-torn station in the border region of Croatia. This area was heavily damaged during the Croatian War of Independence in the 1990s during the break-up of Yugoslavia. Although trains still run, the disused passenger station building is seen in October 2018. *Author*

THE MIDDLE EAST

The strategic position of the Middle East resulted in the military and political value of railways soon being realised. This, in turn, gave rise to some railways being sabotaged, the Hejaz Railway attacked by Lawrence of Arabia during the First World War being a well-known example.

The railways were busy during the Second World War and British locomotives and rolling stock supplemented a number of networks during the war. The creation of the Israeli state in 1948, wars and conflict, some still ongoing, have resulted in many closures. Years of war, insurgency, instability and sanctions have caused endless damage and resulted in the closure of railways. Almost all long-distance international passenger train travel between Middle Eastern countries has also been abandoned.

The railways assisted oil development in some countries and tanker trains originally ran from the oil wells to ports and refineries. Steam locomotives were converted from coal to oil fuel and diesel locomotives were introduced early on. The construction of new roads, cheap oil for road transport and an early use of oil pipelines have also resulted in lost lines, but railways remain.

The headlight on a Turkish locomotive at the museum at Camlik in October 2008. Headlights were required as many railway lines had no fences. *Author*

CHAPTER 10

TURKEY – GATEWAY TO THE ORIENT

The strategic position of Turkey, between Europe and Asia, was recognised by Germany, Russia, France and Britain who were all involved in railway projects in the area. The first railway, in what was originally part of the Ottoman Empire, was the British Ottoman Railway dating from 1860. Lines were also built to push forward competing German colonial interests, including the Berlin to Baghdad railway.

After the First World War, the Ottoman Empire collapsed and was replaced by Turkey and other states. Many lines were in a poor condition and a number of military railways used during the war fell out of use.

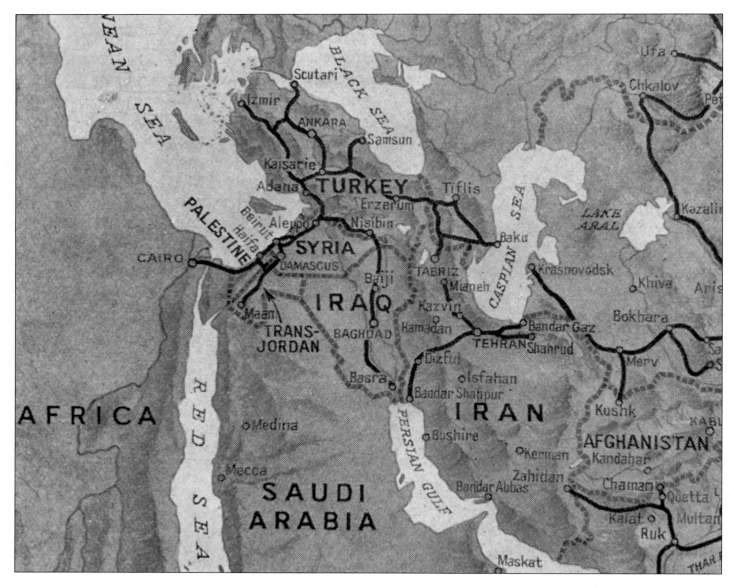

Map showing the pivotal position of the Middle East and Turkey with railway connections to Europe, Asia and Africa in 1945.

In Turkey, the state gradually took over railways and, whilst large areas remained without services, a number of mostly single lines were constructed with the aim of helping to tie the state together.

Crossing the Bosporus

The most famous train from Europe to Turkey was the 'Orient Express' that served Istanbul's Sirkeci station until 1977. Passengers from Europe wishing to travel further east had to cross the Bosporus by ferry to Istanbul's Haydarpaşa station, in Asia, where connecting trains ran through Turkey to countries in the Middle East and Asia.

In 2008, a tunnel linked Sirkeci and Haydarpaşa stations, but the latter station, dating from 1909, was 'temporarily' closed to main-line services in 2013 and long-distance trains currently start from a nearby suburban station. Although there were plans to reopen Haydarpaşa station in 2019, this has not yet materialised and track has been removed for an archaeological dig.

Lost lines of the Taurus Express

Express trains, requiring powerful locomotives, ran trains through Turkey to countries beyond. The train from Istanbul to Baghdad, which first ran in 1930, was known as the 'Taurus Express'. Until 1939, part of the service involved using a bus from Nusaybin to Kirkuk, where a metre-gauge railway line then ran to Baghdad. It was not until 1940 that a through train to Baghdad, on a new direct standard-gauge line, was possible. Links also ran to the Gulf port of Basra, where steamship connections to India were provided.

Restaurant cars were a feature of the Orient and Taurus expresses. The Wagon Lits restaurant cars, towards the end of their service, provided paper tablecloths with scenes from the 'Orient Express'. A salvaged example is seen here. *Author*

Powerful locomotives were required to work on the steep mountainous sections of the Turkish network. Built in 1948, a 2-10-0 No 56337 from the Vulcan Iron Works in the USA is seen preserved at Camlik in October 2008. *Author*

Aleppo was once a junction for international travellers on the 'Taurus Express'. Trains would run to Tripoli in Lebanon, but from here it was also possible to journey much further to Cairo. This would involve a connecting 11-hour bus trip from Tripoli to Haifa. At Haifa, Wagon-Lits ran a connecting service on to El Kantara in Egypt and eventually to Cairo. Other connections included Damascus and Tehran, the latter originally reached by bus running from the north of Baghdad.

A direct coastal line from Tripoli to Cairo, crossing the Suez Canal by a swing bridge, was opened during the Second World War, but political problems after the war, followed by the creation of the state of Israel in 1948, resulted in the cessation of services south of Lebanon. Civil unrest on other parts of the route beyond Turkey first began in 1966 and Wagon-Lits withdrew from the service in 1970. The train continued to run from Turkey to Baghdad via Aleppo with ordinary stock, but after conflict broke out in Iraq the train was suspended in 2003. The 'Taurus Express' still runs on part of the Turkish section.

Other lost international links

A direct line from Turkey to Iran opened in the 1970s and the 'Van Gölü Express' ran from Turkey to Tehran using a rail ferry across Lake Van. With the overthrow of the Shah in 1979, the service ceased its last leg over the lake and into Iran. The optimistically named 'Trans Asia Express' to Tehran was later established but was suspended in 2015. It was replaced by a local train in 2019, but in 2020 the service ceased again as borders were closed due to the coronavirus pandemic.

An international Turkey–Georgia link opened in 2017. This provided a route to Azerbaijan, bypassing the closed link via Armenia. The Kars–Gyumri railway has been closed since the Turkish-Armenia border closed in 1993 and, thus, entry to the former Soviet Union via this route. The railways in this area beyond Turkey have been fragmented due to unrest after the dissolution of the Soviet Union.

Local Turkish closures

Whilst the network was mostly built to standard-gauge, there were two noteworthy Turkish narrow-gauge lines. The 25-mile (41km) Mudanya–Bursa branch was converted to standard-gauge, but it remained uneconomic and closed in 1948, whilst the 23-mile (37km) line Samsun–Çarşamba branch closed in 1971. Today, there are no significant narrow-gauge passenger lines in operation.

Elsewhere on the standard-gauge network, there have also been some local closures over the years. For example, the branch to Fenerbahce, near Istanbul, was closed in 1928, although track was not removed until 1971. Improvements to the rail network in Turkey have also resulted in some temporary and permanent closures. It was deemed too expensive to connect the Izmir–Buca branch with a new tunnel and so the line closed in 2006. Railway improvements also led to the closure of the large Karaagac station in 1971, but the building was restored for new uses. The former station at Izmit is now a museum after the line was diverted, whilst the beautiful station at Edirne survives with a preserved locomotive, but no trains. On the positive side, the line to the Black Sea port of Samsun was refurbished and reopened in 2020 and overall a good service is provided on Turkish railways in what is now called Türkiye.

A narrow-gauge Henschel 0-4-0T locomotive No 97 dating from 1918 preserved at Izmir in October 2008. The locomotive was one of a number used for Turkish construction projects, while others were used on military, or industrial railways. *Author*

Above: Camlik railway station was opened in 1886 on the ex-Oriental Railway. It was located on a now disused loop off the main line that was closed due to a troublesome tunnel. The Turkish station is seen in October 2008. *Author*

Left: Izmir with a disused platform at Alsancak station in October 2008. Dating from 1858, between 2006 and 2010 no trains used the Turkish station. In 2010 some trains returned, but parts remained disused. *Author*

CHAPTER 11

HEJAZ CONFLICT AND CLOSURE

Egypt

Due to the links through Sinai to the rest of the Middle East, for railway purposes I have mostly included Egypt in this chapter. A standard-gauge network developed and, at its peak, luxury dining and sleeping-car trains operated. Egyptian rail travel was once the most similar to that in Britain than in any other African country.

Much of the main Egyptian main-line network survives and, although new investment is underway, parts of the original network are dilapidated and have been accident prone. Links to the west through El Alamein, which were closed during the Second World War, to the Libyan border were reopened and still remain. One line that was only opened in the 1990s ran from the Western Desert area to the Red Sea, but was uneconomic, plagued by drifting sand problems and was subsequently closed. After closure, over 90 miles (150km) of track were stolen by looters, resulting in a train being stranded.

Narrow-gauge was also used and a few sections of 2ft-gauge industrial and sugar cane lines survive, particularly in the Luxor area. At one time, lightly built narrow-gauge lines were also used in this area in connection with archaeological excavations.

Cairo Railway Museum in November 2018, with a British built Robert Stephenson & Company locomotive dating from 1865 on display. Founded in 1933, next to Cairo's Ramses station, it was the first railway museum in Africa. *Dr Alan Grundy*

WORLD'S LONGEST SPAN DISUSED RAILWAY SWING BRIDGE

The line from the rest of the Egyptian network to Sinai involved crossing the Suez Canal. At first, a pontoon bridge for freight and a ferry for passengers was used, but during the First World War a bridge was built at Kantara. The bridge obstructed much of the canal, creating a hindrance to shipping and was removed after the war.

During the Second World War, the military importance of the route across the Sinai desert area was again recognised and a swing bridge was built across the canal in 1942, creating a railway route all the way from Cairo to Istanbul. The bridge was damaged by a steamship and removed in 1947, whilst through trains beyond Sinai ceased at the border with the new state of Israel the following year.

A new double-swing bridge across the canal was opened in 1954 but was damaged by the Israeli invasion of Sinai two years later. A replacement bridge was completed in 1963, but again destroyed during the Six-Day War in 1967. The current El Ferdan bridge was completed in 2001 and does not obstruct the canal, but by 2005 reducing railway traffic and theft of track in the Sinai desert resulted in the line over it being closed.

The construction of a new parallel section of Suez Canal in 2015 had no railway bridge crossing and has further isolated the Sinai railways from the Egyptian network. However, by this time, over three quarters of the track and equipment of the railway across Sinai had been looted and sandstorms had overrun remaining tracks in many locations. The current El Ferdan bridge, with a span of 340m (1,100ft), is the longest disused railway swing bridge in the world.

El Ferdan railway swing bridge in Egypt, seen in March 2004, has the longest span in the world and crosses the Suez Canal. The bridge served a railway that ran into the Sinai Desert and once provided connections to Istanbul but is now closed. *H. Nawara*

Nile delta narrow-gauge

Although standard-gauge lines still remain in the area, the largest narrow-gauge network was the 2ft 5½ins gauge, approximately 620-mile (1,000km) system covering the fertile Nile Delta. Both passenger and freight trains in this fertile agricultural area were originally operated by a fleet of steam locomotives. Decline came during the First World War and an order for new steam locomotives was cancelled. They were sent to India instead, where they were known as the 'Delta' type. Diesels were ordered in the 1930s and the network continued until after the Second World War but is now closed.

The Egyptian Delta Light Railways, with a British built narrow-gauge 0-6-4T No 94 taking water at Tanta in May 1945. At this time the railway had some 130 locomotives. Financial problems led to assets being seized in 1955 and the railway gradually closed. Ray *Tustin*

Iran

The first railway, in what was once known as Persia, opened in 1886 between Tehran and a shrine at Rey. The 6-mile (9km) line was built to 2ft 6in gauge and was used mainly by pilgrims but closed in 1952. The 53-mile (85km) Bushire Railway was a British military supply line that ran from 1918 to 1921 and was constructed using the track and stock from the Powayan Tramway in India.

The bus link to and from Tehran connecting with the 'Taurus Express' was due to the late development of main lines in Iran. The first main line was not opened across the country until 1938, but the network was busy during the Second World War with lines becoming of military importance, including those able to provide supplies to the Soviet Union. Manchester-built Garratts, the most powerful locomotives in the Middle East, once worked the more mountainous sections and, during the Second World War, more than 100 steam locomotives were converted to use oil rather than coal.

The railways were in poor condition after the Second World War, but recovered and new lines were built. The overthrow of the Shah in 1979, the growth in air travel and ongoing tensions have led to the discontinuance of some long-distance sleeper trains, for example from Tehran to Zahedan, although such trains may yet resume. The international link to Azerbaijan, which involved a gauge change, has closed, but links to Pakistan, Turkey and Turkmenistan remain. At a local level, some early British Pacer DMUs were provided to the country for passenger use, but unsurprisingly soon became surplus to requirements.

Iraq

Miles of narrow-gauge line were constructed by the British during the First World War, some using metre-gauge equipment requisitioned from India. Whilst the standard-gauge Berlin–Baghdad railway had begun in 1902, through running to Baghdad was not completed until 1940. As a consequence, the railway network that eventually developed included both narrow and standard-gauge lines.

The narrow-gauge lines had closed, or been converted to standard-gauge, by the late 1980s and only a standard-gauge network of lines survived, including the main line to Baghdad and The Gulf near Basra. Lines linking Baghdad with branches along the Euphrates to Fallujah and Husaybah, near the Syrian border, and a line to the oil-rich area of Kirkuk comprised the main network.

International passenger connections ceased in 2003, as the American and UK-led invasion of Iraq caused disruption. The initial conflict was followed by insurgent activity involving the sabotage of railway, track, bridges and stations. Rail travel became more difficult, and sidings filled with derelict passenger coaches as passenger services were curtailed and some lines closed. Trains continued to run, but problems lasted. The line through Mosul was severed in 2010 by terrorists and the once attractive station was mostly destroyed in 2014.

There has been some rehabilitation. The Baghdad–Basra night train has been reinstated and runs on some days; the journey takes 18 hours, passing derelict intermediate stations on its route. In 2018, a sparse service between Baghdad and Fallujah was restored. The line to Kirkuk remains suspended, but further lines are to reopen, provided stability and peace prevails. Baghdad's large main station, designed in an attractive Moorish style by British architects, still survives and in 2020 plans to rebuild Mosul station were announced.

Iraq with abandoned British built 4-6-0 locomotives at Baghdad East yard, in February 1998. This was the main terminus of the Berlin to Baghdad railway. Closed, along with most railways, due to the war in 2003, some lines are being returned to use. *Colour-Rail*

Israel

Originally, the lines in the area were operated by Palestine Railways but following the Arab-Israeli War of 1948, Israel gained independence. The newly formed country was isolated and all international lines were cut, including to Lebanon at Nahariya in the north and along the coast to Egypt from Ashdod in the south. Links to Jordan and Syria in the east were also closed, and abandoned station buildings and derelict railway structures are still to be found in border areas.

Within Israel, many of the railways were repaired and a good internal network was eventually established. At Jerusalem, part of the original old line to Jaffa has been turned into a park. Elsewhere, some freight-only lines, such as the remaining sections of the ex-Eastern Railway, may be returned to passenger use, but a section to Rutenberg power station has

closed and all lines were closed for a short period due to coronavirus.

Edmondson tickets are found throughout the world, such as this between Jaffa in Israel, then Palestine, and El Kantara on the Suez Canal in Egypt that was issued to my father during the Second World War. The now closed line was important for allied troop movements. *Author's collection*

A tunnel through Rosh HaNikra Cliff on the railway between Beirut and Cairo. A sign in the Israeli tunnel informed 'Beware Border' in Hebrew. The line closed in 1948 due to political problems, although track still remained when seen here in 1959. *Historical Railway Images*

Palestinian Territories

Part of the coastal railway through the Gaza Strip was still used for freight until the 1970s but has since been dismantled and there are no original operating railways in the West Bank or Gaza.

WORLD'S LOWEST-ALTITUDE LOST RAILWAY

The Jezreel Valley line and its branches were completed in 1912. The main route provided a 3ft 5⅓ins narrow-gauge link from Haifa to the junction at Daraa in Syria on the Hejaz Railway. The line closed in 1948 owing to considerable damage to bridges on the route during the Arab-Israeli War. The branch to Nablus, which had only a weekly train, was also closed. The Haifa–Afula section was briefly reopened but closed in 1951 and a number of disused stations still remain, including Haifa East.

A considerable section of line was below sea level, but the lowest point reached by any closed surface passenger railway in the world was on this line where it crossed the River Jordan south of the Sea of Galilee, in an area reaching 808ft (246m) below sea level. In 2016, part of the line within Israel was reopened as a new standard-gauge route running adjacent to the old alignment inland from Haifa.

The Jezreel Valley line in Israel reached the lowest point of any surface passenger railway in world. Remaining sections of line closed in 1948 and Mas'udiya, station, which was a junction on a branch line off the main line, is seen in 2002. *Haggibar*

TEN GREAT LOST RAILWAYS OF THE WORLD – THE ORIGINAL HEJAZ RAILWAY

The most famous lost line in the area was the original Hejaz Railway which once crossed the borders between Syria, Jordan and Saudi Arabia.

The original Hejaz Railway was built by the Ottoman Empire with aid from its German ally and was seen as a strategic link off the Berlin to Baghdad Railway. The main line ran south from Damascus in Syria, through Jordan, with the aim of reaching the Red Sea and Mecca in Saudi Arabia. The line reached Medina, some 809 miles (1,303km) from Damascus, in 1908 and, whilst opposition at that time prevented it reaching its ultimate goal, it provided a considerable improvement for those passengers heading to Mecca.

Although much of the railway ran through hot sandy desert, which produced its own problems, at Ma'an the 3ft 5⅓in narrow-gauge line reached an altitude of 3,700ft (1,128m) and it was necessary to construct several viaducts and tunnels on part of the route. Large and powerful locomotives were also required to work the steeply graded sections of line.

During the First World War, the main line conveyed Ottoman troops and supplies, thus becoming a target for both the Arabs and the British. The activities of Arab Revolt forces in this area led by the British Captain T.E. Lawrence, also known as 'Lawrence of Arabia', destroyed sections of the railway south of Wadi Rum. Indeed, such was Lawrence's success in disrupting trains that the line was only used for its whole length until 1920 when the region was divided up at the Paris Peace Conference.

Most connecting branches gradually closed, but the northern Damascus–Amman-Ma'an section remained busy in the 1960s and, in 1966, an £8 million scheme was announced to reconstruct 566 miles (910km) of line from Ma'an in Jordan to Medina in Saudi Arabia. The old track, which had lain idle since 1917, was taken up and 200 men were employed to upgrade the railway. The Six-Day War in 1967 between Israel and a number of Arab states led to British firms pulling out of the scheme.

The remaining Amman–Damascus services ceased in 2011, although a short passenger service survived at Damascus. New phosphate traffic used some sections of the former route south of Ma'an to reach the port of Aqaba. South of Amman, the line was largely abandoned, beyond Al-Jizah, but tourist trains have run at Wadi Rum. A new high-speed Medina–Mecca line opened, whilst proposals to reopen sections of the original route have been put forward.

Haramain high-speed line to Mecca opened in 2018. Built to standard-gauge (1.435m/4' 8½") and for speeds up to 186mph/300Km/h. The original Hijaz railway was planned to cover this route, but it was never extended beyond Medina

Map of the Hejaz Railway and branches, showing the original proposed link to Mecca.

Damascus station of the Hejaz Railway in Syria with locomotive No 263 seen in September 1980. The imposing building survives, although passenger services were curtailed due to civil war. A local service now uses a suburban station outside the city. *Colour-Rail*

A German Hartmann 2-8-2 locomotive on the Hejaz Railway near Daraa Junction in Syria, seen in October 1986. Much of the line in is closed, but tourist charter trains have run on some sections. *Vincent Corasi*

Daraa Junction locomotive shed in Syria with two Hartmann locomotives dating from 1918 either side of an abandoned Jung 2-6-0 locomotive seen in October 1986. By 2008, the scene here had been cleared of all track and stock. *Vincent Corasi*

Track repairs being undertaken after a steam locomotive had been derailed on the Hejaz Railway, in the Saudi desert by Lawrence of Arabia, during the First World War. One upturned locomotive still remains in the sand. *Historical Railway Images*

Lebanon

The first line to be constructed was in 1895 and ran from the port of Beirut, via Rayak, where there were railway workshops once employing 3,000, to Damascus in Syria. The Rayak–Damascus section joined the Hejaz Railway at Damascus and this section was the same unique gauge of 3ft 5⅓in. French-built stations and Swiss-built locomotives operated the rack sections required to work trains over the heights of Mount Lebanon. On the highest section, concrete snow sheds were added in the 1930s to help ensure winter use was not disrupted.

Further standard-gauge lines built in the early part of the nineteenth century linked to Homs in Syria, allowing through trains from Istanbul to reach Tripoli. During the Second World War, travel south to Egypt was also made possible with a direct railway being opened from Tripoli through Beirut to the Suez Canal, but political problems led to its closure after the war.

The Lebanon Civil War started in 1975 and resulted in persistent damage to the railway network. The northern line along the coast to Homs and the mountainous line from Beirut to Damascus closed in 1976. Remaining sections of line came to a standstill shortly after, whilst the Israeli invasion in 1982 further damaged infrastructure in the south of the country.

A 3ft 5⅓in gauge Swiss rack locomotive from 1906, one of seven that were once in use in Lebanon, seen on the line east of Rayak in 1968. Civil war resulted in the line's closure in 1976. *Historical Railway Images*

Bhamdoun railway station in Lebanon seen in April 2012. Services from the tourist town to and from Beirut were once provided, but civil war broke out in in 1975 and trains ceased the following year. The station eventually became a ruined shell. *Rabiem*

After the civil war, a 'Peace Train' ran at Halat in 1991 for a time. Cement trains worked in the Beirut area until 1997, ending regular rail operations in the country, although a diesel locomotive operating this service was occasionally used on freight trains until 2002. The railway station at Beirut became a private dwelling and that at Tripoli was abandoned, in spite of protest, with locomotives and stock just left to rust away. Attempts to revive key lines have been met with resistance.

Oman

In 1942, a narrow-gauge railway was constructed at the RAF station on the desert island of Masirah, off the coast of Oman. The line carried both staff and freight until the site was vacated by the RAF in 1977.

Syria

The network of lines in Syria developed in two phases – those built in the early 1900s such as the Hejaz line and those built in the 1970s and 1980s. Aleppo developed as a key junction of five lines with links to Turkey, Iraq and Lebanon, together with domestic routes to Damascus, the coast and eastern interior of the country. The routes were once busy and a number of British War Department 2-10-0 steam locomotives, introduced during the Second World War, were used on the lines until 1976, when oil-fired steam haulage ceased.

The international link from Damascus to Lebanon closed in 1976, but a suburban section of the line at Damascus remained. The Syrian railways were in the process of modernising, including the use of air-conditioned coaches, but civil war began in 2011. This put an end to the remaining international passenger links, and as terrorism intensified, the damage to railway junctions and infrastructure eventually led to all lines largely ceasing to function in 2012.

Much track was damaged with some subsequently stolen and the network was severely compromised by the ongoing conflict. However, with Russian help, a new section of freight line reopened from the port of Tartus to Jableh, whilst the Aleppo–Homs–Damascus line has also been rebuilt and more routes are likely to return to use as stability is restored.

Yemen

The 29-mile (43km) Aden Railway was built during the First World War for strategic military purposes. However, in 1922 the line was opened to passengers and the metre-gauge railway had six intermediate stations, with first and second-class seating being provided. The line was, somewhat surprisingly, operated by the North Western Railway of India until closure in 1929.

The lush valley contrasts with the desert as a locomotive and charter train are seen in October 1986 on a surviving section of route from Damascus in Syria to Serghaya, near the border with Lebanon, into which the line originally extended. *Vincent Corasi*

THE AMERICAS

In the USA and Canada, local passenger services have been decimated and long-distance trains severely reduced as the car and plane have superseded most passenger services outside main cities. There are almost no passenger local rural branch lines, other than tourist routes, or in some remote areas of Canada.

A number of long-distance passenger trains still run in North America, although in general the Americas have a sparse passenger network. In the USA, although there has been a huge number of line closures, there were a huge number of railways in the first place. A number of large and sometimes spectacular railway remains are to be found, whilst the remaining freight network is still the largest in the world.

Latin America's railways are a contrast to the north and are generally in a poor way. In parts of Central America and the Caribbean, they are almost extinct. In Mexico and South America, long-distance passenger trains are also increasingly rare. Political instability, tensions between South American countries, severe weather and track gauge differences have assisted in the fragmentation and closure of routes, there being no coherent international passenger network.

Cars and not passenger railways are seen as the priority by some governments in South America. Some railways are crumbling towards extinction, but total abandonment is often postponed and numerous remains are to be found. Mineral and city suburban trains remain, whilst a few tourist passenger trains were making a revival in some areas of spectacular scenery.

An American locomotive electric headlight and tail light seen at the Gold Coast Railroad Museum at Miami in 2016. *Author*

CHAPTER 12

CUTS IN CANADA AND ALASKA

One of the first railways in Canada was opened in 1836 and was a portage line which connected the St Lawrence River to a lake providing a rail and watercourse route to New York. Lines began to be joined up providing railway communications, particularly when the St Lawrence Seaway was frozen, and a network of railways gradually developed. Canada has a sparse rural population, bleak winter weather and enormous remote areas. Although the railways of Canada were only ever about one twelfth of those in the USA, they helped to create the nation.

Two major railways developed. The Canadian Pacific Railway (CP) was privately owned, but heavily subsidised by the Canadian government. The railway once provided a link from London to Australia, its ships crossing the Atlantic Ocean from England, with passengers then crossing Canada on its trains and finally using its ships again across the Pacific Ocean to reach Australia.

The Canadian National Railway (CN) was a publicly owned company formed in 1922 from a number of failing railways that had been kept going during the First World War by government loans, including the transcontinental Canadian Northern Railway. The CN network became the largest single railway system in Canada and once ran its own transcontinental passenger train service.

Québec's Gare du Palais station clock in a distinctive mix of Scottish and French Chateau designs, typical of the many original station buildings in Canada, it is seen in July 2015. *Author*

Lost in The Rockies

By 1885, the CP's transcontinental Montreal–Vancouver route, a distance of 2,906 miles (4,677km), became the longest railway line in the world when first completed. The Rockies were a challenge to railway construction and two original sections of steeply graded mountain line were abandoned as later improvements were made.

The first was at Big Hill, a difficult 4-mile (6km) section of the line with up to 1 in 22 gradients, that opened in 1884. A speed restriction of 8mph was imposed, but the section was prone to runaway trains. Spiral tunnels were opened in 1909, reducing the gradient by half and resulting in the closure of the original, very heavily graded, section of line.

The second was at Rogers Pass, where the worst snow avalanche disaster in Canadian history occurred in 1910, when sixty-two railway workers were killed by an avalanche whilst clearing snow on the line. The route through some of the most dangerous and bleak sections of the Rogers Pass was closed when the 5-mile (8km) Connaught Tunnel opened in 1916.

Canadian National with a section of the old route on the transcontinental line seen in June 2006. This section and others were abandoned after later diversions were built to improve the route. *Author*

World War losses

During the First World War, some lines were closed and requisitioned for the war effort. The two transcontinental railways were seen to duplicate each other for about 100 miles (160km) in the Yellowhead Pass area. As a consequence, the lines were amalgamated into one route and surplus rails were transported to France. This resulted in some settlements on the closed sections simply withering away.

Whilst there had been some rationalisation during the First World War, there was little overall change to the network. The Second World War was to witness the loss of twelve CP ships, the *Empress of Britain,* sunk off Ireland, being the largest Allied liner lost to enemy action during the war. Locomotive works were converted to wartime construction, whilst the Chateau Frontenac railway hotel in Quebec, one of a number of former Canadian railway hotels built to a French-Scottish style and known as 'Castles of the North', was used by Roosevelt and Churchill to plan later events of the war.

Post-Second World War decline

After the Second World War, increased car ownership, followed by government money being poured into roads and a growth in air transport, saw the gradual loss of passenger services. Although diesel traction was introduced, deferred maintenance and lack of wider investment caused branch lines to be closed, whilst increased deregulation made the process of passenger closure easier.

Canadian Pacific's iconic first generation 1,500-horsepower diesel electric locomotive No 4069, dating from 1952, in an earlier livery seen at the Railway Museum of British Columbia at Squamish in June 2017. *Dr Alan Grundy*

WORLD'S SMALLEST COMMERCIALLY OPERATED CLOSED RAILWAY

Ironically, many long routes were closed to passengers in Canada, but in stark contrast the short 1¼-mile (1.8km) Lake of Bays Transportation Company claimed to run the smallest conventional commercially operated passenger railway in the world, until its closure in 1959.

In the 1960s, CN made efforts to attract passengers with cheaper fares, complimentary meals for first class passengers and new trains. This did increase passenger numbers but did not clear the deficit. In 1971, the last of the CP passenger ships were laid up and, in 1978, the company gave up all its passenger trains as the government's VIA Rail Canada was set up to run the remaining and often loss-making passenger services.

In the 1980s, a Leyland diesel bus bodied passenger unit was shipped to Canada from the UK and used over freight tracks with the aim of reviving abandoned passenger services, but this was not a success. In 1981, VIA Rail cut a large number of its routes and many remaining branch lines closed to passenger services. Further cuts were made in both 1990 and 1994. Since taking over, VIA Rail has reduced the passenger network by thousands of miles and closed countless passenger stations.

There are significant stretches of lost passenger lines in New Brunswick, around Quebec, Montreal, Ottawa and Edmonton. The network of branch lines in the Prairie provinces saw passenger services gradually suspended, leaving little more than seasonal freight use for the grain harvest. Between 1962 and 1998, there was a 60 per cent cut in the remaining grain branch lines causing transportation costs increases for farmers, whilst in 2009 a further fifty-two grain-loading sites were closed by CN.

The growth in container rail traffic resulted in the demise of many traditional city railway freight yards, but the abandoned yards were often seen as a redevelopment opportunity. Some former freight yards were huge, even covering several square miles, and a striking part of Vancouver's new development is located on former railway freight yards.

Many Canadian communities are now home to abandoned railways and there are a number of spectacular former railway

TEN GREAT LOST RAILWAYS OF THE WORLD – THE KETTLE VALLEY RAILWAY

The 300-mile (483km) standard-gauge Kettle Valley Railway was a subsidiary of the CP and linked Hope and Midway in British Columbia. Crossing spectacular mountain areas, construction took many years and building costs were high, but mining and fruit traffic used the complete route that opened in 1916. Some gradients were steep and a spiral tunnel and huge loop were needed, whilst engineering feats on the line included the Othello Tunnels, which are particularly spectacular, together with the Myra Canyon Trestles.

Snow could close the line in winter, but ice blocks were collected in the mountains and used to cool produce in summer. This was once a common freight on the line but ceased as refrigeration became widely used. A new highway damaged revenue on the railway and a washout closed part of the line in 1959. The last passenger trains ran in 1964 and the final section closed for freight in 1989. Since closure, much of the route has become a rail trail, whilst a section is used by the Kettle Valley Steam Railway near Trout Creek.

Top right: The Kettle Valley Railway with two of the five impressive Othello Tunnels, cut through solid rock near Hope, seen in August 2009. The line closed and much of the route is now a long-distance trail and cycleway. *Robert Ashworth*

Right: Map of the Kettle Valley Railway, British Columbia, Canada.

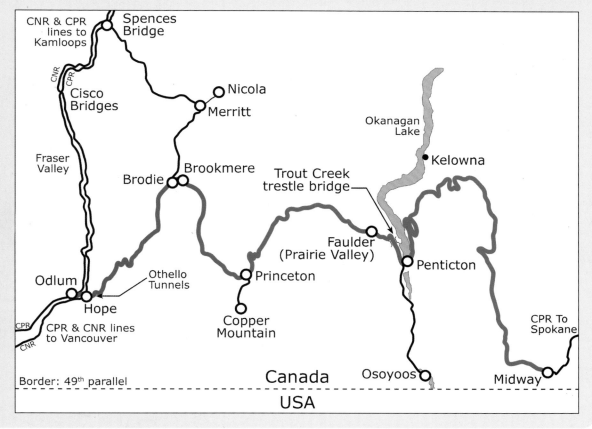

structures. These include some huge disused bridges and viaducts such as the Pass Lake Trestle that was opened in 1916 but has been out of use since the 1990s. The Michigan Central Railroad bridge at Niagara Falls, opened in 1925, has been disused since 1979 and tracks on the Canadian side of the bridge have been removed. Plans to demolish the metal bridge were yet to be implemented in 2022. Mintlaw viaduct is one of the longest disused structures in Canada. Completed in 1912, at 110ft high (33m) and 2,112ft long (644m), the steel viaduct closed in 1981 and the adjoining settlement of Mintlaw became somewhat of a ghost town after closure of the railway.

Some passenger closures continue as government funding reduces and the Algoma Central Railway service was closed in 2015. In 2020, coronavirus was to see many of the remaining passenger services cut for temporary periods, including 'The Canadian'.

The famous 'Rocky Mountaineer' passenger train was also suspended, temporarily.

A number of closed railways have been turned into walking and cycling 'rail trails' and there are a few heritage lines. The trails include disused bridges and it is hoped that this can be achieved at Mintlaw, although there have been many years of no maintenance on the bridge here. Equally, the trails can run through disused tunnels, such as at Brockville, where Canada's first tunnel has been refurbished for use as a footpath.

Abandoned stations

In most cities, there has been rationalisation of the often-huge and duplicated CP and CN passenger stations, with some differing fates awaiting the buildings after closure. A number of earlier stations in cities have been demolished and replaced by newer structures over the

Vancouver's former Canadian Pacific Waterside station opened in 1914 and served as the western terminus of the transcontinental line until 1979. After closure local commuter services have since used part of the building. The huge station frontage is seen here in June 2006. *Author*

Pemberton station opened in 1892 and is typical of many smaller stations in Canada. The line closed in 1969 and the station was preserved and is seen here in June 2017. *Dr Alan Grundy*

years. Bonaventure station in Montreal and Broad Street station in Ottawa were early losses, whilst Toronto's Union station closed in 1927 and was also demolished. Toronto North closed in 1931, but the building remains as does much of Montreal's Windsor station. Place Viger, which was a combined station and hotel, saw the hotel close in 1935 and the station in 1951, but the main buildings have survived.

Fortunately, the attractiveness of railway buildings was increasingly recognised and many declared redundant by later closures and rationalisation have survived. For example, Ottawa Union station closed in 1966, but the building remains. St Thomas station in Ontario closed in 1979 and Parc Avenue station in Montreal closed in 1984, but these buildings have survived. The attractive Union station in Regina that closed in the 1990s also remains, as does Liuna station in Hamilton that closed in 1993, together with both stations in Moose Jaw.

Newfoundland

Canada's island railways have not fared well. Newfoundland once had over 900 miles (1,448km) of 3ft 6in narrow-gauge railways. In 1957, dieselisation was completed and transporter trucks for standard-gauge wagons ferried over from the mainland were provided. However, the 548-mile (883km) journey on the main line was slow, the winter weather was often severe and trains could be marooned in the snow for days on end. On one occasion, the locomotive crew resorted to lowering the fire and clambering into the firebox itself to survive the freezing conditions. Wagons were also on occasions chained to the track during high winds. This was once the biggest 3ft 6in network in North America, but increased road competition resulted in all surviving branch lines being closed in 1984. The difference in gauge to the rest of Canada caused increasing problems and the entire remaining main line was closed in 1988, the longest single closure in Canada.

Vancouver Island

Vancouver Island has significant forests and the movement of timber once resulted in a railway network of mostly forestry lines. Passenger services were sparse and 2011 saw VIA Rail suspend the last

The former railway bridge at Stephenville Crossing was last used by trains in 1988. It is now part of the Newfoundland T'Railway, a 548-mile (883km) long-distance path, the bridge is seen here in June 2018. *Urbanimages/Alamy*

passenger service, the 225-mile (362km) Victoria–Courtenay 'Dayliner', on the basis that track needed upgrading before trains could resume. The suspended service has never resumed; the track has been lifted in part and not been upgraded, so freight has also ceased.

Elsewhere on Vancouver Island, there was a logging railway that was once carried across Bear Creek by a wooden trestle at a height of 254ft (77.5m) and 900ft (274m) long. This was one of the largest wooden bridges in the world but was demolished in the 1950s. However, another survives; fortunately, the magnificent wooden trestle at Kinsol, that closed to railway traffic in 1979, has been restored and is used as a public footpath. The last logging railway in North America survived on the island until it closed in 2017.

Above: The Vancouver Island service was suspended by VIA Rail Canada in 2011 due to lack of track maintenance and has never been reinstated. The railway used old (CP) Budd diesel railcars and one is seen here ready to head out of Victoria in August 1978. The track here has since been lifted. *Drew Jacksich*

Right: The Kinsol Trestle on Vancouver Island is one of the largest and most spectacular surviving wooden trestles in the world. Seen here in June 2020, it was built to convey logging trains over the Koksilah River. Closed in 1979, it now forms part of Cowichan rail trail. *David Stanley*

Prince Edward Island

Prince Edward Island once had through carriages, including sleeping cars from the mainland using train ferries. The ships used also had to act as ice-breakers in winter and were the largest of their type in the world at the time. Originally, the railways on the island were built to a narrow-gauge, but over 310 miles (500km) of line were later converted to standard-gauge. The change to diesel traction was made in 1948, the first in Canada. These improvements did not save the island network in the long term, as passenger services ended in the 1970s and the entire remaining network was closed in 1989. Many of the trackbeds are being converted into rail trails.

Lost Alaskan Railroads in the USA

Alaska is part of the USA but, as lines link directly into Canada and none into the USA, I have included it here. Gold, copper, coal and other minerals led to a number of lines being built, some of which closed during bleak winter periods, whilst the sparse population led to only a few regular passenger services. Of the major closed lines, the 194-mile (312km) Copper River & Northwestern Railway was completed in 1911 to transport copper from the mines to the coast. Almost 130 bridges were included on this expensive and difficult railway route. Part of the line even had to be built across a glacier.

The Million Dollar Bridge

The bridge on this line over the Copper River was known as 'The Million Dollar Bridge' as it was very expensive to build, including requiring the aid of steam jets to sink piles into the frozen Copper River bed. Concrete ice-breaking pillars also had to be installed in the river and placed in front of the main piers as icebergs flowing down the river threatened to destroy the bridge before it was completed. The line made a profit for many years but closed in 1939 when the copper mine supplies were depleted and the recession reduced demand. Parts of the route have subsequently been turned into road tracks, including over this bridge.

The Gold Rush

In 1903, three steam locomotives from the New York Elevated Railroad, that incidentally was not finally dismantled until the 1970s, were sold to an Alaskan company for use on a gold mining line near Nome. The Council City & Solomon River Railroad was intended to serve the mines in the remote area, whilst 43 miles (69km) were used by passenger trains, but due to lack of funds and building materials the incomplete line closed after a short period in 1907. Track remained until 1913, when it was damaged by a storm; however, being a very isolated area, the rusting and stranded locomotives still remain. It is a pity that one of these unique locomotives could not go to a New York museum.

The Council City & Solomon River Railroad with a locomotive, originally from the New York Elevated Railroad, seen near Nome in Alaska in June 2014. The line only operated between 1903 and 1907 serving mining interests in the areas. *Gregory 'Slobirdr' Smith*

Remote lines

A unique 11-mile (18km) steam-operated line was built in 1903, to transport raw salmon from a river to a cannery at the port of Yakutat. The Yakutat & Southern Railroad was only used during the summer fishing season but survived until the mid-1960s and its remains are still to be found. Fortunately, the Wild Goose Railroad was named after the gold mines it served and not its cargo, and part of it survived as a tourist line until 1955.

The Alaskan Railroad survives, although the Chickaloon branch was closed beyond Eska in 1928 and the remaining section serving coal mines in the late 1930s. Other short independent coal and mineral lines were also mostly closed at about the same time. On the 3ft-gauge White Pass & Yukon Route, the Pueblo branch closed in 1918 and the Carcross–Whitehorse section in Canada is out of service. However, the most tangible remnant of the Klondike gold rush of 1898 is that part of this line has reopened as a narrow-gauge heritage line.

American 2-8-2 locomotive called a 'Mikado' until the name was changed to the less Japanese sounding 'MacArthur' during the Second World War. Originally built for narrow-gauge army transport, class S118 No 195 is seen on the White Pass & Yukon Route, stored at Skagway in Alaska, in June 2006. *Author*

Above: The White Pass & Yukon Route closed in 1982, but part of the line reopened in 1988. Former locomotive No 196 has not fared so well having been used for some time as ballast in a local river. The battered and rusting boiler is seen here at Skagway in June 2006. *Author*

Left: A disused viaduct spanning Dead Horse Gulch in June 2006. Built in 1901 following the Klondike Gold Rush it was the largest structure on the White Pass & Yukon Route but was abandoned in 1969 when a new diversionary section of the Alaskan line was completed. *Author*

CHAPTER 13

THE UNITED STATES OF AMERICA

Railroad rather than railway is the word used in the USA, although 'railway' is incorporated into the name of some companies. America's large areas of virgin landscape meant that railroads could go almost anywhere they wished and many of the first lines were built cheaply and quickly. The Baltimore & Ohio Railroad was the first common carrier in USA, with the first section opening in 1830. The line soon developed and, by the 1850s, 20-ton metal coal wagons were introduced to deal with burgeoning coal traffic.

Despite the vast distances, natural obstacles, some areas of hostile indigenous population, limited capital and damage during the Civil War, railroads went on to be built on a massive scale. By the First World War, transcontinental lines and the largest network in the world had developed, with over a quarter-million miles of active line crisscrossing the country.

Standard-gauge was favoured, but many narrow-gauge lines were also built, for example the Denver & Rio Grande in the difficult Rocky Mountains. Narrow-gauge was used by industry and a significant number

developed, for example in Maine, where isolated lines grew into a network offering passenger services. They were also favoured as logging routes and by 1890 about ninety such lines were to be found in Michigan state alone.

The railroads were built by entrepreneurs in the absence of national policy. As a consequence, a large part of the mileage built was not really needed. For example, the Nickel Plate Railroad was built purely to compete with the New York Central Railroad, whilst others were cheaply, or badly, built. By the end of the First World War, costs had gone up, cars and large numbers of trucks were being registered on the roads, and the seeds of future decline had been set.

However, it was the railroads that created the USA and the nation took them to its heart, with some lines running along the main streets of towns to the station or depot. Salem was one such example, whilst until 1936 the 'Empire State Express' ran for over a mile through Washington Street in Syracuse. Such street passenger services have ceased, although freight remains along streets in several urban areas.

A network of steam operated lines once covered the USA. The Oregon Pacific & Eastern Railway with an ex-Yreka Western Railroad locomotive No 19 heading towards Dorena in Oregon is seen in August 1971. The line closed in 1987 and the trackbed is now used by the Row River Trail. *Drew Jacksich*

Steam locomotives played a huge part in developing the USA and many have been preserved. No 26, a 2-8-0 ex-Western Pacific Railroad oil burning freight locomotive, built by Alco in 1918, is seen at the Travel Town Museum in California in September 2004. *Author*

In the 1920s, the line between New York and Washington became the busiest in the world. It was even considered by some that the automobile was just a passing fad and air travel was in its dangerous infancy. The golden age of the American railroads was during this period and by this time a vast railroad infrastructure was in place.

The Streamliners
In view of the huge distances involved in America, a number of famous long-distance named passenger trains, for example the 'Limited', 'Zephyr' and 'Hiawatha', were introduced. The modern design, high speed and sleek lines meant that they were often known as 'streamliners'. They were the highpoint of passenger rail travel in the USA. The most famous was the 'The Twentieth Century Limited' which was introduced in 1902 between New York and Chicago and had new streamlined stock introduced in the 1930s. In spite of a red-carpet service and over thirty members of staff, by 1970 air competition had put it out of business.

Above: Before Amtrak revived the Californian Zephyr in 1983, three railroads ran the train between Chicago and San Francisco. The original train ceased in March 1970, when it is viewed here near Oroville on an ex-Western Pacific section that is now not used by passenger trains. *Drew Jacksich*

Right: The interior of a passenger vista dome car from the Californian Zephyr stock, preserved at the Gold Coast Railroad Museum in Miami in February 2016. The American loading gauge made such elevated viewpoints possible but could not stem the decline in passenger traffic. *Author*

Passenger retrenchment

Whilst improvements to the network had resulted in some early closures of original lines, the impact of the Great Depression was felt by the railroads and, in the 1930s, passenger numbers were less than half what they were in the 1920s. From 1932, passenger services increasingly began to record annual losses. The trucking industry was also making further inroads into freight revenues. This led in 1933 to the Emergency Railroad Transportation Act which enabled the railroad companies to eliminate loss-making services. An upsurge in closures, particularly by smaller railroads, was recorded from this time onwards.

Diesel locomotives reduced costs, but the Second World War, with America fighting on two fronts, added tremendous demands to the railroads. Tracks of little-used lines, including a passenger-only section of the first transcontinental railroad, were removed in 1942 and transported for use on military bases on the Pacific coast. The war also resulted in freight and passenger stock that had been taken out of service being pressed back into use. However, once war had ended, an increase in road and air transport use, together with a decline in heavy industry, was again to result in a further loss of traffic on the railroads.

The problems for the railroads increased after the Second World War and even some legislation hindered fair competition with road transport. Some unions took time to adjust to the financial difficulties and insisted on the minimum numbers of workers on trains. On occasions, trains that could be operated with a single member of crew had a complement of seven. Equally, management were reluctant to invest in the future, such as in new air-conditioned stock, and sometimes seemed to have little understanding of passenger requirements. These issues compounded the general downturn in the railroad industry. Bankruptcies, closures and mergers into new larger companies were the result, and many famous railroad names such as The Rock Island were eventually to disappear.

Problems with local passenger services were even more acute. Troop movements in the Second World War had been heavy, but as war ended railroads increasingly failed to earn a profit from passenger services. By the mid-1950s, buses and cars had killed off the local passenger train and almost all narrow-gauge lines, whilst in the late 1960s, the US Postal Service withdrew the lucrative mail contract from most passenger trains. The interstate highways were built using the railroads to transport the freight required for construction of these

Mergers between railways in the USA were common. A Southern Railway office entrance at Washington in September 1991. The railway operated from 1894 until 1982, when it merged to become the Norfolk Southern Railway. *Author*

new state-subsidised 'freeways'. Indeed, some lines only remained profitable whilst they were conveying concrete and aggregates for the new roads.

The massive growth in car ownership resulted in the loss of more remaining passenger services in the 1960s. At this time, permission to close services was simply required from the Commerce Commission. Once this was obtained, railroads were allowed to stop services immediately, which sometimes even led to passengers being stranded. Branch lines and stations were being abandoned in huge numbers, whilst many companies just collapsed and closed.

In the early 1970s, almost a quarter of the railroads were operating under bankruptcy protection. Closures continued and the finance of the railroads was increasingly weakened. The huge Penn Central Railroad went bankrupt in 1970. The shock of this was to result in government intervention, leading in 1971 to a nationalised corporation, Amtrak, being created to safeguard key surviving passenger services. Amtrak immediately cut about two thirds of the remaining passenger trains.

Legislation passed in 1980 deregulated the freight railroads. The freedom was of benefit, but also made it easier to close lines and triggered further rounds of closures. This was of such concern that, in 1983, 'rail banking' was introduced to preserve abandoned rail corridors for use as walking and cycling trails for public use, but at the same time preserving the corridor in case they should return to railroad use in the future. One of the first was the Elroy Trail, whilst the Katy Trail in Missouri at 237 miles (386km) became one of the longer rail trails following part of the former Missouri Kansas & Texas Railroad. There are rail trails in almost every US state and even plans to link enough trails to create a transcontinental rail trail. Today, requests to abandon railroads are controlled by the Department of Transportation, with consultation periods having to be undertaken before any closure is confirmed.

Even large cities, all with metropolitan populations of over one million, were eventually to lose their Amtrak passenger services. The largest of these cities was Cleveland, which lost services for a time. Others that lost their passenger services include Columbus and Nashville in 1979. Phoenix lost its direct services in 1996, although a passenger station some 30 miles (48km) from the city survives. Las Vegas, where you could only exit the station via a casino, lost its services in 1997 and Louisville in 2003.

A few local US passenger services survived such as on the Monterey branch. Southern Pacific No 3004 hauls the two-coach 'Del Monte' train near Fort Ord in February 1971. Passenger service ceased two months later, but freight continued until 1993. *Drew Jacksich*

Most cities retained freight services, although Columbus has the distinction of being the largest city in the USA with no passenger railroads at all, whilst no passenger trains serve the states of South Dakota and Wyoming.

Currently, less than half of the original network remains and less than 500 passenger stations, all resulting in the largest number of lost lines in the world. There have been thousands of rail line closures and, in every state, disused railroads are to be found. This has left a huge legacy of remains. Fortunately, closures have largely stabilised, and whilst coal and heavy freight, particularly in the 'rust belt', has declined, long-distance freight in the USA has been made efficient with investment in technology, track and stock upgrades. American railroads are no longer a depressed industry.

In early 2020, Amtrak was heading towards breaking even financially for the first time, but then the coronavirus pandemic wiped out passenger numbers and services were cut. In 2021, President Biden, sometimes known as 'Amtrak Joe', may offer hope for the future and plans for some cities to regain passenger services are under consideration.

Elevated lines to Linear Parks

No freight arrives on Manhattan Island by rail ferry, although Brooklyn is still connected. At one time, ferries used a huge freight interchange facility known as Exchange Place station. This was demolished in 1963 and as a consequence, there is also a number of disused freight lines on Manhattan Island. Some remain abandoned, but one of the high-level rail freight lines originally serving riverside industries is now a green elevated linear park on well-restored former railroad infrastructure. It has become one of New York's premier attractions.

The New York High Line was originally built by the New York Central Railroad and opened as the West Side Elevated Line in 1934. It replaced a busy street-level line with numerous level crossings that had been prone to accidents and congestion. In 1980, the last train used the line and property owners wanted to demolish the metal viaducts and this was authorised, but equally a group of urban planners wanted to turn it into a pathway. There was litigation, but support for its retention grew and in 2009 the abandoned line became a linear park.

The High Line in New York in July 2015. The route was once busy with freight to waterside industries but was abandoned in 1980. It opened in stages as a tranquil linear park above the traffic in 2009 and has since become one of New York's most popular attractions. *Author*

Similar urban parks using disused lines are to be found in Chicago where the Bloomingdale Trail runs on an elevated former line for 2¾ miles (4.3km), the second longest in the world. Other similar plans are being developed elsewhere, including Atlanta and Philadelphia.

Union and great stations

The peak of passenger train travel in the USA resulted in a number of spectacular stations being constructed. Different railroads serving a city with their own stations increasingly joined together to build one vast Union station that was used as an interchange by all the railroads, hence the Union name. Because of cold winters, in some parts, the Union stations were mostly designed with a palatial main statement building, with central waiting facilities where passengers were held until trains were almost ready to depart. Almost as soon as many of the stations were completed, rail travel began to be replaced by the car and plane and the imposing buildings have subsequently met with various fortunes.

There was protest, which did not save Penn Central station, but ensured that the same fate did not befall Grand Central station. New York's Grand Central station buildings survived and the station is one of the busiest stations in America. It has a disused line known as 'Track 61'. Mystery surrounds this, but it was built for President Roosevelt. He had polio and in less understanding times he could be transferred from his presidential train to the Waldorf Hotel above by a private lift, thus few would see his disability.

Others large stations have closed, but the buildings remain and have been put to new use. By way of example, Union Station in St Louis once served more than a dozen different railroads and, with forty-two tracks to accommodate the trains, was for a time the largest in the world. Before the First World War, there were 276 arrivals and departures; this number had reduced to 128 at the start of the Second World War and, with the exception of a subway line, there are none today, but the attractive main buildings have been put to new uses. The uniquely designed huge station in Cincinnati once had hundreds of daily trains, but today just three use a small part of the

WORLD'S MOST IMPOSING LOST STATION BUILDING

The demolition of the iconic Pennsylvania Central station buildings in New York in the 1960s is, not unlike the loss of the original Euston station and the Doric Arch in London, now bitterly regretted. Penn Central station was once one of the great landmarks of New York and designed on a massive scale. The eighty-four huge columns and stone sculptures of the building gave great civic pride to the city.

Sadly, the Pennsylvania Railroad's finances became enfeebled and the real estate value of the station's central land was too great a financial opportunity. The airy cathedral-like space of the original station was demolished and a plain office block replaced the original distinctive stone and glass buildings. Someone once said that you entered the original Penn Central station like kings but emerged from the new station like rats. In 2021, the station was made more user friendly when the post office building next door was repurposed as a new train hall.

Pennsylvania station, not the original, but a mock-up of part of the iconic building in a theme park seen here in September 1991. Demolition of the original mighty station in New York began in 1963, causing outrage. *Author*

The Central Railroad of New Jersey Waterside station, seen in September 1995. Dating from 1889 and located on the west bank of the Hudson River, ferry services connected to Manhattan. The terminus closed in 1967. *Author*

former station and the main booking hall has been turned into a museum. Buffalo Central closed in 1979, but again the buildings survived. Worcester station Massachusetts was demolished when the layout was enlarged, but the new station was retained as a historical remnant.

Some station buildings remain but are largely derelict. By way of example, Union station in Gary, Indiana, was closed, but in 2022 the derelict building still remains, whilst West Oakland was damaged by an earthquake and also remains unused. The Central Railroad of New Jersey Terminal station closed in 1967 and required a ferry trip to reach Manhattan Island, and again the huge disused building and train shed remains. Michigan Central station was the tallest station building in the world and looked out over eighteen tracks. Dating from 1913, it was so big that its rentable top office floors were never fully occupied. It was last used for passengers in 1988, but the amazing building remains, has been leased by the Ford Motor Company and is being restored.

Elsewhere, there has been a catalogue of demolition of a number of large and beautiful station buildings. The 1950s witnessed the demolition of both the Southern Railway and Texas & Pacific termini in New Orleans. The 1960s saw the Union stations at Memphis, Portland, Savannah and Milwaukee depots all being demolished, together with Birmingham's ornate terminal station. The 1970s saw both the Grand Central and the Central stations in Chicago demolished, along with Minneapolis Great Northern, Atlanta Terminal and Columbus Union stations.

A particularly impressive, demolished structure was the second Broad Street station in Philadelphia, opening in 1893. The enormous single train shed had a span of 306ft (93m), being the largest in the world and 60ft (18m) larger than St Pancras. The roof was destroyed by fire in 1923 and the huge terminal station closed in 1930, when a new through station was built in West Philadelphia. Broad Street station was eventually demolished in 1953.

Union Station Nashville was built in 1900, decline started after the Second World War and the passenger station eventually closed in 1979. After a period of dereliction, it has since been used as a hotel, retaining many of the original features. It is seen in July 2018. *Hannah Blanchflower Weaver*

Trestles and high bridges

The large wooden trestle was a distinctive feature of North America as the ready availability of timber made its construction relatively inexpensive. Trestles were quick to build and needed little maintenance. They were also flexible and, as the many remaining examples show, long lasting. For example, the Alamogordo & Sacramento Mountain Railway, known as 'The Cloud Climbing Railroad' built fifty-eight wooden bridges including an S-shaped wooden trestle and, although closed in 1947, its remains are still to be found, as are those along the Rollins Pass line which closed in the 1930s. The Camas Prairie Railroad was known as 'The Railroad on Stilts' because on one 5-mile (8km) stretch there were more than a dozen wooden trestles.

As train speeds and weight increased, many wooden trestles were later replaced by steel structures, or spoil was poured over the structures to form embankments. For example, Dale Creek wooden trestle was 150ft (46m) high and swayed in the wind. It was replaced in 1876 by an equally spindly iron structure, which in turn was demolished in 1901 when a diversion made the line redundant.

The 41-span Kinzua viaduct was 301ft (92m) tall and once carried the Erie Railroad on one of the highest metal trestles in the USA. The original wrought-iron work had been replaced by steel, but the viaduct closed in 1959. In 2003, much of the trestle was destroyed during a tornado as the corroded wrought-iron base ties had not been replaced by steel. A short section remaining has been turned into a viewing platform, with a panoramic view of the twisted remains of the collapsed viaduct below.

The huge steel cantilevered bridge over the Hudson River north of New York at Poughkeepsie opened in

WORLD'S LARGEST DISUSED CURVED WOODEN TRESTLE

The San Diego & Arizona Railway was a line that was built through inhospitable Californian desert terrain. Wooden trestle viaducts and tunnels were required on the route, but substantial land movements resulted in closure of part of the original line. This brought about the urgent need for a diversionary route which involved crossing the deep Goat Canyon. This, in turn, required the construction of a curved wooden trestle of 750ft in length (229m) and 200ft (61m) in height. The trestle had a fire-retardant system that was used after steam trains passed over the wooden structure. In 1976, a hurricane destroyed other trestles and the line was closed, but Goat Canyon Trestle still survived in 2022.

Goat Canyon Trestle, located east of San Diego, was built in 1933 due to damage on the original route. Situated in a desert area, efforts were made to avoid fires after trains had passed. It closed to any remaining local traffic in the 1990s and a condensed view of the huge structure is seen here in April 2015. *El cajon yacht club*

The rusting Northern Avenue steel swing bridge in Boston was built in 1908 and was used by both road and rail. The bridge is seen in June 2014, before complete closure later that year due to safety issues. *Author*

1889 as part of the New Haven Railroad. The east-west route over the river closed in 1974 after it was damaged by fire and, whilst it looks rather rusty in appearance, such was the quality of steel that it does not need to be painted. It has since 2009 been used as a walkway some 212ft (65 metres) above the river. The walkway is on the world's oldest disused railroad steel cantilevered bridge, and for a time was also the longest footway on a disused railroad bridge in the world.

The High Steel Bridge is on the Olympic Peninsula that lies across from Seattle. The spectacular riveted single steel truss arched bridge was originally opened in 1929 for a logging railroad, unlocking a previously inaccessible forest area. The line closed in the 1970s, but the steel bridge remains and is 375ft (114m) in height above a formidable chasm. Nearby Vance Creek Bridge is similarly built of steel construction and was also opened in 1929 to carry timber. At 347ft (106m) above the valley floor, it is also one of the highest closed railroad bridge structures.

Subways and freight tunnels

A 2ft-gauge underground freight delivery network was provided in Chicago. Spoil from construction was used to extend the waterfront, whilst coal and ash were original freight, but other goods were conveyed, on a grid pattern of lines, almost all entirely under the streets. At its peak, before the First World War, the network included 150 electric locomotives and 60 miles (97km) of tunnel, whilst a rack section was also provided on a steep part of the network. The network closed in 1959, but many of the tunnels remain and are now used as service ducts or for cables. Taken together, this is the longest non-mining former tunnel network in the world.

The Cincinnati subway was constructed on part of the route of an old canal. Tunnels and seven stations were built, but they were never completed after the First World War due to increasing costs and car ownership, local political infighting and a wider economic downturn. Later attempts to revive the project have not been successful and it remains America's largest abandoned subway.

Finally, on the subject of subways, the City Hall station in New York was on the first line to be constructed under the city. Although closed in 1945, the attractive ornate subway station still survives.

Interurban

Somewhat related to the tram, called streetcar in the USA, and found particularly in the Northeast and Midwest, were what were known as interurban routes. These lines were built mainly alongside roads and it was estimated that about 15,000 miles (24,000km) were in operation before the First World War. Although electrified, many succumbed to the growth of bus and car traffic starting in the 1930s, whilst most of the rest closed after the Second World War. The South Shore Line in Chicago is one of the last remaining, although some lines were converted to diesel operation and survived carrying freight, whilst a few have had their trackbed reused as modern light rail.

Long Beach interurban service with Pacific Electric coach No 1543. Built in 1911 and known as 'Blimp Cars' because of their round windows, this car and the line were last used in 1961. It is seen at the Travel Town Museum in California in September 2004. *Author*

CHAPTER 14

SOME GREAT AMERICAN LOST RAILROADS

It would be impossible to confine to one chapter the numerous fascinating and historic lost lines in the USA. As such, I have selected just a few of my personal favourite lost routes not mentioned elsewhere in this book.

The Denver & Rio Grande Railroad originated mainly due to the discovery of gold, silver and coal in the difficult Colorado mountain terrain. It became the most distinctive and, at one time, also included the largest 3ft narrow-gauge railroad in North America, whilst parts of the mountainous countryside through which it travelled were spectacular.

The first section opened in 1871, penetrating Colorado's steep valleys and pushing engineers' ingenuity to the limit. After developing into a considerable network, 'Western' was added to its name in 1921. The branch to Pagosa Springs was amongst the

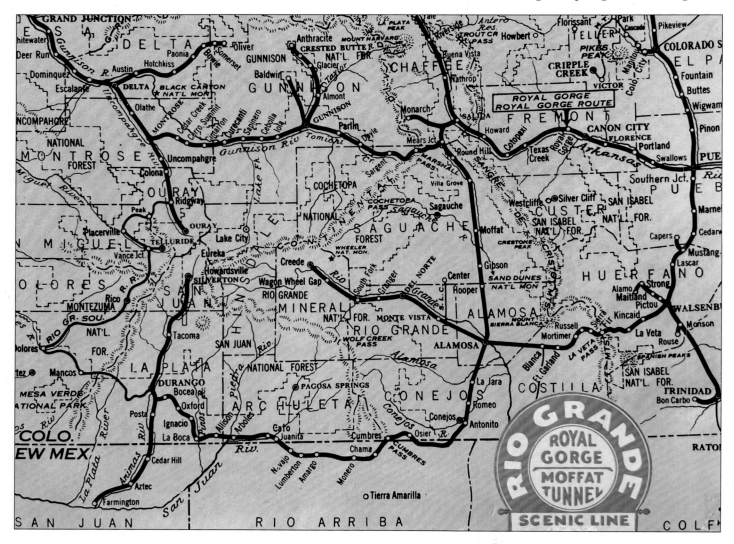

Map of the Rio Grande Railroad showing the narrow-gauge circle of lines. *Author's collection*

first to close in 1935, whilst the branch to Santa Fe and that from Leadville to Ibex, which reached an altitude of 11,512ft (3,509m), closed in the 1940s. Elsewhere, a line twisted and turned through Marshall Pass, reaching an altitude of 10,846ft (3,306m). This section closed, in part, in 1949 and more fully in 1955, breaking the narrow-gauge circle of lines.

The end of the remaining narrow-gauge sections came in the 1960s. Freight on the last 250-mile (400km) Alamosa–Farmington via Durango section ceased in 1967. This was the last narrow-gauge steam freight common carrier in the USA. During the winter of 1964–65, the line over the Cumbres Pass was closed for five months, mostly because of lack of traffic rather than weather conditions, and in 1967 all narrow-gauge working ceased except on the Silverton branch.

The Tennessee Pass line reached a height of 10,240ft (3,121m). Originally opened in 1881 as a narrow-gauge line, it was later converted to standard-gauge. It eventually became the highest main line in the USA until the route was closed in 1997, after a merger with the Union Pacific, who diverted traffic on to an alternative route via the Moffat Tunnel. However, track and the tunnel at Tennessee Pass remain and plans to reopen the route have been considered.

Standard-gauge sections remain in use, whilst the Silvertown branch was sold in 1979 and became a heritage line. The Cumbres & Toltec Scenic heritage railroad runs on a further narrow-gauge section, whilst a standard-gauge heritage line operates through the Royal Gorge, all operating along scenic parts of the ex-Rio Grande.

An original narrow-gauge locomotive from the Denver & Rio Grande Railroad at Knott's Berry Farm theme park, seen in September 2004. At its height there was a considerable network of narrow-gauge lines operated by the railroad. *Author*

TEN GREAT LOST RAILWAYS OF THE WORLD – THE OVERSEAS EXTENSION

One of the world's most famous abandoned routes was the Florida East Coast Railway's extension from Miami to Key West. The 127-mile (204km) section, beyond the mainland, was the vision of the bold industrialist Henry Flagler and the enormous task of building the line was completed in January 1912.

The route to Key West required an amazing number of bridges over the sea between a series of islands known as the Florida Keys, the longest bridge being some 7 miles (11km) in length. So extensive were the engineering works on the line over the stretches of sea that it became known as the Overseas Railroad or Overseas Extension. It was sometimes called an eighth wonder of the world as the route was recognised as the greatest railroad engineering feat in the USA and possibly the world.

The terminus at Key West was used as a connecting port for Havana in Cuba and it was hoped ships using the Panama Canal would also use this as the first port of call in the USA, but this did not materialise. The line was struck by hurricanes and slow speeds were required over some of the bridges. Traffic did not meet expectations and the wider economic situation created by the Depression led the railroad into bankruptcy.

In September 1935, with the lowest barometer readings ever recorded in the Western hemisphere, the 'Great Labor Day Hurricane' tore through the middle section of the line, completely destroying some 40 miles (65km) of track and numerous bridges. A train full of the First World War veterans was also wrecked with the loss of many lives.

The cost of rebuilding was prohibitive, the line closed and the stranded stock was brought back to the mainland by boat. The route was sold to the government, which modified the remaining bridges to accommodate a road. In 1982, new road bridges were constructed, but some sections of the former railroad bridges still survive, including the refurbished Seven Mile Bridge and the Overseas Heritage Trail outlines key features on the former route.

Map of the Florida East Coast Railway Overseas Extension and link to Miami.

Above: An emblem on a coach of the Florida East Coast Railway showing a train crossing the 2½-mile (4km) and 186-arched concrete Long Key Viaduct, seen at the Gold Coast Railroad Museum in Miami in February 2016. *Author*

Right: A timetable board indicating the train times for passengers traveling between New York and Key West and then by ship to Havana in Cuba, recorded at a museum in Key West in February 2016. A hurricane in 1935 caused so much damage the line was never reopened. *Author*

The abandoned Bahia Honda Bridge across the Florida Keys, seen in July 2016. The broken concrete fences on top of the bridge date from the period when, after closure, the rail bridge was converted into road use. *Daniel Chodusov*

It is interesting that from 1932 the Florida East Coast Railway started to substitute bus services on its branch lines, and these gradually closed. Even if the line to Key West had not been damaged, it is unlikely it would have survived until today. A year after the line opened, Henry Flagler slipped, broke his hip and died. Two days later, every employee, every train and every piece of equipment on the Florida East Coast Railway was brought to a standstill and all staff stood at attention for ten minutes to honour Florida's great railroad builder.

Long lengths of closure

The Chicago Great Western Railway covered an area west of Chicago and became known as the 'Corn Belt Route'. Competing with other lines, it specialised in good customer service, innovation and prudent spending. Dieselisation was completed by 1950, but it ran through sparsely populated areas and the last passenger trains ran in 1965. A merger with a rival company in 1968, that only wanted a section of the line that acted as a gateway to Kansas City, was to spell the end of the line. Consequently,

TEN GREAT LOST RAILWAYS OF THE WORLD – THE MILWAUKEE ROAD PACIFIC EXTENSION

The Chicago, Milwaukee, St. Paul & Pacific Railroad became known as the 'Milwaukee Road' and eventually ran from Chicago to Puget Sound on the Pacific coast near Seattle, over what was known as the 'Pacific Extension'. Completed in 1909, the route was the last great transcontinental line to be built. Parts of the route involved steep gradients and, as a consequence, some 656 miles (1,056km) were electrified. Although electrification took place in two different localities, together they made the line the longest electrified route in the USA. Running westward beyond Milwaukee, the route passed through extensive areas of little population and, although there was agricultural freight, the railroad was bankrupt by 1925.

However, services continued and the 'Hiawatha' express passenger trains were introduced. As road and air competition mounted, passenger losses increased and these services were discontinued in 1961. The electrified sections were also decommissioned in 1973, just as oil prices rocketed. Track and other maintenance issues were deferred, but by 1977 the railroad was bankrupt again. This led to the closure in 1980 of the 1,100-mile (1,770km) main transcontinental line section between Miles City in Montana and Cedar Falls in Washington. This was the largest single closure of a main line in the world.

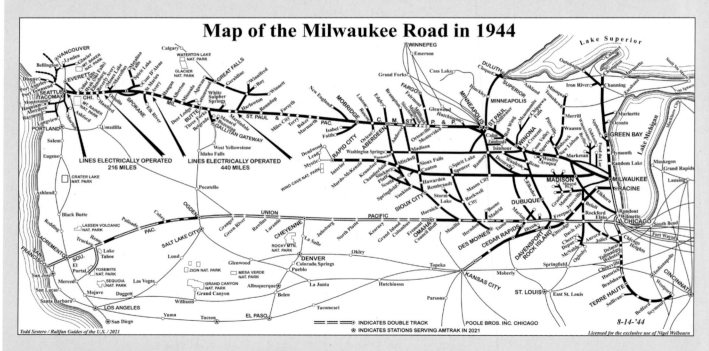

Map of the Milwaukee Road and connecting lines in 1944. *Railfan Guides of the US*

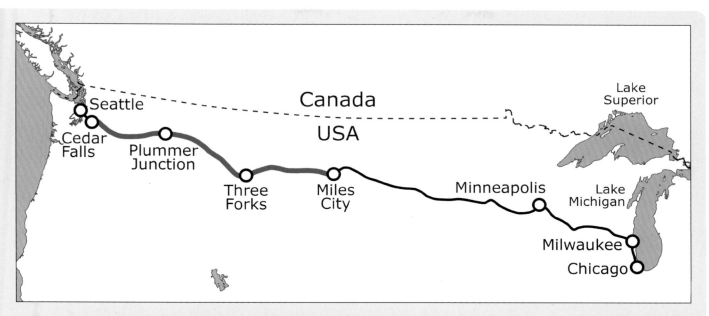

Map of the Milwaukee Road closed transcontinental Pacific Extension west of Miles City.

One of the electrified sections of the Milwaukee Road with electric locomotive MILW E71 arriving at Deer Lodge Montana in August 1971. Originally intended for export to the Soviet Union the locomotives were nicknamed 'Little Joe' after Stalin. Electric traction was abandoned in 1973. *Drew Jacksich*

the early 1970s saw much of its 1,411 miles (2,270km) of lines closed rapidly in stages. Only a few segments of this once large network remain today.

The Colorado Midland Railway closed 221 miles (356km) of line as early as 1918 as the original route had steep gradients, and a shorter alternative route opened. The Fort Smith & Western Railroad closed 250 miles (402km) of route in 1939 as it 'didn't really go anywhere' and it was generally considered that it should not have been built. The Cincinnati & Lake Erie Railroad saw 270 miles (435km) of line abandoned in 1941. The Missouri & North Arkansas Railroad, with 335 miles (539km) of line, was also a large abandonment in 1948.

The New York, Ontario & Western Railway was some 541 miles (870km) in length and closed in 1957. It was one of the larger abandonments and the first to close its main line. A significant later closure included the Buffalo & Susquehanna Railroad, where 254 miles (409km) were abandoned in 1979.

Some remarkable closures

The Central and Union Pacific railroads completed the first transcontinental line in 1869. The construction teams met at Promontory Point in Utah, where the 'Golden Spike' ceremony was conducted to celebrate the completion of the route. In the 1870s, improvements were made to parts of the line and some sections were abandoned. These are some of the first closures in North America that are still visible today. In 1904, a new shorter line bypassed Promontory Point, but the historic site and track remains.

The Green Mountain Railway was a unique 4ft 8in gauge rack line running to the 1,527ft (465m) summit of what is now called Cadillac Mountain, near Bar Harbor, Maine. The line opened in 1883, but to reach the terminus from the coast involved a road journey to Eagle Lake, then a boat ride to the base of the steep cog line. A hotel was provided at the top of the mountain, but the short season and an improved mountain road resulted in the line closing as early as 1890. The locomotives were transferred to the Mount Washington Cog Railway, whilst the summit hotel closed in 1895 and was dismantled.

The Denver, South Park & Pacific Railroad was originally built to a 3ft gauge to serve a mining boom at Leadville. Part of the route involved the 'High Line' over Colorado's mountains. This included the Alpine Tunnel, at an altitude of 11,523ft (3,512m), the highest

The site of the mountaintop hotel served by the Green Mountain Railway seen in July 2015. A road was constructed up the mountain and mischief was known to take place in the hotel. The railway closed in 1890 and the hotel soon after. *Author*

A Heisler locomotive built in 1918 for the Hetch Hetchy Railroad that was used in the construction of the Californian dam across the valley of that name. It is seen at the Travel Town Museum California in September 2004. The gearing mechanism allowed such locomotives to climb steep gradients. *Author*

and longest abandoned narrow-gauge tunnel in North America, whilst Alpine Tunnel station was for a time the highest in the USA. Opening in 1892, the section was difficult to operate, particularly in winter and damage to the line in 1910 resulted in its closure.

The Argentine & Gray's Peak Railway was a 3ft-gauge line in Colorado that opened in 1906, running to Mount McClellan in 1906. Reaching 13,587ft (4,141m), it was the highest adhesion-worked line in America, with Shay locomotives pulling two or three coaches to the summit on grades of up to 1 in 16. Railcars were introduced in 1916 as a cost-saving exercise, but the line closed in 1918.

The Nevada County Narrow Gauge Railroad was a 3ft-gauge line that opened in 1876 and still paid dividends in the late 1930s. Unfortunately, the scrap value during the Second World War of metal viaducts on the line exceeded its transportation value and it was closed in 1942 and stripped of its steel.

The Yosemite Valley Railroad opened in 1907 and made a profit for thirty-two of its thirty-eight years. Pullman and observation cars allowed the scenic route to the National Park to be enjoyed. Passenger traffic was discouraged during the Second World War and the line closed in 1945, just before California's post-war boom and the park's traffic congestion.

The Virginia & Truckee Railroad was built to tap into a silver mining area, and by 1863 there were thirty trains a day between Carson and Virginia cities. The railroad for a time became the richest in the world in terms of return on capital, but it closed in 1950.

The San Diego & Arizona Railway was known as the 'Impossible Railroad' because of the breathtaking but difficult terrain through which it passed to the east of San Diego, through formidable mountains and hot desolate desert. Damage through rock landslides and washouts interrupted services and weakened the financial position of the line, which closed in 1984.

The Asheville & Spartanburg Railroad was the first to be built with large-scale convict labour. The line, which became part of the Southern Railway, included a section of 1 in 20 gradient at Saluda, which was the steepest grade on a main line route in the USA. The grade was infamous for runaway train accidents and closed in 2001.

The Black Mesa & Lake Powell Railroad was the first in the world to use 50kv AC voltage when it opened in 1973. The 78-mile (125km) coal-carrying line closed after a relatively short life in 2019 as shale gas increasingly replaced coal in the USA. The closure also highlighted the vast reduction in electrified freight routes, with just a few short lines remaining in 2022.

WORLD'S CROOKEDEST LOST LINE

The Mount Tamalpais & Muir Woods Railway was described as the 'crookedest railroad in the world'. Opened in 1896, Shay locomotives, geared to travel at about 8mph, wound and twisted their way to a height of 2,353ft (717m) at the Tavern of Tamalpais terminus above the Golden Gate in California. Passengers using the line could then descend entirely by gravity in a carriage with a brakeman. The tourist line closed in 1929 after wildfires had ruined the scenery and a growth in road traffic to the mountain summit.

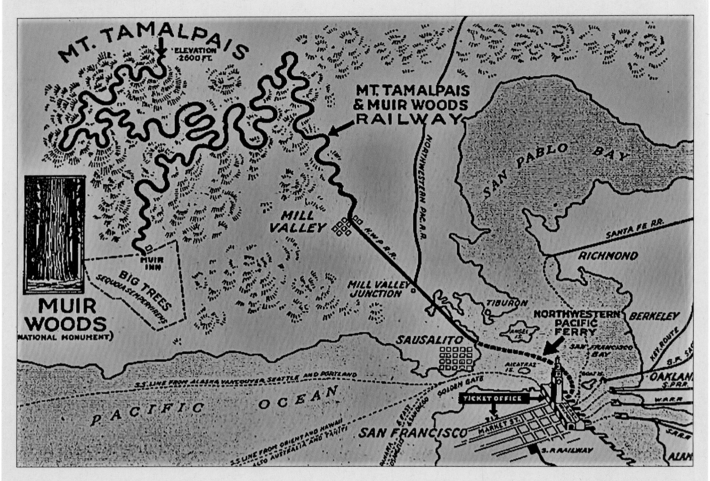

Mount Tamalpais & Muir Woods Railway map, circa 1910, of the world's crookedest railway that closed in 1929. *Author's collection*

CHAPTER 15

MEXICO, CENTRAL AMERICA AND THE CARIBBEAN

Mexico

By the First World War, a network of mostly standard-gauge railways had been established, with main routes fanning out from Mexico City to the coast and United States. Steep gradients were required to reach the central plateau and impressive engineering works to overcome areas of difficult, but often scenic, terrain. A coast-to-coast line was also built across the narrowest part of Mexico. The main line network continued to be expanded until the early 1960s and a comprehensive train service, including Pullman sleeping, restaurant and observation cars, linked major cities.

There has been a decline over many years with the first lines being abandoned in the 1940s and 1950s. Yet, in the 1960s, some 22 million passengers were still using the railways each year and in 1966 new railcars were exported to Mexico from Britain. However, the network was increasingly neglected, steam and ancient stock lingered on some lines and many services were slow and increasingly unreliable. Competition from roads and domestic air routes led to declining revenues, losses increased, and investment dried up. This resulted in significant closures and, by the 1980s, large numbers of remaining passenger and sleeper services came to an end.

A Mexican state-owned narrow-gauge freight train being hauled by American built 2-8-0 No 270 in September 1966 through the San Lázaro Yards in Mexico City, note the mixed-gauge track, all in poor condition. *Roger Puta*

Disused lines on the quay at the port of Manzanillo in Mexico, seen in January 2013. The railway still runs to the town for freight traffic, but not to this particular part of the port. *Author*

By 2000, the last remaining passenger services had ceased, except for a few mostly tourist and commuter services. Freight remains, but the rapid abandonment of remaining electrified lines after the railways were privatised in the 1990s resulted in new electric locomotives ordered from the USA not being delivered. There remain freight links to the USA, but the interchange with Guatemala is currently out of use and today it is estimated that over half of the Mexican network is closed.

Although mostly a standard-gauge network, there was also a number of mixed and narrow-gauge passenger lines of both 2 and 3ft, some of which were later converted to standard-gauge. Of the remaining narrow-gauge lines, the Huatulco branch was abandoned in 1951 and the Zacatlán and Huajuapan branches were abandoned in 1958. The branches were named after towns they never actually served; the final leg of the journey was always undertaken by road.

In the Yucatán Peninsula, twine was produced and an isolated 3ft network of public railways operated until closure in 1975. Several of the locomotives were then sold to the Walt Disney Company and restored for use at theme parks. The main routes in the peninsula were complemented by a huge network of independent plantation even narrower-gauge lines that were used to move sisal, sugar and corn. Passengers were even conveyed on some sections, but all these agricultural railways subsequently closed. Some sections of track remain and are informally used by horse-drawn tourist vehicles.

Central America

Belize
There are a number of disused lines, but the only public railway was the 25-mile (40km) metre-gauge Stan Creek Railway that opened in 1913 from the Middlesex banana plantations to the port of Dangriga. The plantations were destroyed by disease in the 1930s and the line closed in 1937. Some short logging lines survived until the early 1960s.

Costa Rica
The country once had an extensive 3ft 6in narrow-gauge network, even including some electrified lines, much of it designed to transport bananas and coffee to ports

Many lines with their station buildings and railway structures were simply abandoned, not only on branch lines but on more significant routes such as the 300-mile (480km) ex-Mexico North West Railway's loop from Chihuahua to El Paso. Even where lines remained open for freight, abandoned structures such as between Vera Cruz and Mexico City can be found. In the 1980s, parts of the line were upgraded and a number of bridges and viaducts on the route were replaced by new structures. This resulted in the original 1872 curving viaduct known as the Metlac Bridge, towering some 92ft (28m) above the river, being abandoned. The scenic line was known as the 'rail trip of a thousand wonders' before it was closed to passengers in the 1990s.

for export on both the Pacific and Caribbean coasts. Earthquakes in 1991 and 1995 led to the abandonment of much of the network and the link to Panama. Whilst remaining passenger trains mostly ceased in 1995, a few services survived including freight on some sections of line until 2011. An infrequent passenger train continued from San José for a while, but a commuter line was upgraded here and revival elsewhere has been proposed.

One line also reopened, being a section for tourists from a station outside Puntarenas using a section of the ex-Pacific Railroad. The train on the line is sometimes called the 'Tico Tren' and, on the day I travelled, consisted of two well-restored coaches, all hauled by a vintage diesel engine. A note from my diary of January 2013 records:

Although abandoned track and stock remain in Puntarenas, the tourist train now starts outside the port. It slowly ran through a very narrow bored tunnel and over a rusting girder bridge, climbing ever deeper into the Costa Rican countryside. The single line was clearly once very busy as the numerous rusting passing loops and disused wayside stations testify. After over an hour the train arrived at the remote station of Ceiba and blocked the level crossing, but the held-up cars and motor bikes all seemed delighted to see a train.

The Costa Rica Pacific Railroad was originally used to transport the country's coffee harvests from the highlands to the coastal ports. A section of line now stops short of the port of Puntarenas, as seen here in January 2013. *Author*

A disused Costa Rica Pacific Railroad line into the centre of Puntarenas, seen in January 2013. The weakness of Latin American railways has resulted in that they sometimes no longer run to prime locations in the centre of cities. Note the electrification masts which were operational until the early 1990s . *Author*

Ceiba station on the former Costa Rica Pacific Railroad to Puntarenas is now used as a police station and is the terminus of tourist trains. The view here was taken in January 2013. *Author*

El Salvador

In 1975, the two nationalised lines were merged and together covered about 345 miles (555km) of metre-gauge routes. Whilst remaining passenger services became increasingly run-down and all services ceased in 2002, some short sections were revived, but no trains have run since 2013.

The International Railways of Central America was a United States-based company that assumed control of main routes in El Salvador and Guatemala in 1912. It provided links to Guatemala in 1929 that afforded El Salvador access to the Caribbean. The company was purchased by the Guatemalan government in 1968 and the link was closed.

Guatemala

A network of about 550 miles (885km) of metre-gauge lines with links to Mexico, Honduras and El Salvador once existed. A link between the Caribbean Sea and Pacific Ocean was also provided. The railways suffered due to the decline in banana traffic and road competition. They were nationalised in the 1960s but collapsed in 1996 whilst in the course of being re-privatised due to the poor state of the track and rolling stock after years of underinvestment. A few sections of line north of Guatemala City were restored to service, but all remaining services ceased in 2007. The subsequent theft of track and infrastructure makes reopening increasingly difficult, but proposals to regauge and reopen the line to Mexico are ongoing. The main station at Guatemala City is now a museum.

A Baldwin built 2-8-2 No 205 seen between Zacapa and Guatemala City in March 1996. Operations ceased in 2007, but the locomotive has been preserved at the former main station at Guatemala City. *Vincent Corasi*

Honduras

Narrow 3ft 6in and 3ft lines were mainly located on the Caribbean coast and were originally operated by two American-owned banana companies. One network extended to about 370 miles (600km) and the other to about 120 miles (190km). Any remaining passenger services ceased in 2006, with the exception of short stretches at San Pedro Sula and in the Cuero y Salado wildlife park.

Nicaragua

Lines never connected the two coasts and were concentrated on the Pacific coast. The network was damaged by an earthquake in 1972, but about 230 miles (372km) of 3ft 6in line continued in use on the Pacific coast, whilst passenger services ran to and from the capital Managua. Nevertheless, costs were increasing, and passenger numbers and freight were declining; as a result, most lines were closed in 1993 and the last remaining line closed by 2001.

Panama

Part of the approximately 100-mile (160km) Chiriquí National Railroad was also considered for use in a

Above: Santo Tomas station in Guatemala in February 2016 with a disused water crane. Railway services ceased in 2007 and since that time the theft of assets, even including metal bridges, has made the prospect of any reopening unlikely. *Author*

Right: Santo Tomas station with a disused railway box car seen February 2016. Many of the former railway buildings here have been put to new uses. The former main station at Guatemala City is used as a railway museum. *Author*

possible north-south Trans-American railway linking Mexico with Argentina. The grand scheme required a number of new railway connections to be constructed but was never fulfilled and remaining sections of line in Panama were closed by the early 1990s. Two associated 3ft-gauge banana railways, once extending to about 186 miles (300km), also closed by 2008.

The Panama Railway was a predecessor of the canal and remains as one of the few busy freight railways in Central America linking the Atlantic and Pacific oceans. Tourist passenger trains also run, but the original station in the centre of Panama City is closed. The Panama Canal also has a rack railway to tow ships through the locks, but some sections have been closed as a result of rationalisation.

Right: The swing bridge at Miraflores Locks was opened in 1942, as part of a Trans-American Railway, but its condition had deteriorated and it was dismantled in 2018 and transported along the Panama Canal to be cut up. A surviving approach ramp is seen here in March 2020. *Author*

Below: The swing bridge over the Panama Canal at Miraflores Locks in January 2013. This former railway bridge was later surfaced for road use. One of the 'mule' rack locomotives used to haul ships through the canal is also to be noted. *Author*

Caribbean & Atlantic islands

Ascension Island

On the Atlantic Ascension Island, a narrow-gauge line was constructed in the 1860s between a coastal wharf and storage areas. Sadly, giant struggling live turtles were tipped on their back and conveyed on hand-worked wagons to a storage pond before the poor creatures were killed for food. The line had closed by the 1930s and the seas around the island have since become a marine reserve.

Antigua

A narrow 2ft 6in gauge network extended for over 50 miles (80km) serving the sugar mills. After closure in 1971, one locomotive was returned to Britain and can be seen at the Welshpool & Llanfair Railway.

Aruba

A number of short narrow-gauge mineral lines had an equally short life, whilst in the 1920s lines were built in association with two large oil refineries, one surviving until the early 1960s.

Barbados

A 3ft 6in narrow-gauge line ran from Bridgetown to Carrington and was extended to some 24 miles (39km) to Belleplaine in 1883. The 2ft 6in route contained almost 100 bridges and some steep 1 in 33 gradients. The railway became increasingly run-down and passenger services ceased in 1934, largely due to safety concerns. The railway continued to run sugar cane trains sporadically until final closure in 1937. In 2018, a new tourist line opened.

Bermuda

In the Atlantic, a 22-mile (37km) short-lived standard-gauge line ran from end to end of the once British colony. The line opened in 1931 and was well used, as cars at that time were frowned upon on the island. However, after intense wartime use the line was run-down, significant repairs were required, cars were allowed on the island and it closed after just seventeen years' use in 1948. The Astor family had a private railway to connect their estate at Ferry Reach to a main line station. Parts of the line are today used as a walking trail.

Viaduct piers on the sandy shore at Frank's Bay, in May 2013, of the former Bermuda Railway indicating the substantial nature of many of the coastal engineering works. The railway closed in 1948. *Douglas Lander/Alamy*

On closure, the stock was sold to Guyana in South America, but the once busy 60-mile (97km) railway here closed in 1972. However, two petrol-driven freight cars were still extant in 2014, used as stores.

Caicos islands

A 14-mile (22.5km) narrow-gauge network on East Caicos conveyed sisal to a quay at Jacksonville. The lines fell out of use during the First World War and the island became uninhabited, but the ruins of Jacksonville and its railways are still in evidence.

Cuba

The largest Caribbean island is Cuba and the first railways were built by Spanish colonists as early as 1837, to convey sugar cane, tobacco and pineapple from rich farm lands to the docks. The opening date of this railway even beat the first railway in Spain and makes the Cuban Railways the oldest in Latin America.

The construction of lines to both standard and narrow-gauges continued and Cuba developed as one of the world's largest sugar producers, with an extensive railway network. Railway growth was originally in private hands, in particular British and American companies; for example, the United Railways of Havana were once controlled by Britain and run in Cuba by British managers.

Cuba's railways were closely associated with America, but political upheaval in the 1950s, including Che Guevara ripping up track at Santa Clara, resulted

WORLD'S DENSEST RAILWAY NETWORK PER INHABITANT

When measured by total population, Cuba for a time became the country with the most railway track per head of population, in the world. The main standard-gauge passenger lines constituted about a third of the total mileage, and in the 1970s there were about 3,000 miles (4,830km) of public railway and over 6,000 miles (9,650km) of non-public railway mostly running from the sugar cane fields to the sugar mills, much of which was narrow-gauge.

An American 0-4-0T Porter locomotive dating from 1909 No 1122 seen at José Smith Comas sugar works in Cuba in March 1997. Although no longer operating as a sugar railway, some locomotives have been preserved at a museum here. *Vincent Corasi*

in the railways being nationalised by Fidel Castro. A subsequent blockade of Cuba by America had a detrimental effect on Cuban railways, the remaining train ferry to Miami was cut and the network became run-down. Forced to use aging and unreliable equipment, rows of engines were laid up due to a lack of spare parts, and by 2019 no brand-new railcars had been delivered since 1970, but since then brand-new trains built in China have entered service

Cuba's sugar railways have faced a massive decline as the sugar industry contracted. This was due in part to the collapse of the Soviet Union, the main importer of Cuban sugar, and a wider fall in sugar demand. Over 100 sugar mills and their railways have been closed. Many sugar lines were operated by elderly American locomotives until the early 2000s, but most steam had disappeared by 2007, except on a number of tourist sections including the Rafael Freyre system.

Nevertheless, some sugar mills and their lines still remain and spring into action during the sugar harvest.

Lines have also closed due to damage caused by natural events, in particular hurricane damage. In September 2017, a hurricane caused extensive damage to the overhead equipment of the Hershey Railway, Cuba's last remaining electric railway. By 2021, only part of the line had reopened from the former sugar town of Hershey.

Whilst there are closed passenger lines and it is no longer possible to travel to parts of the island by train, a network of secondary lines still remains, including the branch to Guantanamo Bay. However, bus services have a reputation of being more reliable and many remaining branch lines are in a poor state of repair, trains sometimes only run every fourth day, speeds are slow, timetables are virtually non-existent, and services could be unreliable.

Sugar cane is seen arriving at the Julio Reyes Cairo sugar mill, named after a Cuban revolutionary, in March 1994. The locomotive was taken out of service and became derelict and was eventually dismantled. *Vincent Corasi*

The main east-west Havana–Santiago de Cuba line survives, but petty officialdom, unreliability and the poor condition of passenger stock had assisted in reducing passenger numbers. In 2019, new stock from China was introduced and track and stations are slowly being improved. Cuba is the last of the Caribbean islands to retain a worthwhile railway system.

Dominican Republic

Two passenger lines once existed, including the 2ft 6in narrow-gauge railway, which at the port at Puerto Plata involved a section of Abt rack track. By 1908, the line had extended some 62 miles (100km) to Moca, where further lines, built to a different gauge, once provided connections. In 1917, the rack section was replaced by a new, less steeply graded, route that used Shay locomotives. Most of this network closed in 1951 and the only tunnel on the line has been converted into road use. The second 3ft 6in passenger line ran some 77 miles (124km) between Sanchez and La Vega and the last part survived until 1976.

Other lines were built for the sugar plantations and included a standard-gauge central area railway comprising of about 470-miles (757km) of line that was opened in 1911. There was also a network of about 150 miles (240km) of various narrow-gauge sugar cane railways. Many had closed by the 1950s, but a number of sections continued in use.

Guadeloupe

The twin main islands both had narrow-gauge railways serving sugar mills. The sugar industry on the islands declined, in part due to droughts and hurricanes, but in the 1970s there were still some fifteen diesel locomotives working on the island's railways. Sugar cane traffic was gradually replaced by banana traffic, but the last line closed after hurricane damage in 1989.

Haïti

Major agricultural plantations, sugar cane and industries were linked to freight and passenger railways. Two 2ft 6in narrow-gauge lines ran out from Gare du Nord at Port-au-Prince. These were the 27-mile (43km) line to Mannevile, where a lakeside wharf was built to connect with the Dominican Republic, and the 22-mile (36km) to Léogâne, both opening in the 1900s. Regular passenger services ceased in the 1930s, but passenger stock was occasionally used on rural parts of the lines until the mid-1950s. Some remaining sections were used for sugar cane traffic until the 1990s.

A 3ft 6in gauge line, the first section of which opened in 1905, also ran from Gare MacDonald at Port-au-Prince some 90 miles (145km) to St Marc and Verrettes. Proposed connections from this route to two other isolated island passenger lines were never completed. Sections were closed due to hurricane damage in 1963, but parts survived until 1977.

Jamaica

The initial section of what became a 350-mile (563km) standard-gauge railway on the island was the first railway to be opened in the British Empire in 1845. Over forty tunnels were eventually required on the network of lines, due to the mountain terrain in some parts, but lines served most of the key settlements on the island. Bananas, other fruit and sugar were important freight. Much of the equipment was British and Wickham passenger diesel railcars were introduced in 1939.

Travelling mail carriages were withdrawn in the 1960s and a decline in freight traffic and passenger numbers resulted in ever-increasing subsidies being required. In the 1970s, a million passengers a year were still using the network, but two branch lines were closed to reduce costs. The lack of maintenance over many years, together with hurricane damage, saw remaining services being withdrawn in 1992. There have been attempts at a revival and some tourist proposals, but after a short revival of the Kingston–Spanish Town section in 2012 all lines remain closed to passenger services. Apart from a few relatively short mineral lines, associated with the bauxite industry, all the original passenger lines are abandoned.

Martinique

Starting in the 1870s, a network of narrow-gauge sugar railways, serving about twenty sugar factories, developed. A volcano eruption in 1902 caused damage, but there was a general decline in the sugar industry over many years and all the railways had closed by the 1970s, with remaining sugar factories replacing their railways with road tractors and trailers. A short heritage line is to be found on the island.

Puerto Rico

By 1907, the northern and southern metre-gauge coastal railways had been joined up. This created a

Montego Bay station in Jamaica was apparently at this time a tourist no-go area so this view, where the line crosses a road just outside the station, was taken in January 2013. The line remains – rather litter strewn – and any plans to run this section as a heritage tourist railway seem some way off fruition. *Author*

main line around the coast that connected most coastal towns and provided a 168-mile (270Km) link from San Juan in the north to Ponce in the south. Sugar traffic was important, but passengers were conveyed. In 1953, passenger traffic ceased as did the majority of sugar freight in 1957, although some small sections serving the sugar industry remained until the early 1990s. Seven other shorter lines also once operated on the island, all are closed.

St Kitts

A 2ft 6in sugar cane railway opened prior to the First World War and was extended in the 1920s, encircling much of the island to serve just one central sugar mill.

Originally worked by steam, diesel locomotives replaced these in the 1950s. The arrangements were efficient, resulting in the railway being one of the last to close in the Caribbean in 2005. Unlike many islands where the railways were torn up after closure, a scenic section has reopened as a tourist line, using locomotives originally intended for Poland's narrow-gauge systems.

St Lucia

Four sugar mills on the island were each served by narrow-gauge railways that were once busy in the sugar cane harvest season. However, they closed in the 1960s when sugar cane cultivation was replaced by banana plantations, which subsequently also collapsed.

Trinidad

The Trinidad Government Railway was established in 1876 and a mini-railway mania developed, with many small towns insisting on a railway connection. At its peak, plantation lines and a network of standard-gauge lines that ran from Port of Spain to most key towns extended to about 150 miles (240km). Natural asphalt from Pitch Lake was amongst the freight conveyed, whilst secondary sugar routes were also of standard-gauge. The growth of car travel after the Second World War saw the first closures and, in 1968, the last passenger service ran, but a small number of sugar lines survived until 1998. Some steam locomotives, that used the crude local oil for fuel, have been preserved on the island, whilst one was returned to the Middleton Railway in Britain.

A 4-4-0T No 12 locomotive at San Fernando in Trinidad seen in 1973, one of eighteen locomotives built by Kitson in Britain for the island's once extensive network. Closures of lines began in the 1950s with the final passenger closure in 1968. *Colour-Rail*

CHAPTER 16

SOUTH AMERICA

The railways of South America were frequently built with foreign capital. Many were built relatively late on, due in part to political differences, which also resulted in differing gauges and they developed in a somewhat ad hoc way. Originally constructed particularly for mineral and agricultural traffic to reach coastal ports, passenger services outside the main cities were often somewhat an afterthought with little coordination and today passenger services are few and far between. Even by the 1930s, railway shares were becoming worthless and subsequent road and air competition have wrought havoc on the railways. However, the weak economies of some countries have also resulted in a plethora of abandoned tracks, stations, bridges and tunnels all being very much still in evidence long after closure.

Many of the railways in South America that remain open are run-down and some operate very much on the verge of closure. Whilst important freight flows continue, particularly for minerals, international passenger trains are just a memory such as the 'Pan-Americano International Express' which once provided connections between Argentina, Bolivia and Peru. Whilst there are many plans for a railway revival, few have come to fruition and road transport has become increasingly dominant.

Argentina

Argentina initially developed a 5ft 6in gauge network simply because the first locomotives to be used were of this gauge, being purchased as surplus stock after the Crimean War. However, as the network grew, five different gauges developed and about 8,000 miles (12,875km) of metre-gauge line were also once in operation, whilst there were some dual-gauge sections. The railways grew into an extensive network and by the 1930s there were about 30,000 miles (48,280km) of line, the largest network in South America.

An extensive number of lines once radiated to the west from Buenos Aires. The rolling pampas landscape here facilitated the easy building of railways. They were not all of the same gauge, or company, and some were mixed gauge. A huge number have closed and the

remains of disused level crossings, stations and lines are a feature of the area.

The 1930s saw a decline in profits, compounded by political instability during the Second World War, and in 1948 President Juan Peron nationalised the network. Investment dried up, freight services became unreliable and lines were closed. In 1976, some 450 million passengers were carried, but passenger services became increasingly less attractive; for example, trains on the branch to Bariloche were reduced to just once a week. Not only local networks, but main routes were closed, such as that from Buenos Aires to the border with Bolivia.

Argentina had many gauges and was the largest user of surplus Hunslet Leeds built narrow-gauge locomotives after the First World War. Here 4-6-0 works No 1332 is seen at Buenos Aires railway museum in March 2010. The locomotive has been on static display since 1975. *Author*

TEN GREAT LOST RAILWAYS OF THE WORLD – THE CENTRAL TRANSANDINE RAILWAY

The Central Transandine Railway ran from Mendoza in Argentina to Valparaiso in Chile. As a larger part of the closed central section lies in Argentina, it is included here. Completed in 1910, the line once provided part of a longer route of almost 900 miles (1,450km) from Buenos Aires in Argentina to Valparaiso in Chile. Crossing the Andes through the Uspallata Pass, also known as the Cumbre Pass via the Cumbre Tunnel, which was almost 2 miles in length, this was also the highest point of the line at 10,466ft (3191m). A further thirty-five tunnels were required on the mountainous section of route. A number of rack sections using the Abt system were necessary for the steepest parts, snow sheds were also required and a section was electrified. It is the highest closed electrified main line in the world.

The line cut the 11-day sea journey via Cape Horn to about 40 hours and Pullman dining cars once operated on the route. However, in spite of the snow sheds, traffic was regularly disrupted by snow and rockfalls. In 1934, a glacier dammed up a lake of water which, when released, caused so much damage and was so expensive to repair that the line was closed for ten years.

The highest part of the line was built to a metre-gauge and there were two break-of-gauge stations either side of this section at Los Andes in Chile and at Mendoza in Argentina, which reduced the value of the through route. Tensions between the countries also saw closures during the years 1977–8 and passenger services, by this time mostly diesel railcars, ceased in 1979. Apart from a section from Los Andes to the coast, used for copper ore freight, the line has been out of use since 1984 and is deteriorating. A new road has blocked part of the line and the former railway tunnel at Cumbre was used by a road.

Right: On the Argentinian side of the Transandine Railway a railway bridge, now crudely converted for vehicular traffic on this mountainous route that once crossed the Andes, is seen in November 2013. *Bjørn Christian Tørrissen, bjornfree.com*

Below: Map of the narrow-gauge section of the Transandine Railway.

Pacific

Cumbre railway tunnel
(1.96mls / 3.1 Km) under the
Uspallata Pass

Santa Rosa
de Los Andes

Mendoza

Lláy Llay

Punta de
las Vacas

Valparaiso

Chile

Argentina

Santiago

Above: The Transandine Railway at Las Cuevas border station, with overhead electrification decaying at the high-altitude station in September 2011. Unlike the Argentinian section, the track from here to the Chilean town of Los Andes was electrified. *Keith Fender*

Right: The Transandine Railway at the Mendoza Tunnel entrance, seen here in November 2019. The remote mountain line was always subject to damage and here a rock fall has blocked the route since closure. *Miroab*

Elsewhere in Argentina, although much was in poor condition, a considerable network still remained in 1989, but in 1992 President Menem announced plans to scrap the few remaining longer-distance passenger trains. By the late 1990s, the network had been further reduced and, although commuter services continued from Buenos Aries, many remaining lines were in an even poorer state of repair. However, in more recent years investment has increased and some passenger services have been restored.

There were once numerous mineral and logging railways, many in remote areas. The 162-mile (260km) Río Gallegos was a coal railway in Patagonia and was one of the more significant lines. Opened in 1951, the line was busy, but by 2004 there was just one train a day. Today, it is mostly closed and the tracks to the port have been removed, although the mine, some sections of disused track and locomotives remain. Elsewhere, while railways have not been used to transport cattle to market since the 1960s, there has in recent years been considerable investment in new freight stock and track, with grain, mineral and other freight traffic remaining.

A number of tourist railways also survive such as the 251-mile (404km) Jacobacci-Esquel line. Branded by Paul Theroux as 'The Old Patagonian Express', there was an outcry when it closed in 1992, so the provincial governments came together to save the line. Regular trains no longer run over the entire route, but steam trains run either end of the route. The 'Tren a las Nubes', 'Train to the Clouds', using a spectacular high-altitude line and the 'Train of the End of the World' are also scenic tourist lines.

Tilcara in the Andes foothills. The disused station, seen here in January 2016, is on the remains of the line that once ran all the way from Buenos Aries to La Paz in Bolivia, the Argentinian section closing to long distance trains in the 1990s. *Dr Alan Grundy*

Right: Jujuy, with the attractive white painted station, seen in January 2016. The capital of Jujuy province in Argentina the station was closed to passengers, but the building has been put to occasional other uses. The railway here was reopened for freight in 2018. *Dr Alan Grundy*

Below: Río Turbio contained Argentina's only significant coal deposits and a 2ft 6in gauge line was line built to convey coal from the mine to the port at Río Gallegos. A 2-10-2 Mitsubishi built locomotive is seen at Río Turbio in November 1996, the mine remains, but the port line closed in 2001. *Vincent Corasi*

Bolivia

A somewhat piecemeal development of the railways, due to gauge differences, physical issues such as Lake Titicaca and the Andes, together with territory loss, all contributed to two non-connected railway networks developing. The scale of the physical difficulties can be judged from the fact that, at Cóndor, the highest metre-gauge station in the world is to be found.

War with Chile resulted in Bolivia becoming landlocked, so some strategic long-distance links were developed. One line completed in the mid-1920s afforded a 1,553-mile (2,500km) route from La Paz through Argentina to the coast at Buenos Aires. Sections of this route, starting in the 1970s, were closed in Argentina, but in Bolivia the lines at Oruro and Villazón, the latter on the frontier with Argentina, were closed due to flood damage as recently as 2018.

The 284-mile (457km) line from La Paz to Arica on the coast in Chile included rack sections and was built to fulfil the peace treaty between Chile and Bolivia. The line remains in situ, but in 2005 a large section closed to regular traffic. There is a monthly freight train due to a political agreement, but suggestions to invigorate this service have been put forward

WORLD'S MOST UNUSUAL DESERT GRAVEYARD

Eighteen steam locomotives, including some heavy-duty Garratt articulated engines built in Britain, are a reminder of the vibrant railway freight traffic once found in this area. The locomotives, in a serious state of decay, are found at Uyuni, once an important railway junction. The graveyard of assorted steam locomotives and stock was abandoned in the years after the Second World War, due mainly to political instabilities that led to a decline in the mining industry. Being located at a remote and high-altitude area in the Atacama Desert has helped the rusting hulks survive for so many years.

Above: Abandoned locomotives at Uyuni seen in July 2014. In the heart of southern Bolivia and ravaged by salt winds from the adjoining salt plain, a graveyard of British built locomotives, train parts and derelict wagons are to be found. *Mike Atkinson-Smith*

Left: Abandoned trains at Uyuni seen in July 2014. Uyuni was once an important railway junction for four Bolivian lines, but its growth was curtailed due to the collapse of the mining industry and political issues with adjoining countries. *Mike Atkinson-Smith*

The railways were privatised in 1996, more sections were abandoned and there have been instances of asset stripping. The railways are generally in a poor way and only a few passenger services remain, sometimes serving remote areas where roads are poor. At both La Paz, where the handsome station was once connected via the first electrified line in South America, and at Sucre remaining passenger services have been pushed outside the cities and their central stations are no longer used by trains. Long stretches of track are out of use, but a campaign to reopen a number of lines by ex-railwaymen is ongoing.

Brazil

Many different railways with metre, standard, broad and mixed gauge lines developed and new railways were still being built in the 1950s. Lines connected with ports and the main cities, and there were connections to adjoining countries. The huge scale of the country resulted in few railways being constructed in the tropical Amazon rainforest area.

TEN GREAT LOST RAILWAYS OF THE WORLD – MADEIRA – MAMORÉ, THE DEVIL'S RAILWAY

The remote 224-mile (360km) metre-gauge Madeira–Mamoré Railway was built to avoid unnavigable rapids on a river tributary of the Amazon and was said to have a skull under every sleeper due to the death toll of at least 5–6,000 workers by malaria and other causes in the tropical rainforest. It thus became known as the 'Devil's Railway' or the 'Mad Mary'. In the 1870s, work on the railway eventually ground to a halt due to the endless deaths of the workforce in the remote area of impenetrable rainforest.

The discovery of quinine allowed work on the railway to begin again in 1907. A locomotive from the first attempt to build the line was found buried in the jungle undergrowth and the line opened in full by 1912. The line linked Porto Velho on a tributary of the Amazon with the border of Bolivia, thus providing an Atlantic outlet for Bolivia's rubber. An extension of the route was never built and decline came as early as the First World War, but the line remained open with a weekly train due to international treaty obligations until 1972.

The railway terminus at Porto Velho gave trade from Bolivia access to the navigable section of Madeira river, offering a route to the Amazon River, the Atlantic Ocean and beyond. The metre gauge line closed in 1972, but some of the track remains in situ and the two terminus stations have been preserved, along with some rolling stock.

Above: The first passenger train on the Madeira–Mamoré railway pauses on the bridge over the Madeira River in 1910. Although the Brazilian line closed by 1972, a short preserved section is to be found at Porto Velho. *Museu Paulista (USP) Collection*

Left: Map of the Madeira–Mamoré railway in Brazil.

The Leopoldina Railway

The Leopoldina network was once the largest metre-gauge and British-owned railway company in Brazil. It operated over 2,000 miles (3,220km) of line, running mostly to the north of Rio de Janeiro. The railway originally expanded by amalgamating with other routes. It encompassed areas of difficult terrain, with 10,000 bridges and culverts and included some rack sections. The railway ran into financial problems and was taken over by the government in 1949. Today, few sections survive.

A gateway to Brazil

One of the two adjoining lines that linked São Paulo on the Brazilian Plateau with the port of Santos on the Atlantic coast is closed. The original steeply graded 12-mile (20km) 5ft 3ins gauge single line involved cable-worked inclines operated by stationary engines and opened in 1867. Because of the volume of traffic, in particular coffee, a new second double track line with cable-worked inclines was opened in 1901.

Passenger trains operated over the inclines and 'locomotive brake vans' were used to grip the cable and haul the trains on these sections. At its peak, 6,000 tons of freight and 3,000 passengers travelled on the lines daily. The cable inclines of the original line were used until 1970 and the second line until 1982. In 1974, new electric trains saw rationalisation and rebuilding using just the original line. Cable sections were converted to rack working and all passenger services ceased, but freight remains on just the original line.

Decline

Nationalisation first began in the 1950s, but by the 1970s nationalisation of several railways, coupled with political upheaval, resulted in budget cuts and many of the secondary and branch lines were closed. Most remaining narrow-gauge passenger and sugar lines also closed during this period, with one Baldwin locomotive from such a line eventually arriving on the Brecon Mountain Railway in Wales.

By the 1980s, a large number of railways had been allowed to fall into disrepair and this in turn led to long-distance passenger trains being cut, together with the wholesale closure of remaining local passenger services. In the 1990s, the railways were re-privatised, but much track and stock was by this time in an appalling condition, forcing further closures and resulting in the end of almost all remaining long-distance passenger trains.

Narrow-gauge at São João del Rei, north of Rio de Janeiro in August 1994, with No 22 a Baldwin 4-4-0 dating from 1912. The majority of the line closed to remaining traffic in 1983, but a heritage section runs from this station which has been turned into a museum. *Vincent Corasi*

Some examples highlight the loss of lines, while a network of extensive long-distance passenger routes centred on Ponta Grossa are all closed and many fine stations throughout the country are in ruins. Original passenger lines once serving the populated hinterland between Rio De Janeiro and São Paulo no longer exist and even electrified routes are closed.

Three non-suburban passenger services remain, but some new metro lines have opened. Considerable lengths of remaining line are used by freight, in particular by heavy iron ore trains, but in general passenger trains have been marginalised.

Chile

One of the first railways linked the capital Santiago with its port at Valparaiso, but today is disused for passengers beyond a short distance from Valparaiso. The main part of the line once continued eastward climbing over the Andes and crossing into Argentina and is thus included under the latter country.

The railways developed both narrow and broad-gauge routes and a main north-south longitudinal line ran the length of the country. Parts of the main line are in a poor state of repair, particularly north of Santiago, and it no longer serves the southern terminus of Puerto Montt.

Mapocho station in Santiago opened in 1913 and served Valparaiso in particular, but trains were diverted from the centrally positioned station in 1986. The following year the station was abandoned, but the attractive building remains in new uses, as seen here in January 2016. *Dr Alan Grundy*

The disused main Santiago–Puerto Montt line at Frutillar in March 2020. A completely new settlement grew up around the station. Whilst the station and track are out of use, the track still remained clear of weeds at this time. *Author*

WORLD'S MOST SOUTHERLY DISUSED MAIN LINE

The closed terminus at Puerto Montt can lay claim to being the most southerly lost main line railway in the world. Closed in 1992, the line was reopened in 2005 with a new station, increased services and upgraded line, only to close once again by 2014.

Puerto Montt station at the end of the main line from Santiago was completely rebuilt in 2005. It was the southernmost passenger terminus in Chile, but the service was closed a few years after the new station opened. The derelict station is seen in March 2020. *Author*

In 1976, two million passengers were carried on Chile's railways and the main line once had some thirty-five branch lines. Today, all but two are closed. Two other lines also ran from the coast across the Andes into Bolivia, the Antofagasta–Uyuni line and the Arica–Guaqui route, that once extended to La Paz, and both remain open for freight.

The extensive closures in the country have resulted in many abandoned lines, some with buildings and even track remaining. A number of fine metal bridges are also out of use. The Viaduct de Loa, at 336ft (102m), was once the second highest in the world and has been designated as a historical monument.

The town of Humberstone was named after a British chemical engineer and developed by producing saltpetre in the Atacama Desert. The industry declined after the First World War but survived until 1960. The ghostly remains of the town, its station and railways are still to be found rusting in the desert. It is just one example of the many industries and mines that were once served by the railways.

The island of Chiloé had a 60-mile (97km) 1ft 11½in narrow-gauge line running between the main settlements and a port, which opened in 1912. The line closed in 1960 due to a severe earthquake that even sank part of the railway under water and damaged many of the bridges.

Disused track leading to Coquimbo docks in Chile, seen in March 2020. A purpose-made new copper ore dock led to a decline of the original general merchandise dock. Several lines remain in use in this area transporting copper ore. *Author*

Metro passenger services operate at Valparaiso and Santiago, whilst a passenger service runs inland from Concepción. Freight trains run on a number of lines. However, in one instance, a train fell into a river when a bridge over the River Tolten in Southern Chile collapsed, indicating the poor state of parts of the railway infrastructure.

Colombia

A number of isolated fruit railways developed, one using a locomotive that had originally been leased to the Southwold Railway in Britain. Dominated by the Andes, the line from Bogotá to the Caribbean was not completed until 1961 and nationalisation followed in 1962. This line provided part of a wider network that could have even provided a link between Buenaventura, on the Pacific coast, and Santa Marta on the Caribbean coast. The line was eventually all made to a 3ft gauge, but was only ever used in unconnected sections, mostly for the transport of coal, and a substantial central portion was closed.

In the 1970s, some 4.3 million passengers annually were still using the railways, but increasing social and economic difficulties resulted in decline. In the 1990s, the nationalised network ran out of money and all remaining non-suburban passenger services ceased, including a line that ran into Venezuela. Decay and closure of many lines followed, although about half the network remained for freight. Whilst the railways have been neglected as roads were built, increasing congestion has resulted in some lines, closed since the 1990s, being reopened. A tourist train, with steam traction, was introduced from Bogotá to Zipaquirá and, for a while, a 14-mile (23km) steeply graded, disused and overgrown section of track at Cisneros was used by hand-pushed rail carts and became known as 'the longest roller coaster in the world'.

Ecuador

Ecuador's mainly 3ft 6in gauge railways in the 1920s were the lifeline of the country, but roads were built and coffee, like most of that in South America, is now transported by road. The railways, suffering floods and landslides which caused endless disruption, increasingly became neglected. The 1970s saw branch lines and separate sections of line that needed any form of investment closed. By the 1990s, most lines were closed and by 2008 just 10 per cent of the original network was in use by tourist trains.

In 2008, the government announced that the 288-mile (463km) Guayaquil line on the Pacific coast to Quito, high up in the Andes mountains, was to be reopened. It was sometimes called 'the most difficult line in the world' or 'the world's mightiest roller coaster' as it contained the spectacular Devil's Nose zigzag section, where the line climbed to 11,840ft (3,609m) at Urbina. By 2013, the tourist 'Tren Crucero' used steam locomotives for part of the route and ran over this amazingly scenic and spectacular section. However, in 2020 coronavirus resulted in the government closing the entire railway network and sacking the staff, although rehabilitation is being examined.

Guyana

At Georgetown, the first railway on mainland South America opened in 1848. Sugar cane was important traffic on a line sometimes called the East Coast Demerara Railway, but passengers were also conveyed and connections were made to coastal shipping. A disjointed network of lines of differing gauges developed and, in 1948, some stock arrived from Bermuda's closed railways. By the 1960s, the remaining network was in a poor state of repair with just a few services and by 1972 all lines were closed.

Paraguay

A standard-gauge main line ran from the capital Asunción to Encarnacion, where connections by a railway ferry were provided to Posadas in Argentina. The lines were nationalised in 1961, sleeping cars to Argentina were withdrawn in 1972 and passenger services became increasingly sparce. In the 1990s, the remaining lines were still struggling on, carrying freight traffic hauled by elderly steam locomotives that were used until 1999. By 2006, all regular internal services had ceased, although a freight train ran from Encarnacion into Argentina every few weeks. Passenger services between Encarnacion and Posadas resumed in 2014 with a new bridge replacing the train ferry, although services were suspended in 2021 due to coronavirus.

A tourist train was established on a 16-mile (25km) section of the old main line through Areguá. It ceased in 2009, after a bridge collapsed, although a section may reopen. The attractive former station at Asunción has been turned into a museum, whilst some stock of the former narrow-gauge Puerto Casado logging line has also been preserved.

A handsome North British built 2-6-0 No 54 seen on the Asunción–Carmen–Encarnación line in Paraguay in August 1994. Paraguay was one of the last railways in the world to regularly use steam traction until 1999. *Vincent Corasi*

The link from Encarnación in Paraguay to Posadas in Argentina was via a train ferry across the Paraná River. A new international bridge with a railway track rendered the ferries redundant in 1990 and the disused ferries are seen here in August 1994. *Vincent Corasi*

Peru

A number of short, separate coastal railways once existed, but all have long been closed. Two spectacular lines running from the coast high into the Andes have remained open in part. The standard-gauge ex-Central Railway of Peru suffered some serious weather-related damage that caused closure, but has reopened between Lima, Huancayo and Cerro dé Pasco. However, the spectacular 50-mile (80km) freight branch that ran to Chaucha in Bolivia, that left the main route south of La Oroya and was closed in 1998.

Tacna station with a train to Arica in February 1985. The isolated standard-gauge cross-border branch to the coast at Chile was closed in 2012. The station terminus site is now the location of the National Railway Museum of Peru. *Dr James Kus*

WORLD'S HIGHEST LOST LINE

The disused ex-Central Railway of Peru's line near La Cima, that once ran to Morococha, was recorded by Guinness Railway Facts as being at an altitude of 15,806ft (4,818m) above sea level. As such, it is the highest lost standard-gauge line in the world. The line was closed and dismantled in the 1990s.

Ticlio Summit in Peru seen in March 1967, a sign on a building at the summit listing the elevation as 15,680ft, (4,779m). The summit was sometimes closed due to bad weather. The line now passes through the Galera Summit Tunnel which has resulted in the closure of this part of the original line. *Dr James Kus*

The ex-Southern Railway of Peru runs from Mollendo on the coast to a junction at Juliaca in the Andes, where a line continues north to Cuzco and Machu Picchu, whilst one runs south to Puno. The latter once provided connections, via Lake Titicaca, to Bolivia and La Paz. The Arequipa–Mollendo section is closed to passengers. The line beyond Machu Picchu to Quillabamba was not completed until 1979, but a landslide in 1998 destroyed this part of the line. However, tourist trains serve Machu Picchu and South America's only high-quality sleeper train, the 'Belmond Andean Explorer', also provides a tourist service over part of the high-altitude scenic line.

Railway steamers once ran from rail-served ports in Peru and Bolivia, across Lake Titicaca which is at an altitude of 12,500ft (3,810m). The original ships were built in Britain and mostly sailed to South America where they were taken to pieces, loaded onto wagons and eventually reassembled again on the lake. Five ships were once used to navigate the 12-hour lake crossing, and in 1971 a train ferry also served a mine on the coast of the lake. Ferries

The railway to Machu Picchu in Peru commenced in 1914 but was not completed to Quillabamba until 1979. A landslide in 1988 destroyed the northern part of the line, but it still serves Machu Picchu. Locomotive No 102, a 1926 Baldwin 2-8-2, is seen in 1984 at Cuzco. *Dr James Kus*

and connecting train services no longer run, but car floats and one railway ship, mainly for use by tourists, remain.

Suriname

A 107-mile (173km) metre-gauge line opened in 1912 from the coast and ran inland, originally with the aim of reaching gold mining areas. In later years, aviation fuel was conveyed and a hundred tank wagons were provided for this traffic. Diesel passenger railcars were introduced, but all remaining services ended in 1987. In 2012, the government scrapped almost everything that was left of the railway, with the exception of two coaches and a locomotive. There were also a number of plantation railways, all of which are closed.

Uruguay

One of South America's most comprehensive network of lines was built over relatively easy countryside focusing on Montevideo. Construction was mostly by British interests, and much was built to standard-gauge. This resulted in a break of gauge station with Brazil, whilst connections with neighbouring Argentina ceased in 2012.

Most of the original network of single lines had lost its passenger services by the late 1980s, and well over half the network is now closed to all traffic. This includes all but a short section of four narrow-gauge lines. A limited passenger service has been reintroduced on two commuter routes radiating out from Montevideo. However, the centrally located General Artigas station was closed in 2003 and remaining services, operating from a less convenient station, resulted in a further loss of passengers. In 2020, some British-built railway equipment was still to be found and a number of important freight services remain.

Left: Colonia station buildings and abandoned overgrown tracks in January 2016. The Uruguayan station was the terminus of a line from Montevideo and located on the River Plate estuary opposite Buenos Aries, to which it is still connected by a passenger ferry. *Dr Alan Grundy*

Below: Colonia's abandoned turntable and engine shed seen in January 2016. Passenger services to the station were not reinstated after a railway strike in 1985 resulted in the suspension of all services on the line . *Dr Alan Grundy*

Montevideo's abandoned General Artigas station seen in March 2020. The attractive Uruguayan station opened in 1897 but was sold off in 1988 and was closed in 2003. A new, less convenient, station opened, losing 100,000 passengers in the process. *Author*

Venezuela

The country once had about 620 miles (1,000km) of differing and separate narrow-gauge railways that began to develop from the 1870s. What was known as the Bolivar Railway was a 138-mile (222km) 2ft-gauge railway and was the first significant line in the country. The Great Venezuela Railway was a 111-mile (179km) 3ft 6in line that ran from Caracas to Valencia; this was the longest line in the country, but closed in 1966. Whilst several lines had closed in the 1930s and 1940s, remaining lines went into a decline in the 1950s and all narrow-gauge lines had closed by 1967. Standard-gauge lines, of which some sections were electrified, were later built by the government, but all have also closed.

The problems for the railways stemmed from political instability, whilst the government was subsidising oil prices, to the extent that a gallon of petrol was at one time priced at less than a US cent, resulting in car and lorry costs becoming artificially low. By the 1990s, only a single passenger route remained, together with a few iron ore freight lines. A number of new railway projects have been partially constructed, but economic troubles have led to none being completed, although there are three suburban metro railways. The country was rated last in the world in terms of railway infrastructure by the World Economic Forum.

Falkland Islands

There were a number of short tracks laid to jetties, but the main railway on the Falkland Islands was the 3½-mile (5.6km) 2ft narrow-gauge Camber Railway. The line opened in 1916 and ran from Camber Depot in Port Stanley to an Admiralty radio transmitter station at Moody Brook that required coal to generate an electric signal. Two steam locomotives conveyed trains of both coal and workers. Improvements to wireless communication soon rendered the power required for the original transmitter obsolete and the railway was out of regular use by the late 1920s but may have been occasionally used until the Second World War. One of the locomotives was disposed of in a scrap heap and the other was dumped at sea. Both were later recovered and survive in poor condition.

Narrow-gauge track at Port Stanley in the Falklands linking a dock to the former main route in February 2020. The railway was built to convey coal from the port to a wireless generating system which later used diesel fuel and then fell out of use in the 1920s. *Author*

ASIA

The first railways in Asia were mostly built and influenced in their routes by the colonising activities of European nations. Elsewhere, railway development was sometimes initially slow, such as in remote parts of China. Conflicts have seen the closure of lines, whilst a number of later lost lines were built at a dreadful human cost during the Second World War. Some of the world's most spectacular lost lines are to be found in the foothills of the Himalayas.

Asia's population growth led to some passenger trains becoming very crowded, but low fares have sometimes resulted in limited investment and a number of even busy lines have closed, whilst others struggle on with little or no investment. In a number of countries, intercity services have prospered, but where new high-speed lines have been built this has often resulted in the decline of original older routes.

In many Asian countries, rural branch lines have been closed, some soon to become overgrown, but disused stations are often put to new uses, paralleling the trends of Western countries. There are also great contrasts, as many railways are in good health and high-speed railway lines in Japan, South Korea and China in particular, together with busy main lines, has resulted in more passengers being conveyed by train in Asia than on any other continent.

Singapore Tanjong Pagar station. The attractive building, centrally located in the city, closed in 2011. The station clock is seen here in March 2019. *Author*

CHAPTER 17

A PASSAGE TO INDIA

Bradshaw's guide of 1853 suggested an alternative passage to India, other than that by steamer around Africa. The route from London involved a train to the Channel, a ferry to France and then a train across France to Marseilles. From here the next step was by steamer to Alexandria. From the port, a horse-drawn waterway trip to the outskirts of Cairo was to be undertaken. The journey then involved a 70-mile (112km) desert crossing in wagons, or on donkeys, to reach Suez on the Red Sea and finally a further ship to India. The opening of more railways and the Suez Canal simplified travel to Asia.

Afghanistan

The country had an antipathy towards railways, fearing they would be used for invasion, and some lines from neighbouring countries were stopped short of the frontier. One such line included the 2½-mile (3.9km) double-track Khojak Tunnel in Pakistan, one of the longest in the area, that leads to a 'dead end' near the Afghan border.

Within Afghanistan itself, the 5-mile (8km) Kabul–Darulaman tramway was abandoned and track lifted in the 1940s, but the locomotives survived in a museum. A number of narrow-gauge mineral railways opened in the 1950s, mainly to serve coal mines, but are now all closed. Some later freight lines temporarily ceased operation in 2021.

Bangladesh

The many watercourses and low-lying areas resulted in repeated floods and some coastal areas have few lines. The railways originated as part of the Bengal–Assam Railway and the system was basically divided by rivers into Indian and metre gauges, but with some mixed gauge. After many years of neglect, the network has reduced in extent and, whilst jute was an important freight, most individual jute mill lines have closed and this is no longer a rail freight.

After the partition of India in 1947, only one line from Dakar, that connected to India, was used by passenger trains. Services ceased during the 1965 war between India and Pakistan and were not reinstated, even after Bangladesh obtained independence from Pakistan in

the 1970s. The closure of some eight lines that originally connected the two countries caused problems, but a few services were subsequently reinstated. Plans to turn some more lines into dual-gauge routes have also been announced, but in 2021 all passenger services ceased temporarily during the coronavirus pandemic.

India

The Indian railways were laid mainly to four different gauges, from a broad 5ft 6in, through metre-gauge, to the narrow 2ft 6in and 2ft gauges. By the early twentieth century, the Indian railway network was largely complete and included some imposing city stations, together with impressive engineering feats, particularly in the mountainous northern states.

A preserved steam locomotive water crane is seen at Mumbai's station in November 2019. Originally called Victoria station, a statue of the queen was removed in 1947. Some of Mumbai's most imposing buildings are from the railway age. *Author*

My grandfather, Harold Parker, was posted to India in the First World War. He is seen here (right) at Muttra Junction, now Mathura. At this time the station was a junction for a narrow-gauge line, since converted to Indian broad gauge. *Author's collection*

The British were originally involved in creating the railway network to control the country and to extract tea and other commodities, but with further development the railways became the fourth largest in the world. Heavy use of the railways was made during the First World War and they emerged in a poor state of repair, whilst the 40-mile (64km) Powayan Steam Tramway was shipped to Iran in 1918 to help with the post-war effort.

Many lines were very heavily used again during the Second World War, but some twenty-eight branch lines were simply dismantled for use elsewhere in the British war effort. The railways were also called upon to release large numbers of locomotives and stock to the Middle East during the Second World War and many Indian railway workshops were diverted to wartime work.

After the war, independence and the partition of India in 1947 resulted in changes to traffic flows and the Jammu–Sialkot line in Kashmir was closed. The Assam network was cut off from the rest of the Indian system until a new line was built. Links between Pakistan and India were also cut after violence between different religious groups, although one passenger line remained open.

1947 also brought changes to the Maharajas as they were gradually stripped of their lands, wealth and power, making the ornate royal trains used by some to travel around their lands obsolete. Several palaces were converted to hotels, such as that at Jodhpur where a number of disused royal railway coaches still survive on sidings in the grounds, whilst the 'Maharajas Express' is a luxury tourist train evoking some of the style of the earlier royal trains.

Although India still has a considerable network of lines, a number of Indian broad-gauge secondary routes and branch lines have been closed. Closures were more frequent during economic downturns over the years and for a variety of other reasons, but were mainly due to ever-increasing road competition. For example, the Agra–Bah branch opened in 1928, but suffered from early road competition and closed after a short life in 1939. The Dhanushkodi branch on Pamban Island, which is connected to the mainland by a railway bridge, was damaged by a cyclone and the branch closed in 1964. Broad-gauge closures continue, the Patna Junction–Digha Ghat line was kept open just to prevent encroachment on the line, but was closed in 2018, in part due to road congestion caused by its level crossings and the line itself is to be turned into a road. The electrified Chandrapura–Dhanbad line closed in 2017, because an underground coal mine fire undermined the track, but reopened after protest in 2019. In 2021 some 43 miles (70km) of line was approved for closure in the state of Gujarat.

Cochin (Kochi) Harbour station was modernised and restored prior to its closure in 2013. In November 2019, when this view was taken, the booking office was still staffed and open. English, Hindi and the local state language are used on the station sign. *Author*

Once rail served warehouses at Mumbai were designed to reflect the local climatic conditions. They were painted white to resist the heat and provided with large window covers to withstand the monsoon rain and are seen here in November 2019. *Author*

Abandoned railway buildings, from stations, goods warehouses, bridges and signal boxes to former steam locomotive sheds, are found throughout India. Freight remains important, but many industrial complexes no longer use the railways and numerous branch lines and spurs to docks are no longer rail served. In 2020 all passenger services were suspended for a temporary period due to coronavirus, with 20,000 carriages being made available to hospitals.

Narrow-gauges

In addition to the narrow-gauge industrial and mining lines, at one time there were more than 100 narrow-gauge passenger routes. Many were distinctive and were once a lifeline to the areas they served. However, numerous lines, particularly in remote rural areas, have been closed and the traditions associated with such lines have been lost.

In 1992, Indian Railways decided to standardise almost the entire network to the Indian 5ft 6in broad-gauge and this spelt the end of most remaining narrow-gauge lines. Of the once extensive metre-gauge lines, that to Lekhapani was the most easterly in India, but closed in 1997. The seven narrow-gauge lines operated by the Martin's Light Railways also closed, but some have reopened as broad-gauge routes.

The 2ft 6in Satpura narrow-gauge network was one of the largest in India, stretching for more than 620 miles (1,000km). The 'Satpura Express' was once the showpiece of the system, but its average speed was just 18mph and it ceased in 2015. The locomotives and stock had become run-down, but main sections have been converted to the wider Indian broad-gauge. A number of sections remain closed, although a short part of the original narrow-gauge line may be reopened as a heritage line.

Other narrow-gauge lines have also been closed for conversion to India's broad-gauge. Most of the Barsi line was converted by 2008 and the Dabhoi 2ft 6in gauge network of lines closed in 2018 for some routes to be converted. At its peak the narrow-gauge network in the Dabhoi area covered some 435 miles (700km), but conversion of the main sections to broad-gauge has left very few narrow-gauge branches. It has been suggested that perhaps a part could be retained as tourist attractions and to serve local needs, but most lines, such as that at Jabalpur, will either be replaced by new broad-gauge lines on straighter alignments and with fewer stops, or be closed.

Right: An Indian standard-gauge 0-6-0T German built Jung locomotive, in a rather run-down condition, crosses narrow-gauge lines at a former Rohtas Industries site in Dalmianagar and is seen here in November 1981. The lines have since closed. *Colour-Rail*

Below: A Manchester built Nasmyth Wilson F class 2-8-0 locomotive No 720, seen working on the 2ft 6in narrow-gauge ex-Barsi Light Railway. Remaining narrow-gauge lines on this network had been converted to Indian broad-gauge by 2008. *Historical Railway Images*

By 2020, the 123-mile (198km) 2ft Gwalior–Sheopur line was the longest remaining narrow-gauge line, but was closed for conversion, hopefully, to broad-gauge. Complete closures also continue, in 2021 over half a dozen lines involving some 285 miles (460km) of 2ft 6in gauge lines in the Indian state of Gujarat were approved for closure. Coronavirus had reduced patronage and they were considered uneconomic in spite of serving some remote areas and local opposition to closure.

A number of hill railways were built to a narrow 2ft gauge, based on the Ffestiniog Railway's example of relatively cheap and flexible construction in mountain areas. The Darjeeling Himalayan Railway is the most famous of those that remain, but no longer conveys tea and is facing problems through neglect. A branch of the Darjeeling Himalayan Railway along the Teesta River

An ex-Gwalior Light Railway locomotive No 811 rusting in a Bangalore park in March 2019. The locomotive was built in Japan by Nippon in 1959 and was withdrawn in the mid-1990s. The remaining section of this Indian narrow-gauge railway closed in 2020. *Mohit S*

Valley to Kalimpong was opened in 1915 but is now closed. Almost all of India's narrow-gauge industrial and sugar railways are also closed, including three former tea railways in Assam.

Indian Monorails

Whilst the Kundala Valley Railway was India's first monorail, running from 1902 to 1908, of more significance was the Patiala State Monorail. The system was opened in 1907 and a single ground level rail guided locomotives, also fitted with a road wheel, along existing roads, allowing the line to operate around very tight bends. The 50-mile (80km) network conveyed both passengers and freight, but improved road transport led to its closure in 1927. Two of the unique 0-3-0 locomotives survived and one has been restored to working order.

Nepal

The Nepal Government Railway was a 29-mile (47km) 2ft 6in narrow-gauge line that opened in 1927 linking Amlekhganj in Nepal with Raxaul in India, but closed in 1965 after the construction of a parallel road. A second link, the 31-mile (50km) branch from Bijayalpura in Nepal to Jaynagar in India, was the last passenger railway in Nepal to survive. The 13-mile (21km) section from Janakpur to Bijayalpura closed in 2001 after track and bridges were washed away, but services remained from the Indian border as far as Janakpur. The local railway staff, some 120, a high figure for a relatively short 2ft 6in narrow-gauge branch with just a daily passenger train, struggled to keep the line going. However, it was dilapidated, steam engines rusted in sheds, coach interiors were very run-down and there were many derailments due to the poor condition of the track. With just one operational diesel locomotive, the service became increasingly unreliable and staff were not paid regularly. Although well used by passengers, the remaining line closed in 2014, but the section from India as far as Janakpur reopened in Indian broad-gauge in 2018.

Pakistan

Pakistan's railways, once being part of India, were also built to four gauges, but most remaining today are of the broad 5ft 6in gauge. The separation of Pakistan from India led to a number of border lines closing, but in 2019 all international rail travel was suspended. However, unlike India, where a relatively comprehensive network of lines continues, over half the railways have closed in Pakistan.

Declining passenger numbers and the loss of freight to road transport has led to substantial financial losses. A cut in subsidy in the early 1990s resulted in the closure of many branch lines, long links and small stations. It was even rumoured at one time that the entire network could be closed. A few steam locomotives have been preserved, but by 2013 locomotives and rolling stock were poorly maintained, only 180 out of 477 diesel locomotives were operational at this time and none of these were that reliable.

Right: Pakistan Railways steam locomotive No 3157 was built at the Vulcan Foundry near Manchester and dates from 1911. It was used on Pakistan Railways until 1982 and is seen here reimported at the Manchester Science Museum in 1993. *Author's collection*

Below: A 1950s metre-gauge Nippon built Pakistan Railways oil fired steam locomotive departing from Mirpur Khas station, east of Karachi on a loop through surrounding villages in December 1993. All metre-gauge activity ceased in 2006. *Nigel Tout*

WORLD'S MOST SPECTACULARLY POSITIONED BRIDGE – THE CHAPPAR RIFT BRIDGE

The 7-span and 250ft (76m) high Chappar Rift Bridge was an engineering marvel on the 5ft 6in broad-gauge Khost–Quetta line. It was opened by the Duchess of Connaught in 1887 and was thus also known as the Louise Margaret Bridge.

Part of the line in this mountainous area leading to the bridge was built along the almost impossibly rugged terrain of a rift gorge, which is about 3 miles (5km) long with sheer sides up to 300ft (91m) in height. In addition, other bridges were required on the route and no fewer than thirty tunnels, including almost 1¼ miles (2km) of tunnelling in the rift valley itself, either side of the Chappar Bridge.

In 1942, serious damage to several parts of the line, including in the Chappar Rift Valley, was caused by flash flooding. As an alternative route to Quetta, via the Bolan Pass, had been improved, the line over the Chappar Bridge was closed the following year. The complicated task of removing the metal sections of the bridge was then undertaken, for use as scrap during the Second World War, leaving just the stone piers.

The spectacular railway bridge across the Chappar Rift Valley, now in Pakistan, illustrated on a 1931 cigarette card. Much of the line closed in 1942 after serious flood damage and the metal girders of the bridge were dismantled for the war effort. *Author's collection*

CHURCHMAN'S CIGARETTES

CHAPAR RIFT BRIDGE, N.W. INDIA

Closures in Pakistan have included both narrow and broad-gauge, and some extensive branch lines were closed including the Mehrabpur and Samasata lines, which were both over 125 miles (200km) in length. Even in urban areas, much of the Karachi Circular Railway closed in 1999, but parts were being reopened in 2022. A number of rural lines that remained had a sparse passenger service, such as the bi-monthly train on the remote 455-mile (732km) line from Quetta to Zahedan in Iran, although passenger services over this route ceased in 2020 due to coronavirus.

Whilst some improvements have been undertaken, 70 per cent of revenue goes on staff pensions, there have been financial irregularities, as well as delays to new investment and accidents. Although the system was overstaffed, many of the bungalows built along lines for railway officials are today in ruins. Even where lines remained, copper cable thefts have been so prevalent that this led to all electrified lines becoming diesel hauled and, in 2020, the last electric trains ceased.

The Bolan Pass Old Line

Work on the construction of a railway through the Bolan Pass started in 1880 but stopped after the construction of 19 miles (31km) of track due to conflicts in the area. Work restarted in 1885 and Quetta was reached in August of 1886. In 1889, floods destroyed much of the original track which had been laid on the Bolan River bed. A new track was built higher above the river, but much of this also was soon washed away during floods. A third and new all-season track through the pass was opened in 1897 and much is still operational. At a number of locations along the track it is still possible to see the abandoned tunnels and the trackbed of the earlier attempts of building railways here.

The Bostan–Zhob Railway

The first section of this 2ft 6in narrow-gauge line opened in 1916 to serve a munitions factory, but was completed from Bostan Junction to Zhob by 1929, where a connection on another now closed railway could be made to the north of the country. The 182-mile (294km) line made it one of the longest in Pakistan. Kan Mehtarzai on the route was the highest station in Pakistan at 7,295ft (2,224m) and was regularly affected by snow. In 1932, part of the line was dismantled due to unrest and for political reasons. In 1986, passenger services were withdrawn as was most freight the

following year, but formal closure was not until 1991. The line was controversially dismantled in 2007.

The North West Frontier area, because of its high elevation, was one of the few locations in Pakistan where railways regularly required snow ploughs. This is a desolate largely unpopulated area, but railways were originally built for strategic purposes, or to convey minerals and passenger services were somewhat of an afterthought.

Tea Trains
Sri Lanka

With historical links to India, a network of 5ft 6in broad-gauge railways was constructed, with new lines being constructed until 1928. Narrow-gauge railways also developed conveying tea, and a few individual tramways were built from large hill plantations to coastal piers. All the island's tea country narrow-gauge lines are defunct, such as the 2ft 6in Uda Pussellawa Railway that closed in 1948. The remaining section of Kelani Valley lines ceased in 1992, but part of the line from Colombo was converted into broad-gauge.

As road transport improved, there was an increasing loss of railway traffic and lack of investment for many years, resulting in neglect and unreliability. Civil war also damaged the railways and resulted in the line between the cities of Colombo and Jaffna closing in the 1980s, whilst all services ceased on the northern section by 1990. Some lines remained unused for years and became overgrown with disused and damaged stations, such as the old station at Jaffna. However, as stability returned, the Colombo–Jaffna and other lines reopened.

In December 2004, at least 1,000 people on the Sri Lankan coast perished when tsunami waves swept the eight carriages off the track at Telwatta, 63 miles (100km) south of the capital Colombo. Many of the dead were local villagers who tried to escape the waves by climbing on top of the train.

The line was eventually reopened and in 2021 a network of routes survived, some of which encompass scenic parts of the country such as the spiral Demodara loop and tall Nine Arch bridge. Parts still used British semaphore signalling and other equipment, but equally an upgrading of main routes and stock has been undertaken. The temporary suspension of all passenger services in 2021 due to coronavirus may damage future prospects.

TEN GREAT LOST RAILWAYS OF THE WORLD – THE KHYBER PASS RAILWAY

The Khyber Pass Railway was a 36-mile (58km) 5ft 6in gauge line that opened in full in 1926 and was heavily engineered with reversing stations, spirals, thirty-four tunnels and ninety-two bridges. The ascent to the Khyber Pass was one of the steepest non-rack sections of track in the world with sections of gradient up to 1 in 25. It was difficult terrain in the foothills of the Himalayas and the line climbed to over 3,500ft (1,067m) to reach Landi Kotal.

Built to carry troops defending the British Raj against the threat of a Russian invasion from Afghanistan, some stations were built in a fortress style. Unrest in the area had seen the railway close temporarily on a number of occasions and, in 1932, the Afghanistan government insisted that the extension from Landi Kotal to Landi Khana be closed, and proposals to extend the line further towards Afghanistan were abandoned.

In later years, a once busy weekly train ran to Peshawar and was provided free by Pakistan Railways to prove to tribesmen in the area that the line was open and to foster peace. Patronage gradually declined, whilst axle limitations prevented diesel operations and closure came in 1982.

In the mid-1990s, the line reopened as a tourist route, but security issues and serious damage by monsoon rains resulted in service curtailments and the line's final abandonment in 2006. Since closure, there have been washouts that have caused further damage.

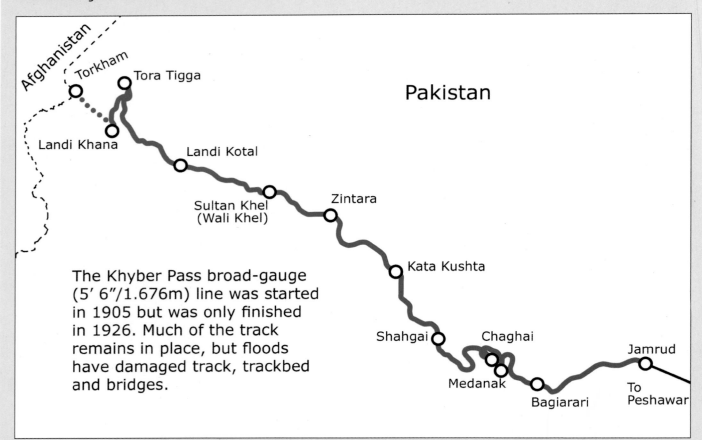

The Khyber Pass broad-gauge (5' 6"/1.676m) line was started in 1905 but was only finished in 1926. Much of the track remains in place, but floods have damaged track, trackbed and bridges.

Map of the Khyber Pass Railway in Pakistan.

Right: The Khyber Pass Railway with a train arriving at Landi Kotal in 1939, after Afghanistan insisted trains terminated here. The mountainous area has been volatile and the station was fortified. Later, tourist trains ran for a while, but the line closed in 2006. *Swiss National Library, Annemarie Schwarzenbach*

Below: Pakistan Railways oil fired Leeds built Kitson 2-8-0 No 2216 on the Khyber Pass Railway with No 2264 at the rear in December 1993. Note the spectacular scenery and local tribesmen asserting their right to free travel. *Nigel Tout*

CHAPTER 18

CHINA & JAPAN

China

WORLD'S SHORTEST LIVED LOST RAILWAY

The Woosung Railway was the first in China, a 5-mile (8km) 2ft 6in narrow-gauge British-equipped line. It was mainly built for freight to avoid Shanghai harbour's sand banks, but also conveyed passengers. The line opened in 1876 but had to be closed the following year when someone was killed by a train. Unrest ensued and people blocked trains as it was considered that the spirits had been offended by the railway.

The Chinese government purchased the line, tore up the rails and, together with the locomotives and stock, ensured that the railway was abandoned.

Sometime later, a locomotive in the Kaiping area was built in secret to convey coal to a canal and the value of the railways was gradually recognised. As a consequence, Britain and other foreign countries became involved in constructing railways. Nevertheless, China developed a relatively small railway network for its size and population, due in part to defeat in the Sino-Japanese War of 1894, but by the mid-1930s the network was expanding.

The Sino-Japanese War in 1937 ended most new railway construction and, as this developed into the Second World War, some parts of the network were dismantled to slow the Japanese advance, whilst other parts were expanded to serve mines and industrial complexes. After the damage caused by the war, 80 per cent of the railways were in an appalling state, and

The clock tower and front façade of the old Zhengyangmen East railway station at Peking seen here in the 1950s. The clock tower was saved in 1979 and rebuilt as part of the China Railway Museum at Beijing that opened in 2008.

even by 1949, when Chairman Mao and the communists took over, only about half were in use. Some provinces still had no rail communications, but the railways were gradually restored and expanded in the 1950s.

Narrow-Gauge

A French-built metre-gauge line ran from Kunming some 530 miles (855km) to Hanoi in Vietnam. Trains would take some 32 hours to travel the route, but deterioration of the track led to the suspension of the twice-weekly service in 2005. Freight trains still ran on a few sections, but in 2017 some narrow-gauge services were replaced by the construction of a new standard-gauge line.

The success of the French line led the British to plan a rival line from China to Myanmar (Burma) that would have also been of metre-gauge, but just 15¼-inch gauge on the most difficult sections. Work began in 1938, but the Second World War intervened and completed sections were destroyed to thwart the Japanese invasion. After the war, the incomplete line remained in ruins and construction was never resumed.

For many years after the war, new narrow-gauge track was still being laid as an alternative to both road building and to standard-gauge lines. Even in the 1980s it was estimated there were still over 1,500 miles (2,400km) of narrow-gauge passenger lines remaining and some lines were even being extended. This policy ended in the 1990s and almost all narrow-gauge passenger services have since been closed and replaced by bus services.

A number of narrow-gauge lines were also earmarked for conversion to standard-gauge, such as the Jijie–Gejiu branch, but the plans were never implemented and the line closed to passengers in 1985 and freight in 1991, with tracks being removed in 2008. In 2003, passenger services on the Meng Bao line ended, together with freight in 2010; a new standard-gauge line followed a similar route to the old narrow-gauge line but was on a straighter alignment. In 2015, an excursion train called 'Jianshui Old Train' ran on part of the narrow-gauge line.

Elsewhere, a few narrow-gauge lines have also reopened sections for seasonal heritage tourist trains. In addition, the Shibanxi system began operating tourist steam trains in 2018. The 2ft Gebishi Railway, opened in 1915, saw the final 24-mile (38km) section closed to regular services in 1990. However, as already mentioned, a seasonal tourist train operated

The closed metre-gauge passenger station of Kunming North in China in December 2016. Remaining passenger services ceased in 2017. The French styled building has been saved from demolition and is used as a railway museum.
Vladimir Menkov

Langxiang was once a junction of a narrow-gauge forestry railway that connected with the main standard-gauge line to Nancha. A 2C class 0-8-0 narrow-gauge passenger locomotive is seen heading a train in March 1988. The Chinese narrow-gauge line has since closed. *Vincent Corasi*

over 8 miles (13km) of the line and a few stations on this route have been restored, but others are in a poor condition.

There were also networks of mineral, agricultural, forestry and industrial narrow-gauge lines of various gauges, with the narrowest being a mere 16inch gauge in width, although 2ft 6in was more common. Most were originally steam worked, but they are now mainly closed. Forestry lines were found including in the Manchuria area, where semi-trimmed logs from the felling sites were transported by narrow-gauge routes to main line stations. A number of narrow-gauge coal mine lines continued, often with ancient stock and locomotives, but few remain in use. The Dahuichang limestone narrow-gauge line on the outskirts of Beijing was one of the last narrow-gauge lines to close in 2005. One of the locomotives was subsequently moved to the Ffestiniog Railway in 2007.

Modern China

China is a huge country and there has been much redevelopment. As a consequence, there are also a considerable number of standard-gauge secondary closed railways in China. They are found in almost every province and many sections are simply abandoned and left to rust away. In Beijing, a linear park is proposed along disused tracks, whilst in rural areas there are a number of lost lines to the north of North Korea. Lines have also closed due to the decline of heavy industry and factory closures. Guangzhou and former coal mines at Tangshan are just two examples of numerous similar instances of railway closures.

Improvements to the network and new high-speed lines have also resulted in the closure of some original routes, although freight remains on a number of these. For example, the original Beijing–Zhangjiakou line was closed to passengers and parts were dismantled, whilst there were once spirals between Turpan and Korla which closed when a new route opened in 2014.

Whilst there are a few heritage lines and the occasional railway museum, a Chinese culture of modernity has seen many old railway buildings demolished, together with the loss of much of the traditional railway culture. Equally, railway remains are to be found throughout the country, including old station buildings, abandoned tracks, bridges and tunnels just as with other countries in the world. Some former railway buildings have even been listed as historical sites.

Finally, in a country with one of the most modern railway networks in the world, it is perhaps unexpected

Steelworks at the industrial city of Baotou in Inner Mongolia with a sturdy 0-8-0T No 5327 simmering at the works sidings in March 1988. The Chinese steelworks were originally constructed with the help of the Soviet Union, steam locomotives are no longer in use. *Vincent Corasi*

that steam traction has survived in some coal-mining areas, after it had largely disappeared elsewhere in the world. The last regular passenger services carrying workers operated by steam came to an end in Baiyin, in Gansu province, in March 2015. Steam could still be found at a handful of industrial sites, but a downturn in 2016 saw a number of industrial plants and their rail networks closed. The Sandaoling open cast coal mine in Xinjiang Province in 2018 had nine locomotives still in daily use, although standard-gauge steam use was likely to end during 2022.

Hong Kong Of China

With its natural harbour and ancient trading routes, it was perhaps surprising how late the railways arrived to serve the area. Whilst a local line ran between 1912 and 1928, the main international link did not arrive until 1908. A large red brick station was opened in 1916 on the southern tip of the Kowloon Peninsula, being the waterfront location adjoining the Peninsula Hotel. With changes of train, it was possible to travel from Hong Kong to London.

The original Kowloon station closed in 1974 and was demolished in 1978, leaving only the clock tower remaining. Today, the station and track to it have been abandoned and built upon, but trains start from the new Hong Kong West Kowloon station, serving Chinese mainland, whilst the new station is, in turn, served by a metro from all parts of Hong Kong. All lines are so busy with passengers that the last freight train ran over Hong Kong tracks in 2010.

Japan

Japan opened its first railway, which was largely built by British engineers, in 1872. However, rapid strides were made and a comprehensive network of 3ft 6in narrow-gauge lines developed on the main islands. A Light Railway Act encouraged country districts to develop branch lines and there were also about thirty narrower-gauge lines than 3ft 6in. The damage caused to Japan's railways by the Second World War was mostly repaired and, by the 1960s, the fastest narrow-gauge trains in the world were running at up to 75mph.

A network of new high-speed lines was developed from the 1960s. This compounded the loss of passengers on the original lines, and in more recent years there has been a continuous quest to cut the railway deficit. As a consequence, there has been an endless catalogue of closures and some are relatively recent. Significant future closures to the network are also proposed, unless local authorities take over loss-making lines. This is a way of transferring unpopular decisions on closure from the central state to the local area concerned.

In some areas, lines have also been transferred to local firms such as the 38-mile (61km) route that was transferred from the West Japan Railway to the Noto Railway in 1988. The relatively modern line, which was not completed until 1964 and contained some forty-nine tunnels, was closed in 2005. Furthermore, increasing car and scooter ownership, together with rural depopulation, are growing problems for many of the rural railways. Some thirty-nine lines covering over 480 miles (771km) were closed between 2000 and 2017.

Closures continue and a large number of lost lines are now to be found throughout Japan's four main islands. For example, the northern island of Hokkaido is crisscrossed with lost railways. Just a few examples include the Haboro line, which was used for coal traffic and closed in 1987. The 92-mile (149km) Tempoku line closed in 1989, the 87-mile (140km) Furusato–Ginga line closed in 2006, and 72 miles (116km) of the Rumoi line closed in 2021.

On the island of Honshu, examples of closed railways include the Shinmei line that closed in 1995, whilst the 67-mile (108km) Sankō line closed in 2018. The latter was not completed until 1975, and the attractive route contained thirty tunnels; such closures do not go unnoticed and some 3,000 people turned up on the last day. There were also closures on the southern island of Kyushu, whilst on Shikoku, the smallest of the main railway-connected Japanese islands, some long-link lines have been closed.

Extreme natural events have caused closures, for example Yokohama's original station was destroyed by an earthquake, whilst the Kobe earthquake caused months of disruption to services. A typhoon closed the Takachiho Railway in 2006. Temporary closures have been caused by the consequences of a tsunami damaging the Fukushima nuclear plant, whilst the 34-mile (55km) Miyako–Kamaishi line reopened in 2019, eight years after it was also damaged by the tsunami.

Ashoro station, seen in May 2010, was operated by the Hokkaido Chihoku Kogen Railway in Hokkaido Japan. The station opened in 2004 but closed in 2006 when buses replaced trains and it has since become a tourist landmark.
221.20

Taushubetsu Bridge in Japan seen in September 2005. The disused railway viaduct found itself situated within a new reservoir. When the reservoir is full the viaduct disappears under the water and is thus known as the 'phantom bridge'.
Fe-Taq

There are some interesting remains on closed lines, including stations, tunnels, bridges and plinthed locomotives, whilst many of the closed stations are surprisingly modern. Taushubetsu Bridge on Hokkaido closed in 1955 and was subsequently submerged, at times, in a new reservoir. Uzui station on the closed Sankō line was known as 'the station in the sky' because it was located on a high viaduct. The Kamioka Railway closed in 2006 and is used by tourist rail bikes, whilst elsewhere similar pedal-powered rail carts use disused tracks. There is even a Lost Line Association to promote the after-use of such lines.

Freight was once important, including coal, whilst live fish were conveyed in water tanks. However, freight volumes are much reduced and many industrial lines have also closed. General freight services are few and far between and, in spite of concentrating on mineral trains over a limited number of routes, rail freight continues to fall, with freight yard closures going back to the 1960s. Tokyo's first station was reused as a freight depot from 1914 but closed in 1986.

Japan mostly adopted a 2ft 6in gauge for forestry and industrial lines. One of the largest networks was the Kiso Forest Railway which had over 250 miles (400km) of narrow-gauge line, with numerous bridges and tunnels, until the closure of remaining lines in 1976. Some passenger lines also ran to this gauge and in 2021 four remained, whilst forestry and industrial lines are mostly defunct.

A network of about 430 miles (700km) of railway was built on Sakhalin Island by Japan prior to the Second World War. After the war, the 3ft 6in gauge network fell into the hands of Russia, which extended the network to the north of the island. Under Stalin, the authorities started to build a tunnel to mainland Russia with forced labour, but this was abandoned on Stalin's death. Whilst Russia also closed a number of lines on the island, it is converting remaining lines to the 5ft Russian gauge.

Finally, the Wakayama–Kishi line was running at a loss and closure was considered. Stations were unstaffed and employees of local businesses near each station were hired to act as part-time railway staff. At Kishi, a grocery store fed stray cats, but one preferred to inhabit the station. In 2007, the cat was offered the position of honorary stationmaster. Patronage on the line increased as tourists used the route to see the cat. The cat saved the line from closure and, when she died in 2015, some 3,000 people turned up for the funeral.

CHAPTER 19

THE FAR EAST

Cambodia

The first line was built by the French during the 1930s and paid for by German First World War reparations. A network of about 380 miles (610km) of mostly metre-gauge line was once in operation, linking Phnom Penh to the coast and to Thailand. The line to Thailand was cut by the French during the Second World War during the Japanese invasion. A troubled theme continued, in the 1960s and 1970s the Vietnam War led to damage and later the railways were used for the forced transfer of people between industrial and rural zones during the revolutionary period of Pol Pot. Train ambushes were not unknown and by the 1970s the railway network had been much reduced by violence and neglect. All services ended by 2009.

Later reconciliation and peace resulted firstly in a single train providing a weekend service from Phnom Penh to the coast; but, with greater stability, the international service to Thailand was reinstated in 2019, after a hiatus of 45 years. Elsewhere, there are many abandoned railway remains, but some sections of disused line were being restored to service in 2019. Others were used by tourists on small individual rail trolleys, known locally as 'Bamboo trains'. The year 2020 saw rail travel grind to a halt for a time due to coronavirus.

Indonesia

Java's first railway opened on the island as early as 1867 and the Dutch colonists built a relatively extensive network of lines, at first following flat coastal plains, but later moving towards the mountains of central Java. Trains originally did not run after dark owing to the hazards of the jungle, whilst large viaducts, steep gradients, some requiring rack and pinion sections, were to be found. Lines eventually developed at a 3ft 6in gauge at each end of the island, but with standard-gauge in the central part between the two narrow-gauge sections. For a while, a third rail was laid over some standard-gauge sections of line to facilitate through running, but the Japanese invasion during the Second World War resulted in 3ft 6in becoming the main gauge used.

At one time the world's longest distance non-stop narrow-gauge passenger train, the 'Surabaya Ltd', ran at speeds of up to 60mph across the island, and in the pre-Second World War period the railways were modern and well equipped. However, after damage and the removal of standard-gauge lines by the Japanese during the Second World War, together with the later disorganised independence of the country, the railways gradually became run-down.

By the 1970s, ancient steam locomotives still operated some passenger services, hauling coaches with missing seats, jammed windows and no lighting. Many stations were oil lit and run-down, and shanty towns were even built on sidings. Fares were so low that no real effort was made to collect them, and the railways became a byword for incompetence, neglect, inefficiency and corruption.

As a consequence, most branch and many secondary lines closed, such as the Labuan line on Java's west coast, also that to Garut (Garoet), which was reached by a branch with some steep gradients of 1 in 26. The 34-mile (55km) Rangkasbitung–Labuan line was built to open up western areas and later included a further branch to coal deposits but closed in 1982 and remaining steam hauled freight trains ceased the following year. After years of neglect there was much old equipment and stock, but there has been more recent investment and a good network now links the main cities. However, a planned heritage revival on the coastal Labuan branch was thwarted by a tsunami on the west coast of Java in 2018.

Most of the narrow-gauge freight railways serving sugar cane plantations and sugar mills, together with palm oil and logging area railways, have closed throughout the Indonesian islands, but a few lines are retained within the confines of remaining sugar mills. It is interesting to note that the sugar cane plantation steam locomotives often ran inexpensively on bagasse, which was compacted sugar cane fibre waste; consequently, in 2010 about thirty locomotives were in use and an occasional steam locomotive was still used until 2020.

Indonesia's sugar industry, once the second largest producer in the world, has seen decline and many lines have closed. A narrow-gauge train to Trangkil Sugar Mill in Java is seen in August 1997. Headed by 0-4-0 No 2, one of four locomotives used on the line that closed in 2002. *Vincent Corasi*

Sumatra's first railway opened in 1876 and was used for military purposes, but three unconnected networks developed in the north, south and west of the island. In addition to passengers, the lines originally conveyed coffee, copra, rubber, tobacco and palm oil.

The Second World War and the Sumatra Railway

Invasion by Japan during the Second World War resulted in damage to some lines and removal of others for use elsewhere. The Japanese also built what became known as the Sumatra or Pekanbaru Death Railway, due to the large number of prisoners of war and forced labourers that died during the construction of the line. The 137-mile (220km) section of narrow-gauge railway was designed to convey coal and military equipment across Sumatra. It was finally completed, through dense jungle, on the day peace was declared in 1945. Consequently, it was only ever used to transport former prisoners out of the area and soon became disused and overgrown. A monument to the railway is to be found at the British National Memorial Arboretum.

Post-war closures

Most of the original lines in Sumatra were restored to use after the war, but closures began in the 1970s. These have included coal railways in western Sumatra that used rack locomotives, and a railway that transported stones from a river bed that were crushed and used as ballast. Whilst many sections of line have closed, parts of the three original passenger networks remained in 2022.

Elsewhere in the archipelago, on the island of Celebes (Sulawesi) there was once a 29-mile (47km) line that closed in 1930. An 88-mile (142km) network of 3ft 6in narrow-gauge passenger lines were to be found on the island of Madura; damaged during the Second World War, parts of the network closed in the 1950s, but the railway remained extant until 1987.

Korean Peninsula

The railways on the Korean Peninsula were once a unified network and Pullman cars ran from Asia to Busan, where there were ship connections with Japan, as between 1910 and the end of the Second World War Japan occupied the Korea Peninsula. During this period, a Japanese company, the largest in Korea at the time, named 'The Chosen Railway' ran broad, standard and narrow-gauge lines.

North Korea was established after the surrender of Japan at the end of the Second World War, resulting in the partition of the Korean Peninsula between the Soviet Union in the north and the USA in the south. Some lines had seen track removed by Japan during the war, but the Korean War that raged between the years 1950–3 led to all lines between north and south Korea being closed, and sections still remain out of use beyond the demilitarised border areas. This includes the standard-gauge 72-mile

(116km) Kŭmgangsan Electric Railway that was once busy with tourists until it was destroyed during the Korean War.

War damage resulted in a decline in rail services, but much was eventually repaired and both standard and narrow-gauge lines reopened. Economic problems in the 1990s resulted in some of the 2ft 6in narrow-gauge railways being closed, whilst flooding and natural disasters have also resulted in lines being closed.

Whilst about half of all narrow-gauge lines have closed, or been converted to standard-gauge, it has been reported that a number of sections of secondary lines are in poor condition with speed restrictions. Yet, a significant standard-gauge network of industrial and mineral lines continues, with far more rail freight being conveyed in the north than south. Whilst rail links to the south are not in operation, in 2022 there were rail connections from the Korean State Railway to China and Russia.

South Korea rebuilt sections of the heavily damaged Gyeongnam Railway after the Korean War and most damaged standard-gauge lines wholly within the South were also reopened. Dorasan station was built in 2002 and was supposed to be a key stop on the route to reunification. Track was laid to reconnect with the Gyeongui Line, that once provided a link between Seoul and Pyongyang. In 2018, for the first time in more than a decade, a train travelled from South to North Korea, but tensions remain and, in 2022, there are still no regular cross-border trains.

A new freight line was built to Gimpo Airport near Seoul in 1951 to transport American military equipment but closed in 1981. Due to the high population levels in parts, there are few disused lines in urban areas, but the long Gwangju–Masan rural link line in the rural south of the peninsular was closed. At Busan, a redundant section of line was rapidly taken over as a walkway by the local population. There are several intermediate closed

Above right: Seoul station in South Korea, seen here in March 2017, was completed in 1925 to a Japanese design, also featuring a Byzantine-style dome and symmetrical layout. It closed in 1988 with the opening of a new station but remains and is seen here in March 2017. *Author*

Right: Sturdy stone columns of the old railway station at Seoul in South Korea seen in March 2017. The station was replaced by a nearby modern building. After closure, the original station was renovated and is now a cultural centre. *Author*

stations on lines that remain open, and many stations and sections on the original Gyeongchun line closed when a new high-speed alignment opened in 2010.

Laos

The first line opened in 1893 on the Mekong River islands of Don Khong and Don Det. It was essentially a river portage route providing links over the islands for freight traffic that could not use the river here. The line closed in the 1940s, although much of the 4-mile (6.5km) narrow-gauge route can still be traced, including an old railway bridge between the two islands which is now used by a road.

Malaysia

Tin was the spur to construct some early railways, and the first lines, largely built through jungle, were opened in the 1880s. By the 1930s, over 1,000 miles (1,600km) of mostly metre-gauge line were operating and air-conditioned sleeping cars were introduced as early as 1936. Whilst road competition had seen the first closure in 1929, during the Second World War Japan invaded and occupied Malaysia. This resulted in branch lines being closed by the Japanese and the track being taken to build the Burma Death Railway. The busy port of Malacca lost its railway at this time, as well as the line to the tin mining settlement of Teronoh. Services were never restored to either destination after the war, but some other lines were reopened.

Kuala Lumpur's original ornate Moorish-designed station survived a Second World War aerial bombardment, but the nearby 28-stall locomotive roundhouse and carriage shed did not. By 2001, many train services had been diverted to a new station in the city, in 2014 the original station hotel closed and the station buildings became a museum.

The 1970s saw the closure of the historic Taiping–Port Weld branch, which had been the first conventional railway to open in the country. A freight branch in the Batu Arang area also closed; such lines once provided coal for the network and regular steam ceased in the 1970s. Later closures include the Port Dickson line in 2008 and the Kerteh–Kuantan petroleum line in 2010.

Two north-south links across Peninsular Malaysia survive, including the eastern 'Jungle Railway'. Although general rail freight has reduced and many industrial railways had closed by the 1970s, a network of narrow-gauge lines still transports palm fruit to oil extraction mills. A link to Thailand remains, but long-distance trains into central Singapore were cut in 2011 and over the Johor Bahru causeway in 2015, but a railway shuttle service remains across the causeway.

In Sabah, the metre-gauge North Borneo Railway's main original traffic was tobacco and by 1903 a network

WORLD'S MOST UNUSUAL RAILWAY MONUMENT TO AN ELEPHANT

The 19-mile (30km) branch to Teluk Anson (now Teluk Intan), a port on the Perak River, opened in 1893 and at the time contained the longest railway bridge in Malaysia. A year after opening, a large bull elephant, whose calf had been killed, charged a train travelling at over 40mph in defence of his herd. The locomotive and tender were derailed and, whilst there were no deaths on the train, the elephant died of its injuries. The courageous animal was buried close to the line and a monument to its brave sacrifice was erected beside the railway. The line closed in 1989 and the monument decayed, but in 2018 the concrete structure was restored and made accessible to visitors.

A North Borneo Railway Hunslet 4-6-4T locomotive No 7 dating from 1912, at Kota Kinabalu in October 1978. Of the disused steam locomotives seen here, No 7 was eventually preserved. The postcard markings inform that UK post codes were introduced at this time. *Jane Blanchflower*

of about 120 miles (193km) of line developed. Although damaged during the Second World War, the 1950s saw considerable sections reopened. In 1963, the Weston branch was closed and in the 1970s the Melalap extension and Kota Kinabalu dock lines were also closed. Eventually, only the Sembulan–Tenom section survived in regular service. Much of this closed in 2007, but reopened in 2011, and in 2019 a Wickham DMU was reported to still be in occasional use. Elsewhere a short freight line ran at Kuching until the 1930s, and three freight narrow-gauge lines once ran in neighbouring Brunei.

Mongolia

The first railway was a 20-mile 2ft 6in narrow-gauge mineral line connecting the capital Ulaanbaatar with coal mines, opening in 1938. Deposits dwindled and the line eventually closed. Elsewhere, coal is still mined, together with other minerals, and is mostly conveyed by rail until deposits become exhausted. The Soviet Union built defence bases in 1943 served by some 250 miles (400km) of line linked to the Trans-Siberian Railway to counter any threat from Japan. Whilst most of these lines are derelict, a small section as far as Choibalsan remains extant. At Mardai, a section of a former railway was reportedly in uranium freight use.

Myanmar

Once known as Burma, the British were involved in railway construction and the first line opened in 1877 between Yangon, (Rangoon) and Pyay. A short 2ft 6in light railway from Mandalay was one of the first closures in 1927 but was later replaced by a metre-gauge line. There were areas of difficult topography and a line from Mandalay included the Goteik Viaduct, the highest in the world at the time. In fear of the viaduct being destroyed, a diversionary line was built, but was never required and was abandoned, whilst the viaduct remains open. By the 1930s, there was a considerable network of metre-gauge lines, together with the 50-mile (80km) 2ft-gauge network of the Burma Mines Railway.

Considerable damage was caused during the Second World War, with the Japanese removing rails from existing branch and secondary lines for military use elsewhere, particularly for the Siam–Burma Death Railway, the bulk of which was built through Thailand.

Elsewhere in Myanmar, much was rebuilt in the 1950s and, although a number of branch lines, link lines and stations have been closed, there remained a considerable network, and in 2020 sleeper services were still provided. Whilst much of the network is increasingly run-down, modernisation and expansion was being undertaken, partly with aid from Japan. However, a military coup has resulted in reduced spending on railways and the targeting of striking railway workers during 2021 resulting in a serious curtailment of services

Philippines

Most of the lines are on the main island of Luzon. At its peak, the network of 3ft 6in gauge lines extended from Manila to both tips of this island, which were once served by long-distance passenger services, including sleeping cars. Decline meant that by 2006 the network had been reduced to less than 300 miles (480km), whilst damage by typhoons in 2012 resulted in further closures and, at one time, only about 48 miles (77km) of original line survived in regular use. Surviving lines mostly formed suburban lines from Manila, where road traffic is congested, but more reopenings are planned. Unauthorised commuter services, run via light rail carts that are pushed along by foot power, use the lines but are smartly taken off the rails to avoid main line trains.

A bagasse-fuelled locomotive No 17 near Manapla on the Philippine island of Negros with a loaded sugar cane train, in February 1983. The line to the sugar mill has since closed and the few remaining sections of sugar lines on the island use diesel traction. *Colour-Rail*

A number of narrow-gauge lines were constructed for the sugar industry and were found on several of the islands, Negros in particular. Many were out of use by 2000 and remaining steam traction on Negros, that used compressed sugar cane waste as fuel, mostly ceased in 2010. Abandoned sugar mill lines are also found on the islands of Cebu, Mindanao and Panay and it is likely that any remaining such lines will close in due course. Some closed railways are also used by self-propelled rail carts, whist a number of steam locomotives survive on the islands in various states of repair.

Singapore

The first railways were local harbour lines, eventually extending to some 16 miles (25km), while a metre-gauge passenger service between Tank Road and Woodlands opened in 1903. Completion of the Johor Causeway in 1923 allowed direct railway links from Malaysia into Singapore, whilst in 1932 the Art Deco Tanjong Pagar terminus station in central Singapore opened.

Long-distance passenger and remaining freight links to central Singapore were cut in 2011 and the central Tanjong Pagar station was closed. This decision seems partly due to the station's redevelopment potential, but also political differences at the time between Malaysia and Singapore. International services, including the luxury 'Eastern & Oriental Express', now run from Johor Bahru station in Malaysia, some 15 miles (24km) outside the central area of Singapore, although a future extension of Singapore's rapid transit system to Johor Bahru will assist connectivity. Much of the abandoned trackbed through Singapore from Tanjong Pagar station has been turned into a rail trail.

In 2011, all services were moved out of Singapore's Tanjong Pagar station, seen here in March 2019. The development potential of the station area and cross border checks with Malaysia conspired to see the closure of this centrally located iconic building. *Author*

The Art Deco Tanjong Pagar station in Singapore. Being located directly opposite the docks allowed easy transfer between steamships and the railway. Marble reliefs represented Agriculture, Commerce, Transport and Industry. The disused station is seen here in March 2019. *Author*

Taiwan of China

From a railway perspective, the mountainous island differs from Chinese mainland and developed routes around the entire coast. There have been closures of parts of the 3ft-6in gauge passenger network, particularly in the south and central areas, and hardly any freight services run. New high-speed and metro lines have been built and a few sections of line also closed due to improvements to the railway network or earthquakes. For example, what was known as the 'Old Mountain Line' was closed in 1999 when a new line was constructed, but part of the old line was reopened to tourist trains in 2010.

Industrial, logging and sugar railways in particular were once estimated to operate about 1,800 miles (2,897km) of mostly 2ft 6in narrow-gauge line, but almost all are now closed. There were over forty sugar mills and a number of railways serving these even ran passenger services. Steam was used on several lines until the late 1970s and even a limited number of local passenger services survived until 1982. Some lines closed suddenly, just two sugar mills remained in 2020 and only one was still served by rail.

A few heritage railways operate and the Welshpool & Llanfair Railway loaned a locomotive to work on the heritage Tai Sugar line. A logging line has also been given over to a tourist operation on part of the Alishan branch, with its triple spiral and steam Shay locomotives used on part of the route.

Thailand

Once known as Siam, the first railway schemes were aimed at linking the then British interests in Burma to China. Thailand remained independent and developed its own railway network, with new lines being built until the Second World War when Japan invaded the country. This led to an alliance between the two countries and enabled the Japanese to build military railways.

Longteng viaduct on the Taiwan Island of China. In 1935 an earthquake damaged the structure beyond repair. In 1999 another earthquake caused one of the remaining piers to collapse and the viaduct was dedicated as a monument to the two quakes. It is seen here in October 2003. *Thomas Lan*

THE WORLD'S MOST NOTORIOUS LOST RAILWAY – THE SIAM–BURMA DEATH RAILWAY

After the fall of Singapore during the Second World War, Japan realised it had captive troops who could be used for railway construction. A plan was devised for a 258-mile (415km) metre-gauge railway from Nong Pladuk Junction in Thailand (Siam) to the coastal Moulmein–Ye line in Myanmar (Burma). The railway would link two existing railway networks, ensure provisions for the Japanese occupying forces and facilitate an attack on India. The route chosen was through dense mountainous jungle and such difficult tropical terrain that the British colonists had decided not to build a railway across this area.

Prisoners of war were used and conditions were brutal as completion of the railway was seen as a matter of ever-increasing urgency for the Japanese war effort. To speed up construction, local Asian workers were also coerced into slave labour. Trees were felled with explosives, cuttings were blasted through rock and also cut by hand, such as that through Hellfire Pass, where sixty-nine prisoners were beaten to death. Many of the 688 original bridges and wooden trestles on the railway were made from unseasoned jungle trees.

Estimates vary, but it is estimated that about 12,000 prisoners of war died building the railway, although local Asian labour losses were much higher and some estimates put total deaths associated with the line at about 100,000. As such, the railway was one of the longest and most deadly of a number of military lines built by the Japanese.

Almost as soon as the railway was complete and joined up with existing railways in 1943, the fortunes of war were turning against the Japanese. The railway was only fully operational until 1944, becoming severely damaged and out of use during the later stages of the war.

After the war, parts of the railway were dismantled and long parts were closed in 1947. Sections have since become walks, are flooded, or have returned to the jungle, but a southern portion of the line in Thailand was reopened in 1957, including a bridge over the River Kwai. Three Commonwealth War Graves are located along the route and a preserved section of original track can be seen at the British National Memorial Arboretum.

The Thai-Burma Death Railway at Hellfire Pass in Thailand in January 2013. The line through here was dug out by hand by Allied POWs and Asian workers during the Second World War, under the brutal control of Japanese guards and at a huge cost of human life. *Stephen J. Mason Photography Collection*

The Kra Isthmus Railway

This 56-mile (90km) line connected the Bangkok–Singapore railway to a west coast port near Victoria Point, thus crossing Thailand's narrowest point. Slave labour was used by the Japanese and the line opened in 1944, but Allied bombing resulted in its closure the following year. For a time, the Japanese managed to get prisoners to move track and equipment to repair other lines, but the tide of war turned against Japan and their brutal railway construction was ended.

Post-war closures

After the Second World War, the country still had a significant remaining railway network of mostly metre-gauge lines. Many rural lines became increasingly lightly used by both freight and passenger services, and in some cases were operated with badly maintained old rolling stock. Over a score of branch and secondary lines have been closed since the 1960s.

The main central station in Bangkok, dating from 1912, was largely closed in 2021 and may be turned into a museum, with most services transferred to a new station. The railways, which have lost money every year since 1951, have come to be perceived by some as slow, inefficient and resistant to change, but investment and improvement in the network continues.

Vietnam

The first railway in Vietnam, which was once a French colony, opened in 1885 and the line ran some 43 miles (70km) between Ho Chi Minh City (Saigon) and Mỹ Tho, but it is no longer in use. Whilst damage to the network began during the Second World War, significant harm was caused by the Vietnam War which dominated the country between 1955 and 1975. The endless years of war resulted in the end of most services, together with a smashed-up railway infrastructure. When peace eventually came, very little of the network was operational.

Although the original central station in Saigon is closed, a new station has been provided and a number of key services have resumed, including the metre-gauge coastal main line unifying South and North Vietnam. The reopening was aided by the use of track from branch lines which were abandoned and dismantled to restore the main line. Some freight trains

A rail and road bridge over the Red River at Pho Lu in Vietnam. The bridge carried the Pho Lu–Xuân Giao narrow-gauge branch line once used by local mines and a fertiliser factory; disused track is seen here in December 2016. *Vladimir Menkov*

run to industrial installations, but parts of the network are still in a poor state of repair, while a sleeper service from Hanoi to the Chinese border in 2019 was limited to 20mph.

Lines remain closed such as the abandoned Cau Giat–Nghia Dan line. Closed in the 1970s, its stations still remain visible through the undergrowth. Vegetation increasingly reclaims such lost lines, but with peace in the area it is hoped there might be more reopenings in the future.

The Langbian Cog Railway

This is one of the most interesting lost railways in Vietnam. It ran on a 52-mile (84km) route from Thap Cham to the cool highland hill station of Da Lat, once known as 'Little Paris'. Completed in 1932 after years of work, the line involved some spectacularly steep cog-working sections.

The railway was eventually forced to close in 1968 as a result of the Vietnam War and the track was removed in 1975. However, several of the stations remain in various states of repair, including the stylish 1920s Art Deco-styled station at Da Lat. Bridges and other infrastructure such as concrete water towers also remain, whilst two of the Swiss-built cog locomotives were reimported to Switzerland after closure and are used on the Furka Pass heritage line. A 4-mile (7km) section has reopened as a tourist heritage railway at Da Lat and further reopening of this attractive line is possible.

The Langbian Cog Railway was on its cog sections spectacular. At Da Lat, an Art Deco station was built in 1938. The Vietnam War sped the line's closure in 1968, but the station, seen here in 2011, remains together with a section of heritage line. *Diane Selwyn*

Right: Da Tho a derelict intermediate French designed railway station on the Langbian line that closed during the Vietnam War. Within the derelict building the old booking office and waiting area still survived, in a dilapidated condition, when this view was taken in March 2016. *Roelof Hamoen*

Below: After closure of the Langbian line in Vietnam some of the original Swiss built rack locomotives were returned and restored in Switzerland for use on the Furka Steam Railway, a heritage line running on a mountain route originally closed in 1982. Class HG 4/4 No 9 dating from 1947 is seen here at Furka in August 2016. *Mario Burger*

AFRICA

frica's original railways were often directed towards extracting its natural resources, or to aid colonial expansion, and not all lines are relevant to today's needs. Some grandiose transcontinental schemes to open up the continent were never realised. Issues such as political instability, civil wars, corruption, theft, natural disasters and impoverished economic conditions have caused endless problems to many lines that were built.

Vast rural areas of sparse population, together with the huge distances between some cities, have led to a decline in passenger routes and Africa has a relatively low number of passenger services. Several networks are but a shadow of their former glory, their transport role has declined and, with little money being spent on track and other infrastructure renewal, they are in an ever-deteriorating condition. There is ever increasing competition from road transport and this has weakened many railways.

Some countries appear to try to fudge the fact that a number of their railways are in fact out of use. Lines survive on maps, but in reality they are often disused or in a semi-abandoned state. On the other hand, a number of new lines have been built, some lines refurbished and reopened and many railway projects have been proposed. Where a good passenger service has been provided, or substantial mineral traffic is transported by rail and there is stability, the railways have thrived, for example in Morocco, whilst just along the coast all the railways are closed in Libya.

No 32-001 one of the first in a series of South African diesels that were built in the USA and introduced in 1959. The locomotive is on display in Namibia and seen here in September 2014. *Dr Alan Grundy*

CHAPTER 20

AFRICAN AMBITIONS

Although some quarry lines existed near Alexandria in 1838, the first significant passenger railway in Africa was the British-built standard-gauge Alexandria–Cairo line. This opened in 1856 and was extended to Suez in 1858. The line was busy until the Suez Canal was completed in 1869. Nevertheless, British influence continued and railway expansion in the Nile Valley was undertaken by F.H. Trevithick, grandson of the Cornish pioneer. Robert Stephenson and Thomas Cook were also associated with Africa's first railways.

Wider railway growth came in a piecemeal way and there developed six different gauges on the continent. Standard-gauge was often used in the north, but the great distances and tight finances also made narrow-gauge attractive, the 3ft 6in Cape-gauge being widely used.

As networks expanded, British locomotives, rolling stock, track and equipment were all exported to Africa. France, Germany, Italy, Belgium, Spain, the Netherlands and Portugal were amongst other European nations also actively involved in Africa's original railway building. Colonial influences can still be seen on many parts of Africa's railways, ranging from elegant French-designed stations to British signalling equipment, with some original installations still in use.

Tropical jungle areas of central Africa and the extreme heat of desert areas caused problems; and, in addition to the often-difficult terrain, there was on occasion fighting with the indigenous population and rampant disease of the workforce. Plagues of locust have been known to cause slippery rails and elephants have derailed trains. The *Spectator* in 1900 included an article entitled 'The Lions that Stopped the Railway' after two lions had killed many Indian and African workers building a line near Tsavo in Kenya; the two lions were eventually shot.

The integration of some lines was originally hampered by different gauges. After African countries achieved independence, the railways were also sometimes broken up according to new national borders. Several international links between countries have been closed as a result and some railways ended up becoming even more disconnected. Parts of the continent have remained volatile and there have been civil wars and instability. Railways have often been one of the first targets for sabotage, which has disrupted services and, on occasion, resulted in closure.

Closures of significance first began in the 1930s and escalated in the 1980s. Concessions to the private sector saved a number of railways from closure in the 1990s; however, in many cases, the new owners did not live up to expectations and several railways have been returned to public ownership in poor condition. Whilst there has been some railway investment, including from China and the European Union, resulting in new or reopened lines, closures continue as the railways struggle in some of the world's poorest countries.

TRANSCONTINENTAL LINES THAT NEVER WERE
The Cape to Cairo Railway

The British colonialist Cecil Rhodes intended to use his vast wealth from gold and diamonds to make Britain the master of Africa. The Cape to Cairo railway was an ambitious project that involved building a trans-African railway, involving about 6,500 miles (10,500km) of track, spanning the entire north-south length of the continent from Port Said to Cape Town. The project was intended to consolidate, support and expand British Empire possessions, particularly in East Africa.

Existing railways, some of differing gauges, the White Nile and lakes Tanganyika and Victoria navigations were all intended to be part of the initial plan. The railway and its connecting lines were planned mainly as a freight route to extract the wealth out of Africa. However, the Thomas Cook Hotel in Egypt, together with the railway-owned hotels at Khartoum and Victoria Falls, would have refreshed weary passengers. It would, if fully completed, have been the longest and most important route on the continent, but would have provided a disjointed and slow long-distance passenger service.

A central section between Uganda and Sudan was never built due, in part, to the death of Cecil Rhodes, economic problems created by the Great Depression in

THE CAPE-TO-CAIRO ROUTE.
Special Supplement to *The Illustrated London News.*

SOUTH AFRICAN RAILWAYS

A stylised view of a train in South Africa on what might have been on the trans-African Cape to Cairo Railway from the cover of a *The Illustrated London News* supplement. The project was abandoned after the Second World War. *C.E. Turner/Alamy*

This twisting line on the outskirts of Cairo near the Mosque of Muhammad Ali is part of link line from the north to south of the city and is seen in April 2009. It would have most likely been used as part of the Cape to Cairo route. *Author*

View from the Zambian side of the Zambezi River of the 420ft (128m) high Victoria Falls Bridge in August 1982. A National Railways of Zimbabwe 15A class Garratt No 407 is standing on the bridge, which is no longer used for regular long-distance services. *Nigel Tout*

the 1930s, the inhospitable terrain and feuding in the area. After the Second World War, the need for such a line was much diminished.

The trans-African line was never completed, but the spectacular Victoria Falls bridge is the greatest legacy of the railway. On completion in 1905, it was the highest bridge in the world. Whilst it was once busy, it is no longer regularly used as a through route and only tourist trains use the bridge. Today, some sections of line that may have provided parts of the transcontinental route are now either closed or semi-abandoned.

The Trans-Saharan Railway

The proposed French line was to counter the British Cape to Cairo railway. It aimed to connect French interests in West Africa and facilitate cotton and agricultural production, which would help pay for the railway. The Mediterranean–Niger Railway was a standard-gauge line that ran from the coast to the towns of Béchar and Abadla in the Sahara Desert.

An approximate 1,300-mile (2,100km) southern extension from Béchar towards Timbuctoo and the River Niger was proposed. Construction was originally thwarted by the Great Depression in the 1930s, but work began in 1941, during the Second World War, and Jewish prisoners were amongst the slave labour force. There were terrible working conditions in the intense desert heat and many died from heat exhaustion, hunger, or typhus.

Construction across the desert required few bridges or engineering works, whilst diesel locomotives were to be used in the extremely dry area. In 1944, the lack of economic, or military, justification and difficulties of obtaining locomotives and equipment during the war were amongst the issues that resulted in the line's abandonment near Béni Abbès, a desert oasis, some 150 miles (240km) south of Béchar.

The abandoned Tendrara station in Morocco, seen in October 2015. This station once served a French labour camp that housed prisoners that worked in the harsh desert conditions to build the Trans-Saharan Railway. The project was halted in 1944. *Brahim Faraji*

CHAPTER 21

ABC AFRICA

North Africa
Algeria

The railways were established by French colonialists and, for a time, the network actually formed part of the French National Railway system. A standard-gauge coastal line was supplemented by several mostly 3ft 5½in narrow-gauge lines running inland. The network declined after the Second World War and independence from France. There were sparse services on western lines, and it was reported that coaches on some services even ended up running with compartments without seats or windows. Several narrow-gauge branches have closed, whilst the border lines to Morocco and Tunisia are closed to passengers, but there has been some rejuvenation of lines.

In the 1880s, the French engineer Lartigue built a 56-mile (90km) network of monorail lines, which were of similar design to the Listowel & Ballybunion line in Ireland. The Algerian lines were worked by animals instead of locomotives to convey esparto grass, used for paper making, and ran across desert areas to the coast for export.

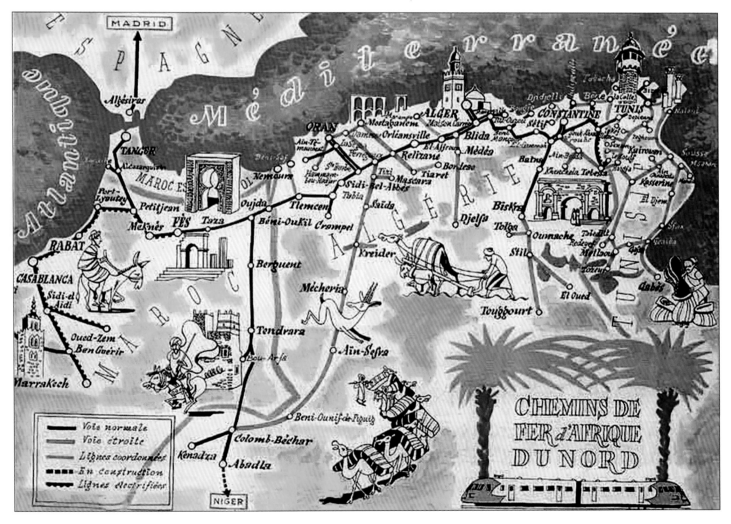

A French map of north African railways showing standard-gauge lines in black and narrow-gauge railways in red. Note the Trans-Saharan link to Niger under construction, dating the map to the 1940s. *Historical Railway Images*

Libya

As with many African countries, new railways were proposed and in 2009 work commenced on a new line, but was suspended in 2011 due to civil war. Some continuing instability has had a detrimental effect on further progress.

WORLD'S LARGEST COUNTRY WITH NO PASSENGER RAILWAYS

Libya once had railways, many of which were built by the Italian colonialists. the Second World War saw new military lines built, but also caused damage to several existing routes. With the exception of a military railway that linked Tobruk with the Egyptian border, which was closed after the war, most narrow-gauge lines continued in use. This included the line along the coast from Tripoli, with a branch heading southwards, together with two lines from Benghazi, but all operated in an ever-declining state. Lines out of Tripoli were closed in 1960 and one was used for a new road. Libya has had no operating railways since 1965 when the Benghazi lines closed.

Tripoli station opened on a line first built in 1912 and was once the busy hub of trains. It is seen here with an Italian Fiat railcar in the 1950s. The Libyan station was built by Italian colonialists and was the largest in the country.

Morocco

Both Spain and France were involved in constructing narrow-gauge lines in Morocco. The French built numerous metre-gauge lines, but by 1935 there were also over 1,000 miles (1,700km) of 1ft 11½in gauge routes. Many original lines were built for military or mineral purposes and, whilst there were isolated sections, a comprehensive network was established. Closures of the narrow-gauge network began in the 1920s and 1930s and today there are no narrow-gauge passenger lines operating. The Spanish-built narrow-gauge Ceuta–Tétouan line was one of the later closures in 1958.

Standard-gauge lines were also constructed and a network of high-quality standard-gauge passenger routes connecting key settlements, together with freight lines, survives, although the international connection to Algeria has been cut. Where improved and new standard-gauge lines have opened, the original disused narrow-gauge remains can often be seen.

Sudan

Military railways from the 1890s formed the origins of the Sudanese railway network and a 3ft 6in narrow-gauge network developed, once running sleeping and dining trains through remote desert areas. In the 1970s, about 2.6 million people used the network annually and new 3ft 6in lines were being built for the transportation of oil as late as 2002.

The railways, which operated some of the longest routes in Africa, have been in decline for many years. For example, the 'Nile Express' running between Khartoum and the Egyptian border could be days late, whilst damage during the civil war of the 1980s resulted in several lines being closed and general mismanagement. There remained deep-rooted conflicts and, fearing labour unrest, thousands of skilled railway workers were dismissed in the 1990s, whilst all passenger services were suspended in 2011 and 2012. A long loop line south of Khartoum, linking with the coast line to Port Sudan, is part of about half of the network that is out of use, whilst much else is in a decrepit condition.

In 2014, some passenger services, with modern stock, were introduced on the Wadi Haifa–Khartoum line and improvements have been promised. Freight survives, but in 2022 it was reported only a handful of locomotives were in working order and all train services were infrequent and slow.

The Sudan railways travelled across desert areas and coaches were specially designed with shaded windows and white paint to mitigate against the heat. Here a Glasgow built 4-8-2 No 509 is seen at the head of a train of such coaches. *Historical Railway Images*

A light railway was used to export cotton from the Tokar area, but closed in 1952. Elsewhere, an approximate 500-mile (800km) network of 2ft lines opened in the 1920s, during the construction of the Sennar Dam and canals, as part of the Gezira irrigation scheme. The lines are used during the cotton-picking season and much the light railway network remains.

South Sudan

This area became independent of Sudan in 2011, but because of its links to Sudan is included here. The railways were left in a poor condition after civil war and the line between the two countries was closed. The line to Wau was subsequently reopened with the aid of the United Nations but was not operational in 2021.

Tunisia

The railways were developed mainly by the French, with metre-gauge and standard-gauge routes. The lines became busy and a fleet of 135 Mallet locomotives were once in use, providing one of the largest concentrations of such locomotives in Africa. During the Second World War, further steam locomotives from the USA and Britain were delivered to help assist the railways with the war effort in North Africa.

Over a half dozen lightly used branches and some difficult-to-operate sections have been closed, including a section through the streets of Sousse. A number of lines in the south and west of the country remain just for freight traffic, whilst international passenger links to Algeria are not in use. In the attractive gorges and rock canyons of southern Tunisia, the 'Red Lizard' tourist passenger train has been run on former mineral lines.

Central and Western Africa
Angola

Four unconnected Cape-gauge railways once ran from ports and mostly served mines located a considerable distance inland. Native eucalyptus trees were originally used for steam locomotive fuel and extensive tree belts were grown near the railways. Steam power, including Garratt articulated locomotives, was extensively used until the 1980s. After Angola and Benguela became independent from Portugal in 1975, civil war broke out and lasted until 2002. This resulted in the destruction and closure of all railways. Whilst routes, such as the 81-mile (130km) Porto Ampoim–Gabela line, closed permanently, when the fighting ended some lines were restored back to use, including the Benguela Railway running from the coast at Lobito into the heart of Africa.

An Angolan narrow-gauge train in 1970. The locomotive is No 63 of the Portuguese Moçâmedes Railway (CFM). It ran on wood and the tanks behind were reserve water supplies. Closed by civil war in the 1970s, the line was reopened in 2015 to a wider gauge. *Colour-Rail*

Benin

A number of metre-gauge lines were opened, including between the port of Cotonou and Parakou, with the original aim of extending to the River Niger, and this remains open for freight. A 66-mile (107km) line also ran from Cotonou to Pobé and a branch ran from Pahou to Segboroué. These lines were both closed in the 1990s, although a short section from Cotonou to Porto Novo reopened in 1999, but passenger services were sporadic and the line subsequently closed again. A number of isolated 2ft narrow-gauge mineral lines had all closed by the early 1950s.

Cameroon

Original lines were built by German colonists prior to the First World War, but after the war France took over the lines. Routes developed from the coast at Douala, and the main line was extended as far as Ngaoundéré in 1974. The main line remains open, although some of the earlier routes including the 31-mile (50km) branch line to Nkongsamba, with its Art Deco station, together with passenger services on the Mbalmayo line, have closed.

Tropical cocoa and sugar plantations were once also served by a number of narrow-gauge railways, all now closed, but some remains are still to be found.

A narrow-gauge Hunslet locomotive from one of the lines was acquired by Statfold Barn and returned to England.

Central African Republic

There were few railways, but a 2ft-gauge line was opened in 1930, some 5 miles (7.5km) between Zinga and Mongo. It functioned as a portage route, bypassing rapids on the Ubangi River. The line was destroyed by conflict in 1960 but remains are still to be found. A rubber factory also once had an extensive network of lines.

Côte d'ivory, Ivory Coast and Burkina Faso

A lengthy metre-gauge line was originally started in the 1900s, during the French colonial period, running from the coast at Abidjan and eventually reaching the capital of neighbouring Burkina Faso by 1954. In 2014, passenger services to Kaya on the very northern section of the line were suspended, together with a mineral branch, but the main line through the two countries remains.

Democratic Republic of Congo

Navigable rivers were an integral part of the transport system and were complemented by the railways, including a number of railway portage routes that were built where the rivers were unnavigable. The lines were

Ponthierville, now Ubundu, with a Belgian built steam locomotive No 28 dating from 1913 on the narrow-gauge portage railway which ran 75 miles (120km) to Stanleyville, now Kisangani, in the Democratic Republic of Congo. An infrequent train may remain in operation. *Historical Railway Images*

of various narrow gauges, but many have since closed, such as the 85-mile (137km) 2ft-gauge Mayumbe line that closed in 1984.

The 58-mile (94km) 3ft 6in Kivu Railway was once even suggested as a possible link in the Cape to Cairo railway but closed in 1958. Elsewhere, some lengthy Cape-gauge routes are still to be found in the south-eastern part of the country, but passenger trains that operate on these lines are infrequent, on occasion running just once a month. Some lines are open in part only, whilst others are in a very degraded condition and derailments are frequent. The line to Lake Tanganyika is closed and only one link to adjoining countries remains in use.

The Vicicongo Railway was a lengthy and remote line operated in the north of the country. The 750-mile (1,207km) 1ft 11½in main line once linked the Congo River port of Bumba with high land at Mungbere and also included three branch lines. It was built by a Belgium company, mainly using surplus First World War military railways. Although parts were reopened in 2004, it is now out of use.

Ghana

The first line was built to serve gold mines, but the once well-used 3ft 6in Cape-gauge network also transported bauxite and manganese to the coast. Passengers were conveyed on trains with restaurant cars and sleeper coaches. In the 1970s, some six million passengers were carried each year, but there was a decline over many years and all services ended in 1985. In spite of an attempt to keep a section as a tourist opportunity, steam locomotives were scrapped and all efforts to revive services ceased in 2007. However, parts of the system have been brought back from ruin, reviving the route from Accra; and, at Sekondi, the line has been refurbished and trains were again running in 2021.

Guinea

A metre-gauge line ran from the capital port of Conakry and, by 1913, had reached Kankan, originally via two river ferry crossings before bridges were built. This 411-mile (662km) line running into the interior from the coast was, for many years, the country's key route; but, apart from a short 22-mile (36km) section from Conakry, closed to passengers in 1986, all remaining services over the line ceased in 1993. In 2011, a commuter service using the original line through Conakry was restored. Two other shorter lines have also closed, but newer mineral lines to standard-gauge, one with a limited passenger service, survive.

The original impressive Takoradi terminus station in western Ghana seen in March 2011. The station was derelict by 2007 and tracks were removed, but a railway remains to the town and runs to a new station. *Ben Sutherland*

Liberia

There were three iron ore mineral lines running inland from the coastal ports. A 3ft 6in gauge line ran 90-miles (145km) inland from the port of Monrovia but closed in 1989 when the iron ore workings were exhausted. Civil war in the 1990s closed the two remaining standard-gauge lines. However, the 54-mile (87km) Bong Mine line also running from Monrovia resumed an intermittent service in 2009, but closed in 2016. The other standard-gauge line ran 160-miles (250km) from the port of Buchanan to Yekepa and was repaired and reopened by 2011, but has since recorded short sections as inoperable.

Mauritania

Shifting sands can cause trouble to railway lines, but a French-built line at Choum involved boring a tunnel through 1¼ miles (2km) of solid granite. This was simply to avoid running on the adjoining flat, but sandy, Spanish territory. The tunnel has been called 'a monument to European stupidity in Africa' as the flat, easy route originally controlled by the Spanish later became part of Mauritania. The tunnel and lines leading to it, that were expensive and difficult to build, were not required after the new line was built on an easier alignment and are disused.

Niger

There were no significant railways during the twentieth century, but a new line including a link to the country's main airport was completed in 2016. Regular train services on the new line ceased in 2017.

Nigeria

One of the first closures was the Lagos Sanitary Tramway which opened in 1906 and ran to a wharf for the onward disposal of human waste to sea, until closure in 1933. On the wider system, Cape-gauge lines were joined up and West Africa's largest network of approximately 2,200 miles (3,540km) was created. Plentiful and cheap road fuel oil, incompetent management and some likely corruption all assisted in the railway's decline. The railway became increasingly run-down, with little new investment in the original network, although second-hand 3ft 6in gauge locomotives were acquired from Newfoundland on the closure of its railways in 1988.

A view from the cab of a 1921 Leeds built Kitson locomotive running on the 114-mile (184km) 3ft 6in narrow-gauge Bauchi Light Railway in Nigeria, which served tin ore deposits. The view was taken before the railway's closure in 1957. *Historical Railway Images*

1988 also saw all Nigerian services cease for a period of six months, but some services resumed where track and infrastructure were in a usable condition. Such was the state of much of the infrastructure that, after a bridge collapse on the Gusau branch, all passenger services were again discontinued for a period in 2002. By 2009, the annual number of passengers had fallen from 11 million in 1963 to just one million. Some steam-hauled rail charters ran until 2013, but in 2019 it was estimated that, of approximately 200 diesel locomotives, only about 15 were in a serviceable condition.

Terrorism in the north-east also resulted in closures, including the line beyond Kano to Maiduguri, but rusting track remained in 2019. Acts of railway vandalism and ticket racketeering have also occurred, but a new standard-gauge railway is being opened in sections and may eventually replace the main routes of the existing narrow-gauge network.

Republic of Congo and Gabon

The line from Pointe-Noire to Brazzaville remains. Built in the 1920s by French colonialists, the original route included the Bamba Tunnel, where carbon monoxide killed many construction workers. In 1985, a 57-mile (91km) new line was opened between Bilinga and Dolisie, bypassing the original tunnel and providing an easier route for iron ore trains. A branch also runs to the border with Gabon, but it lost its manganese ore traffic when a new line in Gabon was built. This also resulted in the closure of a cableway that conveyed the ore from Gabon to the railway terminus in the Republic of Congo.

Senegal and Mali

With independence from France in 1960, the metre-gauge Dakar–Kayes line became part of the Dakar-Niger Railway international route, from the coast at Senegal to Mali and the River Niger. However, in 2003 the line was handed over to a private consortium and little investment was forthcoming. The section between Bamako and the Koulikoro area closed and there were limited local passenger services on just two other sections. Branch lines also closed, together with the line from Dakar to Saint-Louis on the coast, which was the very first constructed in the country. In 2021 Dakar's beautiful historic station was reopened after renovation and new suburban trains started but remaining long-distance services on the original narrow-gauge lines ceased in 2009.

WORLD'S MOST SIGNIFICANT 2FT 6INS GAUGE NETWORK TO CLOSE ALL ITS RAILWAYS

A 2ft 6in narrow-gauge network ran from the capital at Freetown, Sierra Leone, stopping just short of the border with Liberia, together with a branch to Makeni. Almost everything associated with the railway originated from Britain, and in 1955 new Garratt locomotives were supplied by Beyer, Peacock & Co of Manchester. New coaches were also provided for the busy network.

With almost 8 million people, it was one of the most populous countries in the world to have completely lost its passenger railway. Closures began in 1968, but the entire remaining 320-mile (530km) network closed in 1974, a decision at the time supported by the United Nations. Although there have been attempts at revival, significant items of infrastructure have been looted. At Freetown, there is a railway museum, whilst after closure some stock was transported to the Welshpool & Llanfair Railway in Wales. A separate mineral line closed in 2017.

The derelict stone buildings at Hastings station seen in March 2012. Located east of Freetown, the station closed in 1974, along with all remaining lines on the Sierra Leone Government Railway and the building subsequently became derelict. *Joerg Boething/Alamy*

Togo

The railways once consisted of about 350 miles (560km) of metre-gauge line that were mostly completed in the 1930s. Routes were cut back in 1985 and the main Lomé–Blitta line closed in 1999, marking the end of passenger services. Some private freight routes survived until 2014 and a phosphate line was operational in 2022.

East Africa

The East African Railways were formed in 1948 by the amalgamation of Kenya, Uganda and Tanganyika (Tanzania) railways. The system had its headquarters in Nairobi. It comprised about 3,600 miles (5,800km) of metre-gauge track and was so well served by Beyer-Garratt steam locomotives that the inevitable switch to diesel occurred later than on many railways. Disputes between the countries since they became independent have resulted in the abandonment of joint working. The railway ferries on Lake Victoria also stopped operating in a unified way in 1976 and East African Railways ceased as a company the following year.

Eritrea

In Eritrea, a line ran from the Red Sea to the capital Asmara. The section through a mountainous area required many tunnels, bridges and viaducts. The 3ft 1⅜in Italian-built narrow-gauge line was extended further inland to Agordat, giving some 192 miles (307km) of route by 1932. The line was then again extended to Bishia, with unfulfilled plans to extend into Sudan.

Eleven Fiat railcars were introduced in the 1930s and a busy service was provided during that period, there also being a significant fleet of steam locomotives. The section from Asmara to Bishia was closed in 1942 due to war damage and, at the same time, a 45-mile (72km) cableway, running from Asmara, was closed. The rest of the railway survived until it was damaged during the Eritrean War of Independence in 1975.

Eritrea gained independence from Ethiopia in 1993. In 1994, part of the railway from the Red Sea to Asmara was rebuilt and a short-lived diesel service operated, but the attractive route had huge tourist potential. Eleven locomotives and two Fiat diesel railcars survived and

Keren railway viaduct, seen in December 2012, over the dry Ciuf Ciufit riverbed. The Eritrean line here closed during the Second World War; part was reopened, but closed again in the 1970s. A section of the railway reopened yet again for heritage tourist traffic. *David Stanley*

Eritrean Railway Mallet 0-4-4-0T locomotive on a mixed train at Shegerini station in October 2011 on this steeply graded section of line which was still in use mainly for rail enthusiast charters. *Reinhard Dietrich*

rail tours for enthusiasts were provided. Eritrea has seen continued disruption to its railways due to civil unrest, but a tour on part of the remaining line was again provided in 2019.

Ethiopia and Djibouti

The original 487 miles (784km) of the metre-gauge Addis-Ababa–Djibouti Railway, which had been built in stages and completed in 1917, has been replaced by a new standard-gauge line. On the old route, services between Addis Ababa and Dire Dawa ended in 2008 and the section between Dire Dawa and Djibouti closed to passengers in 2014. Whilst the original line has been partly destroyed or abandoned, it was estimated some 200 miles (320km) were still in use, or partly in

operation, in 2017. At Dire Dawa, midway along the old line, a handful of working diesel locomotives survived in 2017, together with a plinthed Fiat-built railcar dating from 1938, but by 2022 it appears the site is a museum. The original French-styled station in the centre of Addis Ababa is out of use. On Djiboutian territory and beyond Guelile, the old railway has also been abandoned.

Kenya and Uganda

The 'Lunatic Line' was the name sometimes given to the original metre-gauge route in Kenya between Mombasa and Nairobi. This was because the railway far exceeded its original budget and was beset with problems. About 2,500 workers perished from disease during the construction of the line, including a number killed by marauding lions.

It was also known as the 'Uganda Railway' as it extended beyond Kenya into Uganda. Firstly in 1901, a branch ran to Port Florence, now Kisumu, connecting with a train ferry across Lake Victoria to Uganda and, later in 1931, a line ran directly to Kampala, the capital of Uganda. Routes continued in Uganda to Kasese, a point close to the Democratic Republic of Congo, and to Arua within 100 miles of South Sudan.

The challenging countryside required the construction of the occasional spiral, such as on the now closed Kasese line, together with many bridges and viaducts, resulting in some branch lines of the metre-gauge railway network not being completed until the 1960s. The lines became busy, once using the most powerful Garrett steam locomotives.

However, in Uganda the once proud railways with their restaurant cars, together with all passenger services, were destroyed during Amin's regime in the 1970s. Branch lines, including two long lines running north from Kampala, remain closed and today large sections of the railways are abandoned. However, there has also been some rehabilitation; the line to Arua was reopened as far as Gulu in 2013, assisted by European Union finance, whilst the short branch to Port Bell on Lake Victoria reopened in 2018. A commuter service was also established at Kampala and operated until the outbreak of coronavirus in 2020 but services resumed.

There were also years of railway decline in Kenya and most Kenyan branch lines, such as those to what was originally called Thompson's Falls, and from Voi to Taveta on the border with Tanzania, have been closed, whilst the line to the pier at Kisumu on Lake Victoria closed in 2007, together with the train ferry connections. On the other hand, some routes are being considered for refurbishment, including the line from Nairobi to Nanyuki near Mount Kenya, and there are trains running again on the line to Kisumu.

The original Mombasa–Nairobi section was closed to passengers in 2017, having been replaced by a new standard-gauge route, built with Chinese finance, running largely parallel to the old line. The original line still conveys commuters from the new standard-gauge station located on the outskirts of Nairobi into the central area, and freight services on the original line remain.

An ex-East African Railways Garratt at the Nairobi Railway Museum in Kenya, which was established in 1971, seen here in November 2010. The heavy weight of the large and powerful locomotive was distributed to many axles thus enabling use on lightly laid track.
S. Shankar

Malawi

Areas of difficult terrain resulted in some lines having tight curves and steep gradients, but by the 1930s a 3ft 6in narrow-gauge network ran north-south through the spine of the country and was connected to the coast at Nacala and Beira in Mozambique. A number of later mineral and other extensions were added over the years, including a link to Zambia, but the latter remains out of use. The line south of Malawi to Beira was closed due to civil war in 1979, but in 2022 was being prepared for reopening. The Lake Malawi (Lake Nyasa) railway steamer service, which bizarrely saw the first naval battle of the First World War, no longer runs or connects with railway services. In 2020, one infrequent passenger service remains on a freight route.

Mozambique

Cape-gauge railways ran from landlocked countries such as Malawi and Zimbabwe through Mozambique to its Indian Ocean ports. The line running inland from the coast at Quelimane, together with sections from Nacala and Beira, were amongst long lengths of line that were put out of action due to the civil war in Mozambique. Lines to the coastal towns of Inhambane, Lumbo and Quelimane remain closed, but after terrorist activities mostly ended in 1992, longer link lines from inland countries to main coastal ports are being reopened. This includes the line to Beira over the 33-span Dona Ana Bridge, which on original opening in 1934 was the longest in Africa.

The Gaza Railway was a 2ft 6in network of lines operating over some 87 miles (140km) in the southern part of the country. Opening in the early 1900s and using American locomotives, the railway conveyed both passengers and freight, mostly consisting of cashew nuts. Parts of the line were damaged by floods in 2000 and, as much of the stock was in a decrepit state, the railway closed at that time. A number of narrow-gauge sugar estate railways have also all closed.

Rwanda

Three separate 2ft narrow-gauge industrial networks once existed but were damaged by civil war in the 1990s and are out of use.

Somalia

A number of railways were built by the Italian colonialists prior to the First World War, with an Italian metre-gauge, 70-mile (114km) main route inland from Mogadishu. In addition to passenger traffic, coffee, cotton and bananas were once conveyed. The lines were dismantled by the British during the Second World War and never reopened.

Tanzania

A metre-gauge line was built by German colonists with the aim to run from the port of Tanga to Lake Victoria, to compete with the British line to the lake in Kenya. The metre-gauge railway reached Moshi, near Mount Kilimanjaro, whilst a 15-mile (24km) 2ft 6in gauge branch wound its way to Sigi, before finance ran out. The branch to Sigi, together with the link to the Kenyan border at Taveta, remain closed, whilst remaining lines fell out of use in the 1990s.

However, cement trains started to run to Moshi in 2019, and in 2020 Dar es Salaam, Tanga, Moshi and Arusha trains were restored on lines that had been defunct for more than thirty years. Other metre-gauge lines survive, and long-distance passenger and sleeper services continued in 2022. The Cape-gauge line from Dar es Salaam through Tanzania to Zambia also remains and new lines are under construction.

The Southern Province Railway was a 170-mile (275km) isolated metre-gauge railway that opened in 1949, running to ports at Mtwara and Lindi in connection with an abortive British groundnut planting scheme. Passenger services operated over much of the network and, in 1952, it became part of East African Railways. The project to grow groundnuts soon ran into difficulties due to the climate and terrain and was sometimes described as 'the worst fiasco in British colonial history'. The railway was gradually deprived of its main traffic but survived until 1962.

Zambia

The rich mineral wealth provided the incentive for the first railways, whilst accidents with elephants and other wildlife were common. The main railway across the country was envisioned as part of the Cape to Cairo route and reached Victoria Falls in 1902. Several branches were built in the 1920s to serve the Copper Belt and the railways themselves became increasingly important to the economy of the country.

In contrast, in 2022 the railways are in a poor state of repair, resulting in unreliable passenger services.

Zambian Railways, ex-South African Railways freight locomotive, at the railway museum at Livingstone in February 2016. The Scottish built locomotive spent its last days on the Zambezi Sawmills Railway. *E. Caminade-Levault*

Even copper traffic has been increasingly sent by road, the Luanshya branch was closed due to vandalism and theft by scrap metal dealers. The Njanji commuter line at Lusaka closed in 1998, was reopened in 2015, but ran at a loss and closed again. The Chipata–Mchinji line provided a link to Malawi and was completed in 2010 but has been out of use for long periods. However, long-distance freight continues and some rehabilitation is promised.

The Mulobezi Railway, once known as the Zambezi Sawmills Railway, at one time operated numerous branches serving teak logging areas off a long route between Livingstone, Mulobezi and Kataba. Whilst the branches and section to Kataba are closed the decrepit Livingstone–Mulobezi section remains and was converted to diesel traction, but not before one of the steam locomotives used on this network was superbly painted by the artist David Shepherd.

Zimbabwe

The discovery of coal determined the railway route north of Bulawayo and the town became a railway centre. Long-distance international trains once ran out of the country to Beira, Cape Town and even Benguela. However, a declaration of independence in 1965, when the country was known as Rhodesia, resulted in increasing isolation. In 1969, international passenger services over the Victoria Falls bridge were suspended and most long-distance freight trains were curtailed until Zimbabwe was established in 1980.

After becoming Zimbabwe, several lines reopened and the country became the one of the last bastions of the Garratt steam locomotives. However, the railways also gradually became impoverished, whilst vandalism and theft to overhead cables resulted in electric services being discontinued. Many lines were abandoned, including branches from Harare, and most of the branch

The arid landscape of the Mbalabala Gorge in Zimbabwe with a class 16A Garratt seen in July 1987 on the West Nicholson branch. At one time, closure looked likely, but the branch line was considerably extended in 1999 to join up with South Africa's railways. *Vincent Corasi*

and secondary lines in the country are now closed. Remaining passenger trains can be unreliable; mostly use old stock, and parts of the railway are in a perilous state with much needing to be renewed. In 2022, some intercity services were operating and a number of suburban services had been reopened.

Southern Africa

Botswana

Botswana Railways announced the termination of all passenger services in 2009, although some trains from adjoining countries still ran through the country, such as the 'Livingstone Express'. In 2017, an internal passenger train was reintroduced, but in 2021 was suspended. Freight services remain.

Eswatini (formerly Swaziland)

The first line was not built until the 1960s, but the closure of the iron ore mine at Ngwenya in 1980 resulted in this line being cut back to Matsapha. Although there are no passenger services, a 186-mile (300km) freight network still survives.

Lesotho

The limited passenger services on the remaining short line in Lesotho ceased in 1989, but freight remains.

Namibia

The first mineral railways were built by German colonists and the 352-mile (566km) Otavi Railway was, at the time of completion in 1906, the longest 2ft narrow-gauge line in the world, traversing arid and remote areas. Conversion to the wider 3ft 6in Cape-gauge started during the Second World War and, by 1961, any sections that remained had either been converted or closed.

The rush for diamonds prior to the First World War resulted in the construction of some lines, including a 74-mile (119km) link from Lüderitz to Bogenfels. The

Above: Swakopmund old station was built in 1901 as the coastal terminus of the line in Namibia, once known as German South West Africa. The line now starts outside the town and the former station has been used as a hotel since 1994 and is seen here in September 2014. *Dr Alan Grundy*

Right: The Namibian war of independence between 1966 and 1990 is highlighted by this armoured rail vehicle displayed at Windhoek station and seen here in September 2014. The Transnamib Museum is located at the station. *Dr Alan Grundy*

lack of water for steam locomotives resulted in the line being electrified. A short link to the town of Kolmanskop was also built, but new, richer diamond areas resulted in the closure of the lines by the Second World War. The terrain is mostly hostile and hot, and the town of Lüderitz was cut off by drifting desert sand on the tracks for sixteen years. Railway links with adjoining countries remain, although passenger services on the branch to Gobabis in the east and to South Africa have been suspended.

South Africa

The discovery of diamonds and gold led to lines being built, and eventually about 80 per cent of all Africa's railways were to be found in this area. However, the immense distances and sparsely populated countryside saw closures that first began during the First World War. Increasing competition from road transport has resulted in over 100 lines now being closed, while some remaining secondary freight lines are little used.

South African Railways (SAR) was established in 1910 by the amalgamation of the main railways. The mostly 3ft 6in Cape-gauge network was once famous for its huge steam locomotives, including the articulated Garratts, which were introduced in the 1920s and were very successful on steep gradients with relatively lightly laid track.

Before the deregulation of freight transport between 1977 and 1990, most freight was conveyed by rail, including on the country's two dozen or so 2ft narrow-gauge lines. Fruit and minerals were important freight, but in the 1980s fruit was increasingly transferred to road and, at the same time, a policy to phase out branch lines, especially narrow-gauge, was introduced. The Minister of Transport at that time just happened to own a fleet of road vehicles.

The longest 2ft narrow-gauge passenger line in South Africa ran 177 miles (285km) between Port Elizabeth and Avontuur. Opened in 1907, the line included the Van Stadens Bridge; at 256ft (77m), it was the highest in the

St Helena gold mine near Welkom in South Africa with ex-South African Railways 4-6-2 Pacific locomotive, seen in April 1983. The locomotive had been withdrawn from SAR in the 1970s and had been snapped up by the mine in the oil crisis. *Vincent Corasi*

world carrying a 2ft line, whilst the route also operated some of the most powerful 2ft-gauge locomotives in the world. The line closed in 2001 and part of it was used for a heritage excursion train known as the 'Apple Express', but this ceased in 2010.

Another interesting railway was the 93-mile (150km) Umzinto–Donnybrook line that was also a 2ft narrow-gauge route and opened in 1908. Closure came in phases, with complete closure in 1987, due in part to washouts. Donnybrook, the impressive steam centre of the line with mostly Garratt locomotives, is no more. After closure, rails were transported to Britain and used on the Welsh Highland Railway, whilst a section of the original African route may reopen as a heritage railway.

Parts of the main Cape-gauge railway network involved mountainous areas. A significant length of lost line is to be found on the old Natal main line through the Drakensberg Mountain range, after the original steeply graded route was largely replaced by a new line in 1961. The Aliwal North–Barkly East branch, which closed in 2001, also required no less than eight zigzags to cross the Drakensberg range.

In 1990, many long-distance passenger trains were withdrawn, whilst in 2010 all the remaining state-run long-distance passenger trains were suspended; however, after an outcry, a number of services between main centres were subsequently restored. Outside urban areas there are no regular branch passenger services and no regular international passenger services, although some luxury trains do travel further afield to other countries and a number of heritage and tourist services survive.

The 'Banana Express' ran on part of the 2ft narrow-gauge Port Shepstone–Harding line until 2006. Subsequent damage to the South African line resulted in services being suspended. A Garratt articulated locomotive No 88 and called *Snowy* at that time is seen in April 1985. *Vincent Corasi*

Above: Hopefield station in the Western Cape is located on a branch that ran from Saldanha through Darling to Kalbaskraal. The line was regauged from 2ft to Cape-gauge in 1926. Whilst out of use, the rusting track remains and is seen in February 2020. *Dr Alan Grundy*

Left: Franschhoek station opened at the end of a branch from Paarl in 1904. The line closed to regular traffic in 1992 and rail tours ceased in 2002. The South African station building survives as a restaurant and the concrete station sign is seen in February 2020. *Dr Alan Grundy*

Groot Drakenstein station in February 2020 on the Franschhoek line. The South African branch had a limited passenger service and all traffic ceased in 2002. Overgrown track remained in 2006, but part has since been used by vineyard sightseeing trams. *Dr Alan Grundy*

Freight was deliberately manipulated off some lines by government officials and many remaining freight lines see an infrequent service. Unfortunately, when lines are little used, thieves have sometimes caused damage by the removal of track and railway infrastructure. In the Cape Town area, in 2019, arson on eighty suburban trains curtailed services, whilst in 2020 large amounts of copper overhead wires were stolen during a coronavirus lockdown, again curtailing services. It is clear that the railways in South Africa certainly face some challenges.

Africa's amazing and increasingly threatened wildlife has, since the 1920s, seen the tourist use of lines to visit safari parks. The Kruger National Park in South Africa once had a line that ran through its heart. Opened in 1912, the line closed in 1973, but the huge Selati Bridge was not demolished. In 2020, the innovative idea of returning carriages to the railway bridge to create a luxury high-level hotel was undertaken. Elsewhere, the 'Blue Train' and Rovas Rail provide luxury passenger services.

Outeniqua Choo Tjoe was the last continually operating passenger steam service in South Africa running over the scenic Garden Route until 2009. A class 24 locomotive 2-8-4 is seen at Knysna in April 1986. Although still closed in 2022, reopening is a possibility. *Vincent Corasi*

CHAPTER 22

AFRICAN AND OTHER ISLANDS

The Azores

There was once a 7ft broad-gauge railway line on the island of São Miguel, originally to construct and then operate on a harbour breakwater at Ponta Delgada. The line was worked by equipment previously used for breakwater construction at Holyhead in Wales. The short line connected to a quarry and remained in use until 1973. Two of the ex-Great Western Railway broad-gauge locomotives used on the line survive.

Equatorial Guinea

On the island of Bioko a standard-gauge line opened in 1913. It ran to villages from the main town of Malabo (Santa Isabel) and was extended to the harbour by means of a short section of Abt rack railway. However, the 11-mile (18km) line was never expanded as originally proposed and the final section closed in 1931. There were also some forestry railways, the last closing in 1963.

Madeira

Madeira had a rack railway that was completed from the capital Funchal to Monte in 1894 and was extended further to Terreiro de Luta at a height of 2,845ft (867m) in 1912. A lack of tourists and a need for steel during the Second World War resulted in the closure and dismantling of the line in 1943.

Above: The station at Monte, on the island of Madeira, provided a cooler area in summer and was a health resort. The derelict station and sales booth, which closed in 1943, is seen here June 2011, but has since been refurbished. At Terreiro de Luta station original ticket machines still survive. *Author*

Left: A tile picture of part of the Monte Railway at Madeira seen in June 2011. The island suffered from a lack of tourists during the Second World War and the rack railway closed in 1943, but the tourist toboggans that followed part of the route remain. *Author*

The derelict southern terminus of the Monte Railway at Funchal in Madeira seen in January 2017. The station closed in 1943 and although appearing not to be in any alternative use at this time, the building still remains in quite good condition. *Author*

Madagascar

Two separate metre-gauge networks still provide rail services, from a number of attractive French-designed stations, but are run-down and have a sparse passenger timetable. In 2019, weather damage resulted in the closure of a line for a period of time. Sugar estate railways on the island of Nosy Be are closed.

Mauritius

A network of about 155 miles (250km) of standard-gauge lines once existed, fed by many more narrow-gauge sugar plantation railways. The network which served much of the island was once busy, and new Garratt locomotives were ordered from Beyer Peacock in the 1920s. After the Second World War, traffic declined,

passenger services ended in 1952 and all services ceased in 1964. A few narrow-gauge lines survived for a longer period, but sadly, the railways are as dead as the last Dodo seen on the island.

Réunion

A 54-mile (87km) metre-gauge line between Saint-Benoit and Saint-Pierre opened along the western coast in 1878. A 23-mile (38.8km) line was also opened on the eastern coast to St-Benoit. A proposal to link the two lines would have almost encircled the island with railways. Sugar was the most important freight and some fifty steam locomotives were used over the railway's lifetime. Passengers were also conveyed and diesel railcars were introduced. Most passenger services

The coastal lines on the island contained many tunnels, including one of the longest tunnels on a metre-gauge line at some 18,635ft (5,680m) in length. Some of the tunnels were of restricted bore and later railcars used on the island had to be cut down in size to travel through them.

St Helena

At Jamestown, a funicular opened in 1829 to serve a fort, but termite damage to the sleepers caused the line to close as early as 1871. The route also included a long staircase that remains and became known as 'Jacob's Ladder'.

São Tomé and Príncipe

On São Tomé, an 11-mile (18km) narrow-gauge line ran inland from the coast, opening in 1913. It transported both freight, in particular cocoa, and passengers. Officially closing to regular services in 1931, the line remained in occasional use by plantations until the 1950s. Even after this, the line was occasionally used for conveying rocks and building materials, whilst a short section was used by a tourist train until 1978. The remains of Trindade station are still to be found.

Numerous plantation railways also developed to transport cocoa, coffee and palm oil and by 1910 about 155 miles (250km) of line were in use. A number of lightly built plantation railways also once existed at nearby Príncipe, the largest being over 25 miles (40km) in extent. From the 1960s, lines began to close and none remains open on either island.

Zanzibar

A 2ft-gauge 7-mile (11km) line was opened in 1879 by the island's Sultan to connect his palace with Zanzibar Town. The private line closed with his death in 1888. A public railway also 7 miles (11km) in length was opened from Zanzibar Town on the island in 1905, closing to passengers in 1922 and to remaining freight in 1930.

In La Réunion, St Denis Tunnel cut through a coastal headland and is seen here between 1879 and 1891. This section survived until 1976, after the general closure of lines in 1963, in case the coastal road was closed by storms. *Henri Georgi*

were suspended in 1956 and freight in 1963, but a section of track retained for possible emergencies was not taken up until 1976 when a new road was built. A railcar and other stock survive and an occasional tourist train runs on a preserved section of track at La Grande Chaloupe.

CHAPTER 23

OUT OF AFRICA

The British involvement in Africa resulted in locomotives, rolling stock and railway equipment being produced in Britain and exported to Africa's railways. As a consequence, many of the railways had somewhat of a British appearance. In today's modern world, this shared historic colonial legacy can sometimes lead to questions being raised about the preservation in Africa of former British Empire-built locomotives. Conversely, there has been a surprisingly high number of British locomotives reimported out of Africa and back to Britain.

Whilst British-built steam locomotives are still to be found in Africa, those from other countries, in particular Germany and America, also remain. Some are rusting, and in an ever more derelict condition, in many African countries. Equally, some steam locomotives can be found in good condition, a few even in working condition. Others are preserved as static open displays, including at a number of railway museums.

There are also some heritage railways, including the Sandstone Heritage Trust which, in addition to Cape-gauge main line locomotives, also has about fifty narrow-gauge locomotives, many originally supplied by European manufacturers. A number of narrow-gauge industrial steam locomotives that have escaped scrap are also found throughout Africa. One pair of locomotives are of particular interest to me, due to my first name! They are No 1 and No 2 of the Sub Nigel Mining Company. Of these Leeds-built 2ft 6in narrow-gauge locomotives, No 1 is plinthed in the township of Nigel and No 2 can be found at a former gold mine located near Johannesburg.

Whilst they have not been reimported, one was portrayed by the renowned artist David Shepherd and, as such, has found itself admired on many a rail enthusiast's wall. Furthermore, it is to be noted that when the Mulobezi Railway ceased using steam in the 1970s, a locomotive was donated by Zambia to David Shepherd and transported to the UK.

Originally built in Glasgow, this locomotive was used on South African Railways before working on the Mulobezi Railway. The locomotive was presented to the artist David Sheppard as a gift from Zambia and is seen here in 1998 exhibited at Bristol Temple Meads rail yard. *Author*

WORLD'S LARGEST SINGLE LOSS OF HISTORIC STEAM LOCOMOTIVES

In 2010, some twenty-seven steam locomotives belonging to the South African National Rail and Steam Museum were stored in an open area near Johannesburg. The collection included the last survivors of several classes of locomotives dating back to the late nineteenth century. Unfortunately, they were confronted by a large gang of armed metal thieves. They did so much irreparable damage, by cutting into the frames to get to the brass bearings and removing other valuable metal items, that the entire collection had to be scrapped.

Before the end of steam on South African Railways (SAR), modifications to a steam locomotive in 1981 demonstrated that they could use 28 per cent less coal and 30 per cent less water, whilst increasing output by 43 per cent. This positive development was unfortunately too late to save steam and South Africa continued to buy new diesel and electric locomotives. However, after the official end of regular steam on SAR in the 1990s, a number of locomotives was retained for rail tour use.

In East Africa, over thirty oil-fired Garratts were still in operation until the 1980s and were the most powerful locomotives to run on the narrow-gauge lines. Two were retained but are both out of use. Steam locomotives survived at a number of coal mines, where fuel was virtually free, for longer periods with some locomotives working in Zimbabwe in 2017.

Over the years, over a dozen Garratt locomotives, of various gauges and sizes, have returned from Africa to Britain. Of the larger locomotives, SAR No 2352, built by Beyer, Peacock & Co in Manchester, is preserved at a Manchester museum. At Summerlee in Scotland, SAR No 4112, an ex-North British locomotive built at Glasgow, is to be found. Exposed to the elements in 2019, the St Rollox depot was given the task of refurbishing the

Springbok engine. Other Cape-gauge locomotives have found new homes in Britain. For example, locomotive SAR No 3007 returned from South Africa to the transport museum at Glasgow, and the Mizens Railway in Surrey has a smaller SAR locomotive No 196.

Of the narrow-gauge, a number of steam locomotives that once worked in Africa can be found at Statfold Barn. The Welsh Highland Railway has no less than six ex-SAR narrow-gauge Garratt locomotives, together with two other steam locomotives that were once used in South Africa. The Vale of Rheidol Railway in Wales also has a South African Garratt.

There are reimported diesel locomotives at Statfold Barn, and two diesel locomotives, originally from a diamond mine, are also part of the Ffestiniog and Welsh Highland ex-African stock, whilst wagons from South Africa are also to be found. A diesel used for an abortive groundnuts scheme in Africa found its way to the Great Whipsnade Zoo Railway in 1972. Other narrow-gauge locomotives that once worked in Africa are to be found elsewhere in Britain.

A locomotive from the closed Sierra Leone network was transported in the 1970s to the Welshpool & Llanfair Railway, together with four coaches. The coaches were

The Beyer Garratt class GL 4-8-2 2-8-4 were some of the most powerful narrow-gauge steam locomotives ever built for the Cape-gauge South African Railways. No 2352 is seen here in 2000 after its return to Manchester, where it was originally built in 1929. *Author's collection*

South African Railways class 15F, built in 1945 in Glasgow was donated back to the city by South African Railways. Part of the motion of the huge North British locomotive is seen at Glasgow's transport museum in October 2011. *Author's collection*

Ex-Natal Government Railways, later South African Railways class A 4-8-2T No 196 at the Mizens Railway in May 2021. The locomotive was withdrawn in 1962 and plinthed at Pietermaritzburg before arriving at the Surrey location in 2011. *Author*

originally ordered from the Gloucester Carriage & Wagon Company in 1961. Sierra Leone's National Railway Museum at Freetown came within a week of having its stock scrapped, but all were saved and the collection and museum remain.

In 1988, a number of narrow-gauge locomotives arrived in England from Mozambique. It was suggested that the private purchaser was really intent on buying traction engines, but was obliged to buy the locomotives as well to secure the deal. Most of these and other imported smaller locomotives, some from sugar railways, have found their way to a number of British heritage locations.

A number of locomotives have also been transported to other countries. Two ex-South African locomotives are to be found in Germany. Steam locomotives from Africa have also been exported to new homes in Switzerland, the USA and New Zealand.

The story is yet to be completed. In 2019, the British-based North British Locomotive Preservation Group successfully purchased one of the last heavy duty 4-8-2T locomotives in Africa. The group actively supports former British locomotives in Africa including a Hendrie designed locomotive, built in Glasgow in 1909. Hendrie worked for the Highland Railway but joined the Natal Government Railways in 1903. There he led the world, designing South African locomotives that were more powerful and with more advanced features. The locomotive links between Britain and Africa remain, are surprising and many.

This 2-6-2T Hunslet locomotive was built in Leeds in 1954 for the Sierra Leone Government Railway. It was saved after closure of the network in that country in 1974 and is now at the Welshpool & Llanfair Railway in Wales, where it is seen at Llanfair in September 2018. *Author*

This diesel locomotive on the Welsh Highland Railway, at Caernarfon in September 2003, originally worked at an African diamond mine and later at a cement works in Port Elizabeth in Africa. It is one of several locomotives from Africa now used on the Welsh railway. *Author*

A 4-8-4 locomotive No 3432 stored in the open at Auckland in January 2018. Originally from South Africa it was saved from scrap in 1996 and shipped to New Zealand, with the aim of restoring this and two other steam locomotives for main line use. *Author*

The A4 Pacific class locomotives, designed by Sir Nigel Gresley, hold the world steam record for speed. Here *Union of South Africa* is seen in 2019 at Weymouth with the springbok plaque donated by a Bloemfontein newspaper proprietor in 1954. *Author*

The Welsh Highland Railway fully reopened in 2010 and has made good use of some repatriated ex-South African Railways Garratt locomotives, such as this 2-6-2+2-6-2 class NGG16 No 87 dating from 1937 and seen here in May 2012 at a road crossing at Porthmadog. *Author*

Above left: A British built Bagnell 0-4-2T *Isibutu*, dating from 1945, originally supported a spark arresting chimney when it ran on the 2ft gauge Tongaat sugar cane lines in Natal in South Africa. It is seen here at Statfold Barn in Staffordshire in August 2020. *John Carter*

Above right: Not all locomotives were lucky enough to be saved and most ended up for scrap. This tank locomotive, that was particularly used for coal traffic, is seen in 1980 rusting and being taken over by vegetation at Enugu in Nigeria. Once a busy junction of four Cape-Guage lines, by 2018 there were no trains operating. *Rob Higgins*

OCEANIA

The gold boom of the 1850s saw a vast programme of railway construction in parts of Australia, but separate local lines were built and any idea of a national network was not foreseen. As a consequence, uncoordinated railways developed to different gauges, as did later state-backed networks. Subsequent work was undertaken to create more standardisation, allowing all mainland state capitals to be connected by standard-gauge.

There is a sparse rural population with huge areas of wilderness, and today very few rural branch lines continue to provide regular passenger services. As a consequence, there are a large number of closed branch lines and secondary routes. Of the truly narrow-gauge lines, only heritage railways survive. A number of lines remain just for grain freight and there are long-distance passenger and freight trains on standard-gauge routes, together with suburban services in main cities.

In New Zealand, the lessons from Australia's differing gauges resulted in a unified 3ft 6in gauge network being established; however, with many stretches covering difficult topography, some lines were not completed until the 1940s. Rural areas are sparsely populated and there has been a massive closure of branch lines. No regular long-distance passenger trains run, other than for tourists, but freight and city suburban services survive.

On the smaller Oceanic islands, all the railways have been closed except for some sugar cane lines in Fiji.

The ornate tiled ticket office window at Dunedin station in New Zealand in January 2018. *Author*

CHAPTER 24

AUSTRALIA

Australia's first lines were individual routes, often leading inland from coastal harbours; they were once the lifeblood of the areas they served and helped develop the country. The individual states were responsible for their railways and built lines to different gauges. At one time, there were said to be over twenty gauges in operation and this inconsistency became increasingly problematic as a national network developed.

South Australia and Victoria originally built most lines to a broad 5ft 3in gauge, on the advice of an Irish engineer. New South Wales used standard-gauge, on the advice of a Scots engineer. The picture was further clouded when, with large expanses, Queensland and Western Australia decided they could only afford to build most railways to a narrow 3ft 6in gauge. As the network expanded and the first transcontinental lines were envisioned, a break of gauge at most state boundaries caused increasing problems as long-distance traffic increased.

Gladstone Junction in South Australia demonstrated the problems caused by the differing gauges, ending up with triple-gauge track. It was originally a four-way junction station with all 3ft 6in narrow-gauge lines. In 1927, the line to the south was converted to 5ft 3in broad-gauge. Then, as part of the standardisation project, the main line through Gladstone was converted to 4ft 8½in standard-gauge in 1969. Thus, Gladstone became a junction for three gauges, and sections of triple-gauge track once existed in the freight yard. Gladstone station closed in 1991 and, by 1993, the broad-gauge line to the south and narrow-gauge line to the north had closed, leaving just the standard-gauge line running through the station.

Silverton station seen in October 2010 on the Silverton Tramway. The 36-mile (57km) 3ft 6in line was a missing link between two standard-gauge lines connecting Sydney and Perth, but in the end a new line was built and the tramway closed in 1970. *John Mewett*

Long-distance routes

In spite of the gauge problems, long-distance trains developed and helped bind the nation together, although changes at state borders were required for many years. For example, the old Sydney–Brisbane mail express once ran on a winding inland route through the New England Range. The standard-gauge train from Sydney would arrive on the Queensland border at Wallangarra, where a 3ft 6in narrow-gauge train to Brisbane awaited to continue the journey through the scenic Darling Downs. An alternative coastal route that did not involve a break of gauge was built and eventually led to the narrow-gauge route being closed, whilst a considerable length of the original standard-gauge line to the Queensland border was also abandoned in 1989.

The standardisation of gauges began in the 1920s, and steam locomotives built after the Second World War for the Victorian Railways were designed so that they could be easily converted from 5ft 3ins to standard-gauge. Although all of the mainland state capitals have been connected by standard-gauge since the 1990s, secondary routes have not always been converted.

Decline after the Second World War

Just as in Europe, after the Second World War the Australian railways were mostly run-down and neglected. Whilst the network peaked in size at this time, since then most of the truly narrow-gauge and secondary lines have been closed. The 1950s saw the first loss of a number of short branch lines, particularly where traffic had mostly been timber or livestock. Many such lines had been unprofitable for a number of years, sometimes running slow, mixed trains, and the growth of the trucking industry saw closures in ever-increasing numbers. Although some lines remained for seasonal grain freight, few original timber railways survived beyond the 1960s.

The 1960s witnessed increasing car ownership; as a consequence, railway passenger numbers continued to decline and financial losses mounted. In 1963, the Road & Railways Transport Act of 1930 was repealed, exposing the railways to intense competition from road transport. More closures ensued, large areas began to end up without any passenger branch lines and smaller stations on main routes were closed.

The late 1970s saw the replacement of local railway goods services with road transport from regional rail hubs. This resulted in the closure of more freight branch lines and wayside stations, particularly outside the grain-producing areas.

In the 1990s, many of the smaller rail-served grain silos were closed in favour of larger centralised silos. This resulted in the closure of a number of grain branch lines and smaller grain stations on general freight lines that remained open. Any lingering rural branch lines outside city suburban areas were by now mostly closed, but grain branches and mineral lines remain. In addition, state-connecting standard-gauge main lines now convey long-distance passengers and huge amounts of freight. This is quite a contrast to the original short and unconnected local lines all with different gauges.

Railcars from bus bodies were introduced on some little used Australian branch lines. This railbus dating from 1937 was later used to pay staff in cash, before more modern methods were employed. It is seen preserved at the New South Wales Rail Museum in March 2019. *Dr Alan Grundy*

Western Australia

The first government-built line in this huge state was from the town of Northampton. It opened in 1879 to convey copper ore to the coast and survived until 1957. The state went on to develop a substantial network, most of which was 3ft 6in narrow-gauge and, at its peak in the 1930s, over sixty overnight passenger services were provided. The first closures began in the 1940s and buses replaced many passenger services, whilst the separate network of Kalgoorlie Woodlines associated with the timber trade survived until the 1960s.

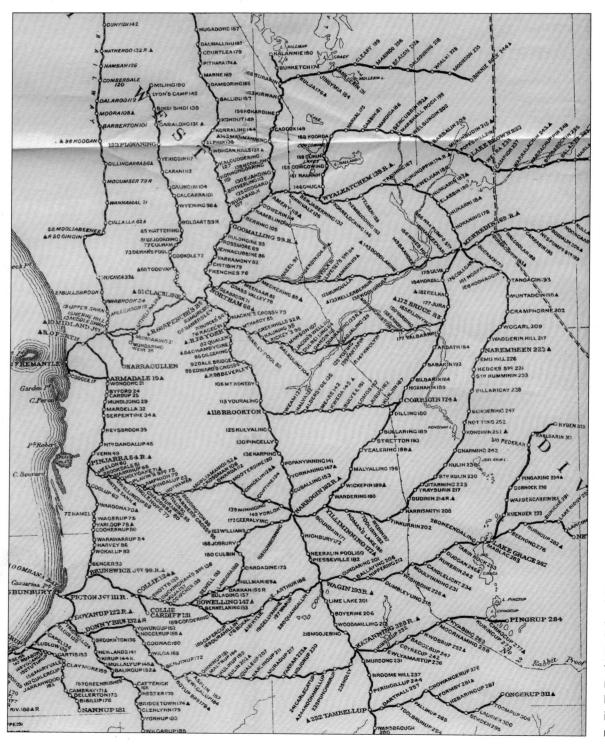

Part of a map produced by the ex-Western Australian Government Railways, showing the once extensive network of branch lines that existed in 1935; note the rabbit proof fence.

Western Australian Government class Fs 4-8-0 freight locomotive No 365. The British built locomotive dating from 1912 was superheated in 1930 and is seen withdrawn from service in October 1970, at the end of the steam era and at a time of line closures in the state. *Historical Railway Images*

The railways also served the wheatbelt and the original plan was to ensure that no major harvest area was more than 15 miles from a railway. Large areas with a scant rural population resulted in a large mileage of lightly used branch lines, while some lines simply linked railway locations that were already railway connected. In 1957, over 800 miles (1,290km) of line were closed which had less than one scheduled passenger train per week.

Today, almost all the original rural branches are closed to passengers, except for a number centred on Perth and some heritage sections. Busy mineral lines remain to some coastal ports, but the 114-mile (184km) Port Headland to Marble Bar line, the 94-mile (151km) line from Flinders Bay and 66-mile (106km) line from Geraldton Wharf all closed in the 1950s. Of the more unusual lines that have closed, the Kalamunda Zig Zag was part of the Upper Darling Range Railway that closed in 1949. Throughout all the closures, several lines were retained for the annual grain traffic, but many of these were closed in 2014 and, despite protests, they still remain closed.

Queensland

The railways of Queensland were mostly built to a 3ft 6in gauge with the aim of opening up vast, undeveloped areas and to serve mines. Copper ore and coal were conveyed by rail to the coast and at Urangan a now-closed coal pier, almost ¾-mile (1.1km) in length, was completed in 1917. The railways reached their peak in the 1930s, when the last significant line was opened. Sugar cane railways were built and there were also some fifteen light railways. Just as the last lines were being opened, the Ravenswood branch became the first to close in 1930.

There were areas of difficult topography that presented a challenge for the railways. By way of example, the remote Cooktown line featured 1 in 24 grades and was worked by a weekly railmotor until its closure in 1961. The Amiens branch reached the highest railway point in southern Queensland, closing in 1974. The Boolboonda Tunnel had to be driven through solid granite; having closed in 1961, it is now home to a colony of bats. Over the years, the railways have

Dickabram Bridge over the Mary River, seen in April 2010, was a combined rail and road bridge dating from 1886 and is one of just two such remaining in Australia. The railway branch over the bridge to Kingaroy closed in 2011. *Kgbo*

suffered many closures of branch and secondary lines, although a network of mostly 2ft-gauge sugar cane railways remains in use.

Of particular loss was much of the Tablelands Railway that ran inland from Cairns. Some sections were difficult to build, not only because of the steep and challenging topography, but also because of the climate and disease, with stretches having to cross swamps and dense rainforest. The lines were originally built to extract minerals, in particular tin, but timber was also transported and a network of private lines connected with the main network.

The railway in this part of Australia was extensively used during the Second World War, as an invasion by Japan was anticipated in North Australia. The railway helped to fortify the area and soldiers were transported to gain experience of tropical combat conditions. The railway also facilitated the construction of roads in the area and, by 1980, parts of the Tablelands Railway were closed. However, the Kuranda Scenic Railway runs on a picturesque part of the line from Cairns, whilst a weekly Savannahlander railcar continues on an 18-hour trip to Forsayth.

The Mount Morgan rack railway used the Abt system and had grades of 1 in 16.5. It was bypassed by a conventional line in 1951, itself closed in 1987, after the mine it served ceased production. Most of the line was dismantled in 1989, but the station at Mount Morgan and a short section of original rack railway were retained as a tourist attraction. There are also over two dozen other railway heritage sites.

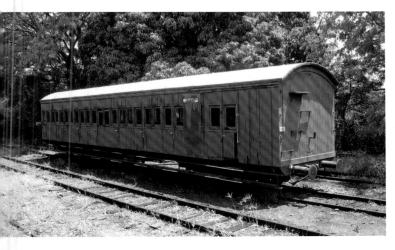

The Mary Valley Rattler is located at Gympie. Originally closed in 1995, part of the route reopened as an Australian heritage railway. A wooden bodied guard and passenger carriage is seen here in February 2015. *Dr Alan Grundy*

Northern Territory and South Australia, linked by The Ghan

In the Northern Territory, the North Australia Railway was a 3ft 6in narrow-gauge line. Opened in 1889, it ran 316 miles (509km) from Darwin to Birdum, the latter effectively just a tin shed in the middle of nowhere. However, the line was busy with troops during the Second World War, whereas cattle and, more latterly, iron ore traffic in particular kept the line open until June 1976. Adelaide River and Pine Creek stations on the line have been preserved on this most northerly of lost lines in Australia.

In South Australia, the state had both 5ft 3in broad-gauge lines and 3ft 6in narrow-gauge tracks. Little investment had been undertaken since the railways were first opened and losses became heavy as early as the 1920s. As a consequence, a programme of modernisation was undertaken and, by the 1930s, the network had been much improved. This all helped to reduce losses, but the inevitable road competition eventually led to closures.

There has been an endless list of branch and secondary line closures and the truncation of routes starting in the 1920s. Many survived until the 1970s, when a large number of lines in the south eastern area of the state were abandoned. Closures of lines that remained for goods have also continued. In 1990, the Waikerie and Peebinga lines closed, whilst in 2015 the Pinnaroo and Loxton lines were mothballed, which means they are out of use, but track and infrastructure are retained for possible future use. No country passenger branch lines, outside Adelaide's commuter services, have operated services in South Australia since the 1990s.

Belair station seen in April 2018. The disused shelter on the platform was once provided for visitors from Adelaide to Belair National Park. Until 1987, the station provided services beyond to Bridgewater, but today is a terminus. *Dr Alan Grundy*

TEN GREAT LOST RAILWAYS OF THE WORLD – THE OLD GHAN ROUTE

The old 3ft 6in narrow-gauge Ghan line stretched some 767 miles (1,235km) from Port Augusta to Alice Springs. Completed in 1929, originally one passenger train a week used the line, averaging just 12mph. The train became known as 'The Afghan Express' in homage to the previous camel route traders but was shortened to 'The Ghan'.

Steam locomotives were replaced by diesels in 1954, and in 1957 a new section of standard-gauge line that had been built from Port Augusta to coalfields was extended to Marree. The new route broadly followed the original narrow-gauge line which was then closed between Marree and Hawker. The new line resulted in all passengers having to change trains at Marree.

Unlike the current train, the old Ghan would have taxed the toughest of passengers. Running through a significant length of Outback, on occasion extreme heat, wildlife and locust plagues caused problems, but sand drifts and washouts also made the route impassable, sometimes for several weeks, before repairs could be completed.

As a consequence, a new standard-gauge line was completed on an entirely revised route. The new standard-gauge line to Alice Springs opened in 1980 and brought an end to the old line. The very last old Ghan ran in November 1980 and the remaining narrow-gauge section between Marree and Alice Springs was closed in 1981.

This also resulted in the abandonment of some settlements along the old line that had been established to serve the railway. Being in the Outback, structures were not bulldozed and much of the route can still be traced. Abandoned diesel locomotives that used the line are also to be found. The Algebuckina Bridge also remains, with nineteen spans, once the longest in South Australia. It crossed a dry river bed, which turned into a torrent when rain appeared.

Today, 'The Ghan' still runs on the new standard-gauge route from Melbourne to Alice Springs and on to Darwin. At Port Augusta, the original narrow-gauge line remains as the heritage Pichi Richi Railway, which runs along part of the old route.

To Darwin
Alice Springs

Central Australia Railway narrow-gauge (3' 6"/1.067m) line built by the South Australian Railways from Port Augusta to Oodnadatta in 1891. It was finally opened to Alice Springs in 1929. The express that ran on the line was nicknamed the 'The Afghan Express'. The the line closed in 1981 and the track was removed. The trackbed is now "The Old Ghan Railway Trail" for walkers.

Northern Territory
South Australia

The standard-gauge line opened in 1980 from Tarcoola to Alice Spings to replace the Central Australia Railway. It took until 2004 for it to be opened all the way to Darwin. 'The Ghan' train is still run on this line for tourists.

The standard-gauge line from Port Augusta to Marree (shown in black) was opened in 1957 for transporting coal and livestock, but closed in 1987.

Oodnadatta

Marree

To Kalgoorlie

Tarcoola

To Sydney

Port Augusta
Port Pirie

Southern Ocean

Adelaide
To Melbourne

Map of the original narrow-gauge route of the Old Ghan that ran from Port Augusta as far as Alice Springs.

Above left: Poster of the Commonwealth Railways publicising winter holidays on the Old Ghan route of the Central Australia Railway, circa 1940. *Dr Alan Grundy*

Above right: NSU class diesel locomotive used on the Old Ghan route, seen at Alice Springs in February 2009. Capable of operating on light track and in extreme heat they were built in Birmingham in the UK. The last was withdrawn in 1987. *Reinhard Dietrich*

Right: Algebuckina viaduct, on the Old Ghan route; opened in 1892 the wrought iron bridge is 1,927ft (587m) long. Once the longest in South Australia, it was last used in 1981 and is seen here still with rusting rails in April 2008. *Craig Terry*

Cattle were transported on the line, but their welfare was not always a high priority as they were mostly being transported to be slaughtered. During one period of extreme heat in the 1970s, an entire train of livestock died and, at the end of the journey, about 400 head of dead cattle were buried at Marree.

New South Wales

New South Wales was home to Australia's first railway with iron track at Newcastle, opening in 1831 and serving a coal mine. Standard-gauge lines developed that followed British railway practices, and a network of branch lines grew over the more settled eastern part of the state and also to serve mines. The coastal area was originally disconnected by rail from the rest of Australia by the Blue Mountains, but this was overcome by the Zig Zag railway that was able, via a number of switchbacks, to gain height and traverse the mountainous area, until this was replaced by a 10-tunnel deviation in 1910. Part

of the original section has since been preserved as a heritage railway.

The state policy was to run the railways as a public service, holding down charges, retaining lines, and introducing a number of branch line railcars in the 1920s, sometimes referred to as 'Tin Hares'. For a period up until the early 1970s, relatively few lines were closed. However, this reduced the capital to provide investment for improvements and maintenance, which in turn was to lead to later closures. Many rural passenger lines were replaced by bus services, and today a web of closed branch and secondary link lines are to be found.

Of the many closed branch and secondary lines, some of interest include the Campbelltown–Camden line, which had the steepest adhesion-worked incline in the state at 1 in 19, until closure in 1962. The Dorringo branch, which included two tunnels and was one of the costliest lines to build, closed in 1972. The former line

Ben Lomond station name board, seen in May 2014, informing of the height above sea level, making this the highest station in NSW. The station, on the ex-Great Northern line closed in 1985, whilst most of the remaining route closed shortly after. *John Mewett*

Above: Deepwater station, in May 2014, is one of many stations in Australia with a rather British appearance. Opened in 1886, on the original main route between Sydney and Brisbane, the station closed in 1972 and the remaining section of line in 1989. *John Mewett*

Right: Sydney Mortuary station conveyed funeral trains to Rookwood Cemetery, in the same way as London–Brookwood services in England. Funeral trains ceased in 1938 and after being used for other purposes the station was largely disused in February 2019. *Author*

to Hay, with its grand station buildings, was closed in the 1980s. A section of secondary line that once served Byron Bay was reopened in 2017 as a heritage railway using solar power.

At Sydney, the Central Station has some interesting lost features. Platforms 26 and 27 were built on the site of a cemetery next to the station, as part of a proposed new line to Bondi, but it was never completed and the platforms lie dormant. Also, beside the station a separate mortuary station once ran funeral trains to the outlying cemeteries until 1938 and was then used as a parcels depot until the 1960s. The Sydney Goods Line, which closed in 1984, opened in 2015 as a linear park. Parts of the track and some railway fixtures from the line have been incorporated into the new walkway.

Victoria

The smallest mainland state was well served by a network of 5ft 3in broad-gauge lines, whilst there were also standard and narrow-gauge lines. Some routes were built on the insistence of politicians, where traffic levels could have never been justified and a few closures began in the 1930s. The 1950s saw a number of short and uneconomic branch lines close and by the 1960s there had been considerable further losses. By the 1980s, rural branch lines had all but disappeared apart from the freight lines in grain-growing areas.

The truly narrow-gauge lines were also amongst the first to close, with all lines having ceased operation by the early 1960s. For example, the Walhalla Railway was located in the mountains east of Melbourne and was one of four 2ft 6in narrow-gauge lines built by Victorian Railways. The 26½-mile (43km) line from Moe to Walhalla reached goldfields in May 1910, just as the gold was largely worked out, but timber traffic survived until 1954. Narrow-gauge heritage railways have been established on parts of the old lines, including the famous Puffing Billy Railway.

In Melbourne, an outer circle railway line closed as early as 1893, whilst the inner circle line closed to passengers in 1948. Together with other passenger railway lines in the city area, they were early victims of tram competition. In the 1980s, a report written by those with vested interests in roads recommended consideration be given to further significant rail closures; fortunately, criticism of the report led to only a handful of more lines closing.

Beechworth station, seen in March 2019. Closed in December 1976 after a century of use, a footpath today uses the old trackbed, whilst the buildings are now used as a youth centre. *Dr Alan Grundy*

Right: A section of the Yarra Valley Railway, to the north east of Melbourne, which was closed in 1980, survives and a heritage railcar is operated at weekends. Healesville station ticket office on the line is seen here in March 2019. *Dr Alan Grundy*

Below: The famous Puffing Billy heritage railway is located in the Dandenong Ranges east of Melbourne. The 2ft 6in narrow-gauge line originally closed in 1954 but reopened later as a heritage railway. No 14A a Baldwin 2-6-2T dating from 1914, is seen in March 2019. *Dr Alan Grundy*

Conversion to standard-gauge has continued, but the broad-gauge line to Mount Gambier has not been converted and was mothballed. Today, surviving passenger services are centred on Melbourne, but grain freight lines still remain.

Tasmania

There were some unusual island lines. The first was a 5-mile (8km) route laid across a peninsula to Port Arthur that allowed ships to avoid a notoriously stormy area. Trucks for passengers and freight on wooden tracks were pushed along by convicts from 1836 until the 1870s. Also of interest was the Grubb's Tramway, a horse-drawn line that conveyed passengers; the journey took over 90 minutes upgrade, but just six minutes by gravity downgrade, until its closure in 1927.

The first significant passenger lines date from the 1870s, and the passenger network was eventually built to a 3ft 6in gauge. This was considered to be the most cost-effective due to areas of dense forest and mountain terrain, but still resulted in a number of lines having steep gradients, tight curves and low speeds. Nevertheless, passenger services developed and Hobart once witnessed some seventy passenger trains a day.

Today, there are no passenger services and almost all branch lines are closed, with the first loss being in the 1920s. Passenger trains had never been that financially successful, but they became increasingly less used as road transport improved. Because of the ever-declining state of the track, all remaining suburban and local passenger services ceased in 1974. Even 'The Tasmanian', the last remaining passenger service on the main line train from Hobart to Launceston and Wynyard, ceased in 1978, but freight is still transported on the line.

Coal, tin and copper ore deposits on the island resulted in several mineral lines being built across the

Westerway was on a branch line that ran to the forests of Mount Field Park. Opened in 1909 remaining freight services ceased in 1995, but the Tasmanian station has been restored by volunteers of the Derwent Valley Railway and is seen here in March 2019. *Dr Alan Grundy*

Right: There are no railway passenger services in Tasmania, other than heritage lines. The substantial stone built former Hobart station, seen in March 2019, saw its last passengers in 1978 and the site has since been incorporated into film studios. *Dr Alan Grundy*

Below: The Tasmanian Strahan–Queenstown line served mines and incorporated gradients of up to 1 in 10, using rack sections, until closure in 1963. Now reopened as the West Coast Wilderness Railway an original rack locomotive *Mount Lyell No 3* is seen at Lynchford in March 2019. *Dr Alan Grundy*

harsh terrain of the west coast. The North East Dundas Tramway was a 2ft-gauge line that used the world's first Garratt locomotives but closed in 1932. One of these locomotives was saved and returned to Britain. The Abt rack system was used on the Mount Lyell Railway; after closure in 1963, much of it was reopened in 2002 as the West Coast Wilderness Railway. The Emu Bay Railway ran across the north-west of the island and closed in 1998.

A legacy of lost Australian structures and lines

Closed railways have certainly left their mark on Australia, not only where tracks have recently been pulled up, such as on the Moolort line that closed in 2004, but where lines had tracks removed decades ago such as the Maldon extension that closed in 1976. Numerous country stations have also survived, some looking remarkably British in style. After closure, many were sold to private owners, some were demolished, whilst a few remain derelict and unkempt.

Improvements to the network resulted in early tunnel closures. The two Sleep's Hill tunnels on the Adelaide–Melbourne line opened in 1879 but were abandoned in 1919 as the bores were too narrow for new stock. The Otford Tunnel opened in 1888 south of Sydney. On a gradient of 1 in 40, engine crews suffered smoke and fumes, so a deviation was built and the original tunnel, together with others at nearby Helensburgh, were abandoned during and after the First World War.

Examples of disused railway bridges and trestles are also found throughout Australia, built in wood, iron and steel. Examples include the Stony Creek Bridge, a wooden trestle 906ft (276m) long and 61ft (19m) high. The long metal Parramatta River and Algebuckina bridges are also fine remaining examples. The St Laurence Creek bridge in Queensland was demolished in 2010, but examination of the cast iron piers, after 90 years in salt water, showed remarkably little corrosion.

There are many Australian heritage railways and numerous railway museums. Elsewhere, disused railway lines have had their trackbeds turned into rail trails; for example, the Kilkivan–Kingaroy Rail Trail follows some 55 miles (88km) of old railway line, and the East Gippsland Rail Trail runs for some 60 miles (96km) using disused trackbeds.

Bush fires have historically caused damage to Australia's railways, the Noojee branch and its wooden trestle being closed by fires in 1926 and 1939, before official closure in 1958. Unfortunately, some heritage railways, such as the Zig Zag line and others, have seen some stock damaged beyond repair by Australian bush fires which became particularly ferocious in 2020.

A small wooden station at Lowood on the Brisbane Valley Railway line from Ipswich in Australia, seen in October 2010. Closed in 1991, much of the trackbed has been turned into the Brisbane Valley Rail Trail. *Shiftchange*

CHAPTER 25

PACIFIC ISLANDS

Banaba (Ocean Island) Nauru (Pleasant Island)

On the small island of Banaba, a 2-mile (3km) 2ft narrow-gauge railway opened in 1906, running from a phosphate mine to a coastal port. The line became very busy, operations were expanded in the 1920s and new locomotives were required. In the 1930s, a further new set of locomotives were again ordered and the gauge widened to 3ft. After the Second World War, the line was widened yet again to standard-gauge and diesel locomotives introduced. The line closed in 1979 after 90 per cent of the island surface had been stripped away.

A similar 2ft narrow-gauge 4½-mile (3.9km) phosphate mineral railway was provided on the island of Nauru in 1907. It was upgraded to a 3ft-gauge in the 1920s and diesels eventually replaced steam, but the deposits became depleted and the line closed in 2011.

Christmas Island

A 12-mile (18km) standard-gauge phosphate mineral railway ran between Flying Fish Cove and South Point. It was opened in 1914 and originally contained an incline that was later replaced by a conveyor. In the 1950s, the line conveyed passengers, mainly workers and their school-age children, in small Wickham railcars. The line closed in 1987 when phosphate mining ceased.

Christmas Island with the station waiting shelter at South Point railway terminus. Mainly Chinese phosphate mine workers and their families living in the area used the station until closure in 1987. It is now one of few buildings remaining and is seen in June 2015. *David Stanley*

Cook Islands

On Rarotonga Island, a short narrow-gauge railway ran from warehouses onto a wooden pier that contained three tracks and several loops used by hand-operated trucks up until the Second World War. The pier was once served by the Union Steam Ship Co of New Zealand. A later tourist line on the island using an ex-Polish narrow-gauge steam locomotive has also closed.

Fiji

Fiji once had an extensive network of mostly 2ft-gauge sugar cane railways, dating from the 1880s. During the sugar cane cutting season, from mid-June to mid-January, the railways were busy, often working 24 hours a day.

There is a catalogue of sugar mill railway closures in Fiji, starting in the 1920s, with the Nausori Mill and its railways closing in 1960 and the Nausori mill closing in 1959. The closures were due in part to rainfall which, in some areas, was too heavy for the successful growing of sugar cane. Cyclone damage has also caused closures and world sugar demand has fallen, but this is the only Pacific archipelago to still retain some sugar cane railway lines, including a closed section used by rail bikes, whilst two steam locomotives were exported to Britain for preservation.

WORLD'S MOST FAMOUS FREE PASSENGER TRAIN

The most significant railway was a 2ft-gauge line that ran along the coast of the largest island, Viti Levu, for some 142 miles (229km). Working over much of this line was what became known as the free passenger train. It was operated as part of an agreement with the British colonial government to compensate communities in the area who agreed to the railway being built, rather than out of the goodness of the railway's heart. Passenger trains were not given priority over freight trains and a twice-weekly service was run. Commencing in 1914, the passenger train was withdrawn in 1973 after Fiji's independence and the line becoming state owned. A section of railway on which the free passenger service once ran closed in 2009.

Fiji's railways were built to transport sugar cane, but a free passenger train was provided and is seen near Rarawai Mill in 1947. The free service ceased in 1973, but a few steam locomotives escaped being scrapped. *Noel Butlin Archives Centre, Australian National University*

French Polynesia

On the island of Tahiti, from the 1890s a number of short horse-worked lines opened in the Papeete area serving wharfs and warehouses, but all had ceased operation before the First World War. A 2ft narrow-gauge railway opened on the island of Makatea in 1920 to convey phosphates to a pier on a rocky outcrop that allowed larger vessels to dock. The railway was originally steam operated and new diesels were introduced after the Second World War, but the line closed in 1966.

Hawaiian Islands

The first section of the standard-gauge Hawaii Consolidated Railway opened in 1899. Passengers and freight were conveyed and, by the 1930s, there were over 106 miles (171km) of line, including two main routes across the largest Hawaiian island. Part of the routes travelled through daunting topography and the railway had been costly to build, with numerous bridges, viaducts and tunnels on some sections. The end of the lines came suddenly, after sections were severely damaged by a tsunami in 1946.

Pearl Harbor was the main US Pacific navy base on Oahu, and in 1959 the Hawaiian Islands became the 50th USA state. At the same time, many of its once over fifty surviving sugar lines were closing. This included the 3ft network of lines found on the island of Oahu, the Kahului Railroad on the island of Maui and over 200 miles (322km) of line on the island of Kauai. A few sugar routes survived until the 1960s and today there are some short tourist lines.

The Hawaiian Railway Society's Alco 0-6-0 steam locomotive No 12 from Oahu's sugar railway. The line ceased operation in 1947, but the American navy continued to use some of the track for military transport until 1969. The locomotive, seen in August 2006, was last used between Honolulu and Pearl Harbor in 1953. *David W. Dellinger*

Micronesia Federated States

A phosphate plant was served by a railway on the small island of Fais. It was opened when the island was under Japanese control after the First World War. The line was destroyed during the Second World War and never reopened.

New Caledonia

An 18-mile (29km) originally metre-gauge public passenger line connected Nouméa and Païta until its closure to passengers at the outset of the Second World War, although it was used for military purposes during the war. Remains of the station and a locomotive are still to be found at Païta.

Papua New Guinea

Whilst earlier logging lines and mineral tramways once existed, in the run-up to the First World War copper mining in the Port Moresby area led to the construction of a number of narrow-gauge lines. Due to the war, some lines were never completed, whilst others fell into disrepair. In 1921, a line was built to connect a copper mine to smelters at Bootless Bay but closed in 1926. The 1920s also witnessed a number of cocoa and coconut plantations establishing short 2ft-gauge lines, the most extensive being at Bougainville, extending to 14 miles (23km). Some later palm oil lines were also built, but by the 1990s the once numerous lines had all closed.

In 1920, a 7-mile (11km) 2ft line opened on Misima Island connecting gold mines to the coast, using a second-hand steam engine from Australia. The gold was soon exhausted, and the locomotive was returned to the mainland when the short-lived railway closed in 1922.

Samoa

An 8-mile (13km) narrow-gauge railway was built by Germany during the First World War on the island of Upolu to provide coal to a wireless station and also included links to some of the island's coconut and banana plantations. During the course of the war, the line was taken over by New Zealand forces and the main route was upgraded. The German plantation branches had closed by 1916, but the railway remained until military forces left the island in 1920.

Solomon Islands

A 1½-mile (2.4km) monorail on the island of Guadalcanal was used prior to the First World War to transport bananas from the Berande plantation to a dock at Tetere Bay. In the 1920s, a 1¾-mile (2.8km) logging railway opened on the island of Vanikoro and used a Shay steam locomotive. A cyclone damaged the line in 1935 and it ceased operation. During the Second World War, a military railway was built to construct and then supply an airfield on Guadalcanal; whilst this closed after the war, some short sections of plantation lines survived elsewhere on the islands until the 1970s.

Tonga

A narrow-gauge freight railway once conveyed mostly copra, which is the dried meat of coconuts. It ran from a shallow central lagoon through the town of Nuku'alofa to a deep-water quayside. In 1942, part of the line was reinstated at Nuku'alofa by American forces to facilitate wartime supplies to naval ships. The railway fell out of use after the war, but parts of the course of the line, including along Railway Road, can still be traced.

CHAPTER 26

NEW ZEALAND

When the railways were first constructed, after witnessing the problems the number of different gauges were causing in Australia and seeing a similar situation starting to develop in New Zealand, in 1870 the government set down that a 3ft 6in gauge was to be used for all future government lines. In spite of this somewhat narrow gauge being used, long tunnels and high viaducts were required through many areas of beautiful, but difficult and precipitous, terrain. A large number of branch lines, including timber and mineral railways, fed into main routes.

The railways did much to develop the economy of New Zealand, but tough economic conditions of the 1930s and increasing competition from road transport led to a reduction in freight and passengers during this period, but most lines remained open. New carriages and railcars were introduced to boost passenger traffic, whilst the government brought in legislation to protect the railways from competing road freight transport, although this was gradually eased and later abolished.

By the 1950s, New Zealand had more than 1,350 stations, whilst the network included many branch lines. However, financial losses were mounting and, although increasingly efficient and handsomely styled railcars had been introduced on some lines, passenger revenues were only amounting to a small part of total earnings.

In 1952, a report was commissioned by the government to investigate the operation of New Zealand Railways. The report had undergone a consultation process and the road transport lobby were keen to see lines close, suggesting that the money saved by closures could be put into roads. The report unfortunately included lists of lines that should be closed, together with those that should remain under review. The effect was to produce uncertainty and this, in turn, lead to a significant decline in traffic as customers abandoned the railways in fear of closures.

View of a British points lever from Rotherham, seen at the Museum of Transport and Technology (MOTAT) near Auckland in February 2018, with the firm's name on the cast iron weight. Much of the original railway equipment in Australasia was exported from Britain. *Author*

Railcar, RM 31, *Tokomaru* was built in 1938. The semi-streamlined units were withdrawn in 1972, but this heritage unit is still used for excursions and is seen at Napier in February 2017, after the station had closed to regular passengers in 2001. *Jacquie Wakeford*

There were protests against closures and a few reprieves, although in some cases this was for a limited time only. Several lines were retained for freight, but in the decade between 1953 and 1963 over 300 miles (485km) of branch line were closed completely, with a higher number of lines being closed on the South Island.

Numerous rural stations were constructed, mostly of wood. Once vibrant centres of the community, after closure many became increasingly vandalised and large numbers were demolished. Today, only about 100 mostly suburban stations remain with passenger services and less than 40 of the original wooden stations survive.

Coastal shipping made some inroads into rail freight, but railway freight remains important, particularly container and timber traffic, whilst a number of the freight lines are lightly used, or used for timber only. Privatisation in the 1990s saw some freight reclaimed from the roads, but the railways were eventually returned to state ownership in a worse condition. Today, over one third of all the track has been closed, but a report commissioned in New Zealand in 2017 showed that the government subsidy for railways was dwarfed by the benefits to the economy, and in 2022 investment in the railways continued.

Bush Tramways

It is estimated there were once hundreds of logging lines operated by the timber industry for transportation and using a variety of narrow gauges. These were called bush tramways in New Zealand, the last traditional line closing in the 1970s. One of the longest was at Mokai, which had a main line of 50 miles (80km) and some 25 miles (40km) of 3ft 6in gauge branches. Steep grades and tight curves were common on such lines, one being known as the 'Corkscrew Railway'. The Ellis & Burnand Tramway was a 23-mile (37km) 3ft 6in logging railway that included a spiral of line in a tunnel and two trestle viaducts. It closed in 1955, but much of the route is now a walking trail. Other disused bush tramways have also been turned into walking and cycling routes.

North Island

Although there was more population on the North Island, passenger services were cut back, particularly from the 1960s to the main lines and a few branches. There has been a long catalogue of closures over many years. For example, the 48-mile (78km) Moutohora line, the passenger services of which were replaced by buses in 1945, closed completely in 1959. The 89-mile (144km) Stratford line, with its 24 tunnels and 91 bridges, was closed to remaining passenger services in 1983, but may just possibly reopen in part as a tourist route. The 38-mile (61km) Okaihau branch, the most northerly in New Zealand, lost its passenger trains in 1976 and was closed in 1987.

Regular public long-distance passenger services have also ceased, including the 'Silver Star' sleeper service between Auckland and Wellington that ended in 1979. Most regular passenger trains, excluding the suburban

Above: Waitakere station became one of the least used and the suburban service from Auckland ceased in 2015. The original wooden station building, dating from 1881, had been relocated to MOTAT in 1972 and is seen in February 2018. *Author*

Right: Auckland Central station was built between 1927 and 1930. It displayed ornamentation and grandeur at the height of the railway's domination, as seen by the large clock in February 2018. The station closed in 2003, being replaced by a station in a new location. *Author*

Auckland station now provides accommodation for students and is seen in February 2018. The huge building was designed in an American style as this was considered to be the most fashionable and luxurious at the time. *Author*

The Karangahake Gorge line, which originally transported minerals and gold, closed in 1978, but part of the trackbed is now used as a walking trail. This uses a disused tunnel and bridges on the line, as this bridge over the river, seen in February 2018, shows. *Author*

services at Wellington and Auckland, were eventually withdrawn, except the 'Northern Explorer' tourist train between Wellington and Auckland.

Closure of some remaining freight-only lines has also continued. The huge Mohaka Viaduct over a river gorge opened in 1937 and at 312ft (95m) in height is the tallest viaduct in Australasia. It was mothballed in 2012, along with the Napier–Gisborne line, but is now used by occasional logging freight trains. Mothballing is where out-of-use track and infrastructure remain in place, as opposed to removal after closure, allowing the railway use to return if required. Some such lines are used by tourist rail carts, for example over the mothballed 31-mile (50km) Dargaville branch tracks.

The Rimutaka Incline

The Rimutaka Incline opened in 1878 using the Fell central rail to overcome a steep 3-mile (5km) 1 in 15 gradient on a remote and gruelling part of the Wellington–Auckland main line. For 77 years, Fell 0-4-2T locomotives were used, and sometimes as many as five locomotives were required to be spaced out along the train to reduce draw bar strain and to provide braking on the descent. Loads were still limited; the operating costs were high and conditions in tunnels poor.

The main line became busier, and remarshalling trains at the top and bottom of the incline to add or remove locomotives, together with speed being limited to 10mph, caused long delays. Specially adapted diesel

Mangaroa Tunnel, on the abandoned North Island Rimutaka route, viewed in January 2018. The line through the tunnel opened in 1878 and closed in 1955. The tunnel is now part of a rail trail.
Russell Street

railcars improved timings for passengers, but in the end a new tunnel to cut out the incline, the deviation, was opened in 1955 at the same time as closure of the incline route. After closure, much of the trackbed of the original route is now used as a walking trail that highlights the steep gradients.

The incline was an example of some original lines being economically built, which then required improvements to be made as traffic increased. Elsewhere on this main line, a steep and winding section, with tunnels that were subject to earthquake movements, was closed in 1981 when a diversion between Mangaweka and Utiku was opened.

South Island

There was less population on the South Island and many of the settlements are some distance apart. This resulted in the construction of numerous secondary and branch lines, but as passenger numbers decreased, service cutbacks, due in part to an inability to finance new rolling stock, frequently proceeded to closure to freight.

An early closure that provoked upset at the time was the Nelson Section. This was an isolated 64-mile (103km) line that closed in 1955. There was a six-day 'sit-in' at

Kiwi station on the line; although consideration was given to reopening and linking the route to the national network, due to the backlash the closure caused, the line remained closed and today has the longest disused tunnel in New Zealand.

A number of branch lines have closed in the far south, for example the Wyndham branch which closed in 1962 and the Tokanui line that closed in 1966. The Catlins River branch stations were originally established at saw mills; the line closed in 1971 and has the distinction of having the most southerly closed railway tunnel in Australasia. The 59-mile (95km) Roxburgh branch, which was one of the more protracted construction projects, beginning in 1874 and not completed until 1929, closed in 1968. The 87-mile (140km) Invercargill–Kingston branch, with its 34 stations, had closed by 1982.

Passenger closures were to continue and 'The Southerner', the last main line service, was withdrawn in 2002. Fortunately, a tourist train had made its first run from Christchurch to Greymouth in November 1987. The 'TranzAlpine' train was a last-ditch attempt to retain long-distance travel and was a success. Tourist trains with huge windows have become increasingly popular and, in addition to this route on the South Island, coronavirus permitting, they also run between Picton and Christchurch.

The Little River branch trackbed is seen in January 2018. The rural line, one of a number centred on Christchurch, was used by mixed passenger and freight trains until 1951, whilst freight continued until 1962. Much of the route has since been converted into a footpath and cycleway. *Author*

The 'Kingston Flyer' with AB class 4-6-2 Pacific locomotives that once worked the 87-mile (140km) line, seen at Kingston in January 2012. The South Island line closed in 1979 and a heritage service was restarted on a short section, although this has not operated since 2012 in 2021 services resumed. *Bernard Spragg*

Rails from Dunedin

The Otago Central Railway ran some 147 miles (236km) broadly westward from Dunedin to Cromwell, via Middlemarch, and in some ways is typical of many lines. The first section was opened in 1889, but being constructed through difficult terrain, requiring many bridges and viaducts, completion to Cromwell was not until 1921. Gold was an initial spur, but the line was also built to open up Dunedin's hinterland. Oat and chaff traffic combined with rabbit, sheep, wool, cattle, fruit and timber were once important goods on the line. Mixed freight and passenger trains ran at first and again towards the end of the railway's life.

Diesel traction for freight was introduced in 1968. Railcars were also introduced and increased passenger numbers, but the poor state of the track resulted in derailments and, on Anzac Day (25 April) 1976, the passenger services were suspended. Complete closure of the Cromwell–Clyde section came in 1980. However, tourist excursions were run through the spectacular Taieri Gorge and when complete closure of the remaining line was announced in 1989, the local council bought 40 miles (64km) of the line from Dunedin to Middlemarch, together with Dunedin station. Tourist services continued on this section, run by Dunedin Railways, until 2020 when the line was temporarily mothballed due to coronavirus.

The surviving station building at the seaside settlement of Waitati, near Dunedin, in January 2018. Although closed to regular services, some tourist trains operated by Dunedin Railways terminate here and the line remains open for freight. *Author*

A mosaic dating from 1906 featuring a goods wagon at Dunedin in January 2018. At its peak there were extensive freight services and over 100 passenger trains a day served the station. Suburban services ceased in 1982 and long-distance trains in 2002, but some tourist services continue. *Author*

CHAPTER 27

WORLD'S END

Being on the ground, railways have been subject to physical damage and lines have been permanently closed by everything from floods in Australia, a volcano in Italy, a tsunami in Haiti, an earthquake in Chile to hurricanes in the Americas.

Endless wars have also resulted in closures. The massive damage and degradation to some lines during two world wars led to permanent closures. The railways are often perceived as a soft target and have been closed by sabotage in more local conflicts, within and between countries. Even robbery and looting have resulted in some closures.

In terms of management, everything from lack of vision, incompetence, vested interests and outright corruption have resulted in closures. Governments interfere, or fudge closures with an inference that reopening may be a future possibility. They may also take a dogmatic approach, operating a mostly nationalised or privatised network. Governments sometimes flip flop between approaches, or use a mix of the two, but there seems no magic formula that prevents closures.

Throughout the world, one of the main reasons for closure is the result of years of previous underinvestment. Lack of track renewal forced the Donegal Railways to close in 1960. Investment in new high-speed services in France has resulted in neglect elsewhere. In Britain, whilst Network Rail invested in safety, they ignored the proper

An 0-6-2T locomotive No 805 seen on a charter train in September 2000 on the surviving section of the Damascus–Serghaya route, near the border with Lebanon, into which the line originally extended, before civil wars ended the service. *Nigel Tout*

Even when railways remain open, parts of the infrastructure are sometimes in a poor condition. The signals seen here at Mechita in Argentina in June 2013, originated from Liverpool and highlight the investment required on some lines that remain open. *Miroab*

maintenance of other infrastructure. Small savings now will result in massive costs, or closures, in the future.

Many railways were originally built to convey coal, and coal-fired steam locomotives survived for many years. Some could also run on almost anything that burns; the Zambezi Sawmills locomotives used sawmill waste, Asian sugar locomotives used sugar cane waste, and those in the Middle East were converted from coal to oil. Yet, flexibility and durability were not to save what increasingly looked like an antiquated form of motive power. In North America, steam had mostly been replaced by diesel traction in the 1950s, and in Europe during the 1960s, but pockets of steam survived throughout the world for much longer and have become tourist attractions.

If railways are not competitive with other forms of transport, particularly in terms of cost, speed, convenience and technology, then this is another potential factor in their closure. In parts of the world, trains are being run remotely. For example, some freight trains in Australia operate with no drivers in the cab, as does the rapid transit system in Singapore. However, worldwide railway staff numbers have been slashed and a wide range of economies implemented.

In global terms, every year sees a reduction in the overall mileage of railways. Yet, passenger numbers and tons of freight hauled were, until 2020, increasing. Container traffic and heavy freight are generally buoyant, whilst on the passenger side intercity, commuting and tourism trains had all seen growth and investment in most continents. Furthermore, the reopening of closed railways has been proposed in Europe, North America, Africa and many other parts of the world.

Sadly, railways have also more recently been closed by an invisible enemy. Coronavirus can be spread by

In Britain the steam age ended in the 1960s, but the *Flying Scotsman* was saved from scrap at this time by Alan Pegler. The firebox is seen here in February 2020 when the locomotive visited the Watercress Line and attracted large crowds. *Author*

close contact and, as a consequence, passengers deserted the railways. Passenger services were reduced in every continent. Multiple countries suspended passenger services for temporary periods and a few services may never reopen, but others such as Ecuador took the opportunity to completely close their railways and sack the staff.

Rail travel is safe, and the fact that about 3,500 people are killed on the world's roads each day is largely ignored. It is also a green and sustainable transport. Looking at the number of closed railways in this book and the huge numbers of passengers and freight that once used them, subsequently mostly transferring to road transport, it is clear that railway closures have even had an effect on global warming.

Some closed lines have reopened as heritage railways, others have been of benefit to both nature and recreation. Bats have colonised disused tunnels, and overgrown routes crossing barren countryside have acted as wildlife corridors. They have also been used as new routes for physical recreation and a large number of rail trails are to be found throughout the world.

Many of the weaker lines were closed as a result of the economic downturn in the 1930s and some after the banking crisis of 2008. I sadly fear the coronavirus pandemic will result in a further decline in railway finances, resulting in more lost lines. Yet, sixty years ago, it was confidently predicted that the railways, like the canals before them, were finished as a serious transport mode. Clearly, the future is difficult to predict.

Above: The reduction in use of the railways and modernisation resulted in huge numbers of unwanted passenger carriages. Many were just abandoned in sidings to await their fate, as seen here with a smashed window of an Austrian coach in November 2019. *Author*

Left: A blue Wagon Lits coach with the original crest. Once the ultimate in luxury travel, the coaches gradually became dilapidated and were withdrawn. Many have since been restored for new tourist use, as seen here in France in 2010, recreating a most civilised way to travel. *Author*

End of the line, a simple but elegant buffer stop seen in Germany in May 2014. *Author*

BIBLIOGRAPHY

Balkwill, R. and Marshall, J., *Railway Facts & Feats*, Guinness, 1993

History of Railways (magazine series) 1972

Hollingsworth, B., *Atlas of the World's Railways*, Bison Books, 1979

Lambert, A., *Lost Railway Journeys from Around the World*, White Lion 2018

Ovenden, M., *Railway Maps of the World*, Viking, 2011

Railway Wonders of the World (magazine series) 1935

The World's Railways, Odhams Press, 1949

Wolmar, C., *A Short History of Trains*, Penguin Random House, 2019

INDEX

NORTH AND CENTRAL AMERICA